Customers that Count

FINANCIAL TIMES

Prentice Hall

In an increasingly competitive world, it is quality
of thinking that gives an edge – an idea that opens new
doors, a technique that solves a problem, or an insight
that simply helps make sense of it all.

We work with leading authors in the fields of
management and finance to bring cutting-edge thinking
and best learning practice to a global market.

Under a range of leading imprints, including
Financial Times Prentice Hall, we create world-class
print publications and electronic products giving readers
knowledge and understanding which can then be
applied, whether studying or at work.

To find out more about our business and professional
products, you can visit us at **www.business-minds.com**

For other Pearson Education publications, visit
www.pearsoned-ema.com

Pearson
Education

Customers that Count

*How to build living relationships
with your most valuable customers*

Tony Cram

FINANCIAL TIMES
Prentice Hall

An imprint of **Pearson Education**

London · New York · San Francisco · Toronto · Sydney
Tokyo · Singapore · Hong Kong · Cape Town · Madrid
Paris · Milan · Munich · Amsterdam

PEARSON EDUCATION LIMITED

Head Office:
Edinburgh Gate
Harlow CM20 2JE
Tel: +44 (0)1279 623623
Fax: +44 (0)1279 431059

London Office:
128 Long Acre
London WC2E 9AN
Tel: +44 (0)207 447 2000
Fax: +44 (0)207 240 5771

First published in Great Britain in 2001

ISBN: 0 273 65431 4

British Library Cataloguing in Publication Data
A CIP catalogue record for this book can be obtained from the British Library.

10 9 8 7 6 5 4 3 2 1

Typeset by Pantek Arts Ltd, Maidstone, Kent
Printed and bound in Great Britain by Biddles Ltd, Guildford & King's Lynn

The Publisher's policy is to use paper manufactured from sustainable forests.

To my mother and in memory of my father

TONY CRAM is Programme Director at Ashridge designing and delivering development programmes for clients including Marriott Hotels, St Paul International Insurance, BBA Group and Rockwell Automation. He is a visiting professor at Universitatsseminar der Wirtschaft Germany, works with the Swedish Institute of Management and teaches on company programmes for the University of Michigan, USA. He contributes to the work of the British Red Cross as a member of their National Communications Panel. He is a Fellow of the Chartered Institute of Marketing.

The *Financial Times Handbook of Management* (2000) includes a chapter from Tony on the consequences of Customer Relationship Management. His first book, *The Power of Relationship Marketing*, was published in 1994.

He joined Ashridge Management College after twenty years experience as a manager and director in marketing, sales and general management. He worked initially in the motor industry and subsequently for a French company in the leisure sector. He spent eight years with Grand Metropolitan at operating company board level, later moving to TSB Bank, where his final position was Director of Marketing Services.

He speaks internationally at conferences and seminars and has an enthusiasm for helping organisations create competitive advantage through long-term customer relationships.

Contents

Acknowledgements

My first acknowledgement is to the participants I have met on development programmes and seminars, especially at Ashridge Management College, Universitätsseminar der Wirtschaft at Schloss Gracht in Germany, the Swedish Institute of Management, the University of Michigan USA and OSDE Binario in Buenos Aires, Argentina. For all your questions, challenges, suggestions and contributions, I thank you warmly.

My second acknowledgement is to the busy and successful practitioners who have taken time away from their exemplary relationships with customers to talk to me about their formulae in this elusive skill. In particular, I must thank the following people: David Blohm of Smarterkids, Lynne Roach-Hildebrande and Stephan Chase at Marriott International, not forgetting the contribution of Dawn Booth and her colleagues, Randy Freeman and Kieran Coulton of Rockwell Automation, Mike Foley and Lora Flewelling of REI in Kent, Washington State. I also want to thank Remko Goudappel of DSM in the Netherlands, George Levvy, Jane Burns, Laura Simons and Brian Dickie of the MND Association, Stuart Turnbull and Kim Ashford of Kwik-Fit, Martin Hudson of St Paul International Insurance and Mats Nordlander of Papyrus, Gothenburg, Sweden.

My third acknowledgement is to David Hennessesy of Babson College, Wellesley, Massachusetts who gave guidance, hospitality and introductions to support my research in the USA. I must also thank my Ashridge colleagues, including the team in the Ashridge Learning Resource Centre who trawled journals on my behalf and proposed suggestions for further reading.

I appreciate the permission of Peter Barker of PricewaterhouseCoopers to quote the results of the Financial Times/PricewaterhouseCoopers World's Most Respected Companies survey and also Hilary Osmend of The Gallup Organisation who allowed me to quote the copyright 'Q12 advantage'.

Richard Stagg and Stephen Partridge of FT Prentice Hall have given me encouragement and solid advice throughout.

Chris, my wife, again has proved a linchpin in researching examples, developing the themes with me and reading and revising every chapter. Thank you.

Finally, despite all the teamwork, advice and support, the views expressed and the mistakes are entirely my own.

R elationships based on reality are essential for long-term business success. This section identifies eight characteristics of real personal relationships and uses them to provide a model for building a living commercial relationship. It recommends focusing this approach on the most valuable customers

There are four chapters;

- Relationship reality: an introduction and overview.
- Business challenge, relationship solution? How long-term relationships can address business challenges.
- New relationships – hidden costs: the costs involved in new relationships and how to gain a payback.
- Existing customers – hidden value: applying Pareto's Law to identify the Customers that Count.

It is 2 January. The Chief Executive Officer puts down his copy of *The Economist*'s annual publication of predictions for the world in the next 12 months. He gazes out of his panoramic window in the John Hancock Tower and reflects on the competitive pressures. He wonders: 'How the heck can we stay ahead?'

The challenge: complexity, choice and competition.

The solution: building long-term customer relationships. As a solution, it is easy to say and hard to deliver. New thinking is needed.

Securing customers through long-term loyalty is a key driver for organizational profit streams, and the value of repeat business is clear. Organizations now need practical steps to help them achieve that loyalty. A new spin on loyalty is coming from an interest in customer relationship management (CRM), or data-driven optimization of customer relationships. This book builds on current thinking in CRM and goes further to provide two practical approaches:

1 **Living relationships.** We can learn from living relationships between individuals. The human characteristics that we seek in our personal dealings can be applied to customers to provide a rich interchange for both parties that is mutually beneficial. We all enjoy the companionship of like-minded folk. Customers will naturally appreciate an involvement with like-minded suppliers. In the future, customers will be captivated by human characteristics, rather than simply captured through database technologies. This book presents an eight-point life plan to make relationships real.

Building relationships on a human model is resource intensive. Therefore, how can it be applied to every customer, and still provide a realistic return? The answer is simple: you do not need to apply the approach to all customers.

2 **Focus on the most valuable customers.** Most businesses discover that the top 20 per cent of their customers normally provide 75–90 per cent of profits. This approach uses the 80/20 principle to focus loyalty,

building on the small number of customers who provide the bulk of the profits. Note that the most valuable customers may not necessarily be the largest customers, some of whom may be contributing very slender margins. For 80 per cent of the customers, the performance must be good. For the priority 20 per cent of customers, the performance must be brilliant (*see* Fig. 1.1). This book is dedicated to brilliance for the most valuable customers.

- **Brilliance**
  for the most valuable
  20% of your customers

- **Good performance**
  for the remaining 80%
  of your customers

Figure 1.1 Focused brilliance

Using the quantified 'hard' data from CRM to distinguish the best customers, enlightened organizations will turn to 'soft' virtues to develop beneficial relationships with these 'Customers that Count'.

The structure of the book

The book is structured in four sections (*see* Fig. 1.2).

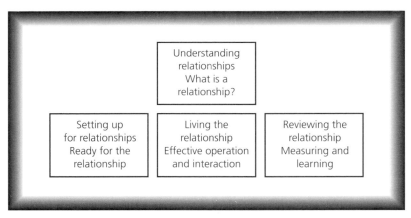

Understanding
relationships
What is a
relationship?

Setting up
for relationships
Ready for the
relationship

Living the
relationship
Effective operation
and interaction

Reviewing the
relationship
Measuring and
learning

Figure 1.2 Customers that Count

What is a relationship?

In Part I we focus on understanding relationships. This first section explains relationship reality and uncovers customers' expectations of a relationship on a personal level. We identify translatable requirements for a commercial context. There are examples from Recreational Equipment Inc., leading retailers of outdoor gear in the USA, and Kwik-Fit, one of Europe's best-regarded car service centres. This section also identifies costs of acquiring new customers and contrasts them with the value of existing customers.

Setting up for relationships

In successful human interactions, there is normally some forethought and preparation before embarking on a relationship. Part II covers setting up for the relationship. This implies detailed attention:

- strategic preparation: establishing the right pattern with stakeholders, including employees, investors, distributors and suppliers;
- selecting the right customers: the identification and matching process.

We see how Milwaukee-based Rockwell Automation – world leaders in factory automation – focuses attention on its best customers.

Living the relationship

Then there is the experience of the relationship itself, with all the involvement and interchanges that this entails. Part III is about living the relationship and applying lessons of real personal relationships to the aspects of commercial relationships:

The customer wants	How the organization meets this
Reliable performance	Training and retaining staff; systems and standards for consistency and recovery
Trust	Respecting confidences and privacy
Recognition	Full customer introduction, updates, database and training
Accessibility	Convenience and two-way communications
Service/assistance	Respecting time, expertise and responsiveness
Education	Anticipating needs, and providing guidance and advice
Preference	Fair pricing and appropriate priority
Individuality	Reassurance and unique brand values

We see examples of best practice from Marriott International and Smarterkids.com in the USA, Papyrus, a major paper merchant in 13 European countries, and Horlicks in India.

Reviewing the relationship

And finally, to ensure that harmony continues, there are periods of review and reflection. Part IV is an overview describing:

- measurement of growth, stimulating word-of-mouth marketing;
- barriers to exit: how to build switching costs;
- lessons from failed relationships, including when and how to sack customers;
- mutual interest.

This section is illustrated with examples from Dutch-based DSM Polypropylene and the UK charity, Motor Neurone Disease Association.

The conclusion is that success comes from focusing on business-critical customers. Focus means building relationships. The quality and history of your relations with your customers is your only true competitive advantage – everything else can be copied. Successful relationships are non-exploitative and exemplify large aspects of mutual interest.

The quality and history of your relations with your customers is your only true competitive advantage.

How to use the book

Each stage of the book is illustrated with examples from different industries and markets. These are designed to demonstrate good practice. Often the best learning comes from another industry, so a case example concludes each chapter. Examples enter memory faster than principles. They are also easier to share and can convince others of the wisdom and worth of the idea – the fact that it works in the real world speeds acceptance elsewhere.

My experience at Ashridge Management College has shown me that ideas root most effectively when they are applied in a practical context. The more quickly you can link an idea to a live business issue, the faster it will be understood, absorbed and implemented. Therefore each chapter ends with a suggested exercise. It is an immediate way in which the conclusions of the chapter can be applied to the reader's business. You have the option to skip the exercises, but I recommend instead that you take time to work through the exercises and envisage the concepts in practice in your organization.

Different aspects of the theme of the book will intrigue different readers. I have therefore suggested follow-up reading for particular sections so interest can be taken further.

Theme: Relationship reality	Case example

Kwik-Fit

Sir Tom Farmer opened the first Kwik-Fit centre in MacDonald Road in Edinburgh in 1971. Now, owned by Ford Motor Company and with Sir Tom Farmer as Chairman, Kwik-Fit is one of the world's largest automotive service operations with more than 2300 service points across Europe. Over 10 000 employees replace the tyres, exhausts and brakes of 8 million motorists in England, Wales, Scotland, Ireland, Holland, Belgium, Switzerland, Germany, Poland, Spain and France. Growing rapidly, the target is 5000 outlets by 2005.

Kwik-Fit was rated the best firm in the UK for managing relationships with customers, according to research sponsored by CRM consultants, Round. The survey, published in February 2000, was conducted by the market research organization AC Nielsen MEAL and took the opinions of 300 CRM professionals. Kwik-Fit outperformed Amazon, Citibank, Tesco Direct and Direct Line Insurance to take the top slot in the survey.

Kwik-Fit is well prepared for a relationship with customers. Historically the reputation of the automotive after-market has been tarnished by back-street car mechanics, exploiting the ignorance of motorists. Kwik-Fit has worked tirelessly to counter this by developing and training staff to deliver absolute reliability, in an open and transparent manner. Stuart Turnbull, a director of Kwik-Fit, explained to me that through Kwik-Fit's three training centres in the UK and Holland and a purpose-built hi-tech multimedia training academy, Kwik-Fit people can work towards nationally recognized qualifications that complement Kwik-Fit's bespoke training programmes.

Service centres are well located with easy access. Availability of tyres and components is impressive, courtesy of ISO 9002 accredited systems. Every member of staff knows the company objective: 100 per cent customer delight.

To delight customers in a living relationship, Kwik-Fit encourages interaction. In all my own dealings with their centres, I note that the fitters rapidly acknowledge your arrival and make you welcome. Promises are kept, and on subsequent visits I am recognized. It is easy to get in touch; the care-line 0800 number is answered promptly, and prepaid cards addressed to Chairman Sir Tom Farmer are readily available in Kwik-Fit centres for those customers who prefer to make written contact.

Kwik-Fit publicizes a code of practice (*see* Fig. 1.3), which is displayed in service centres and on its website, www.kwikfit.com. This is designed to address all the concerns of the motorist, male or female, young or old, confident or novice, and to set realistic expectations against which they can be judged.

The people in our centre will always:
- Treat your vehicle with care and always fit protective seat covers.
- Ensure your vehicle is inspected by a technically qualified staff member.
- Examine the vehicle with you and give an honest appraisal of the work required.
- Give you a binding quotation which includes all associated charges prior to work commencing.
- Ensure you are aware that an non-exchange part or component removed from your vehicle is available for you to take away.
- Ensure that all work is carried out according to the company's laid-down procedures.
- Inform you immediately of any complications or delays.
- Ensure that all completed work is checked by a technically competent staff member.
- Offer to inspect the finished work with you at the time of delivery.

Figure 1.3 Kwik-Fit code of practice

Kwik-Fit also conscientiously reviews its relationships. Each week it calls customers to check that it is delivering consistently against its code of practice and achieving customer delight. Stuart Turnbull told me 'Our customer-service unit contacts more than 7000 customers a day, within 72 hours of their visit to a Kwik-Fit centre to ensure they were fully satisfied with the service they received'. Sir Tom Farmer (2000) has written: 'Feedback indicates that 98.2 per cent are satisfied with the service. From the other 1.8 per cent, most people are not critical of the service, but have some valid observations to make.'

Such is Kwik-Fit's reputation that it has been able to build on this relationship and extend its services by offering car insurance. The success of this business extension is proof that it has taken trust in its trade to a new height.

Finally, the advertising brings the relationship to life by highlighting the expertise of the people that customers will meet: 'You can't get better than a Kwik-Fit fitter'.

Exercise 1 How strong is your loyalty edge? — Exercises

1 List your customers in value sequence (by profit contribution).

2 Focus on the top 20 customers.

3 Consider each customer in turn.

4 Rank the customer on a 1–5 scale:

- Certain to be a customer in three years' time: 5 points
- Likely to be a customer in three years' time: 4 points
- No reason why this customer should move: 3 points
- Hard to assess this customer's loyalty: 2 points
- Unlikely to be a customer in three years: 1 point
- Customer future in jeopardy: 0 points

5 Add the points and score out of 100 maximum points. How strong is your loyalty edge?

Further reading and references

Cram, Tony (1996) *The Power of Relationship Marketing*, Financial Times Pitman.

The Economist (2000) *The World in 2001*.

Farmer, Sir Tom (2000) 'The Quest for Customer Delight', *Market Leader*, Spring.

Hamel, Gary (2000) *Leading the Revolution*, Harvard Business School Press.

She furrowed her brow, and pondered. 'Loyalty', she said out loud. She thought some more. These questionnaires could be tricky. 'Who am I loyal to?' she asked, reading the question again. Then she began to write some family names, paused, and then she added two school friends. She wrote the trading name of her employer, reflected, and then erased this, replacing it with her boss's name. There were a good number of lines remaining. Who else? Aha, her doctor, her dentist and another professional. A thought flashed through her mind: how about the guy who services her car, and her travel agent? No, that was a different issue.

Businesses are facing challenges from new market forces, increasing competitive intensity and changing customer needs. Loyalty from customers can support companies through the maelstrom. New techniques like customer relationship management (CRM) seem to promise higher levels of allegiance, and build on current loyalty marketing schemes. However, loyalty is a result, not a process, and therefore difficult to manage. Alternatively, by focusing on characteristics of effective personal relationships, we can build a living commercial relationship.

Business challenge

Many businesses see the first decade of the twenty-first century as a time of opportunity and threat. Companies must either take the high ground with new approaches, revitalized strategies and enterprising initiatives, or they risk perishing. The safe middle ground has disappeared. Growth through new ideas is one extreme; takeover, bankruptcy or market exit is the other extreme. Therefore companies must take account of any new development, lest it provide their competitors with a knockout blow. Currently, customer relationship management is the new idea.

Customer relationship management

Customer relationship management is defined by Wundermann Cato Johnson (part of Young & Rubicam Inc.) as 'an integrated approach to maximizing customer value through the differential management of customer relationships'. Essentially CRM has two aspects: analysis and action. It is a data-driven approach to identify and profile customers. Often data warehouses will be deployed to analyze huge number of transactions to determine in which group a customer should be placed. The result is that the company is able to manage customers in different ways. The communication with the customer will be integrated across all the points of contact. Resources will be deployed effectively and so generate maximum profit for the company (*see* Fig. 2.1).

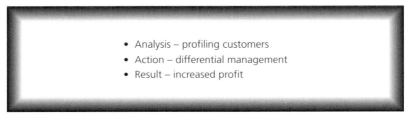

- Analysis – profiling customers
- Action – differential management
- Result – increased profit

Figure 2.1 Customer relationship management

CRM advocates claim that it provides the answer to business security and success through achieving customer loyalty. For example, Siebel is working very hard to convey business benefits of applications and services. In an advertisement for its applications software, in *The New York Times* of 11 July 2000, Siebel published a convincing survey. Between January 1995 and December 1999 organizations that had purchased at least $500 000 worth of 'Siebel e-business application', outperformed the Standard & Poors 500 index by 85 per cent. A separate survey showed improvements in customer satisfaction, revenue growth and employee productivity.

Solutions to big challenges are normally expensive. CRM is no exception. A survey by Cap Gemini and International Data Corporation reported in *Premier Content* (18 January 2000) by Dermot McGrath, found that large companies spend an average of $3.1 million on hardware, software and services for CRM projects.

Taking on political and economic threats

The CRM solution promises to minimize the threat of more competitive markets brought by political change, including the expansion of the

European Union, the growth of Mercosur in South America, promises of a North American Free Trade area and burgeoning potential of Asean (Association of South-East Asian Nations). How better to respond to newer, bigger trade groupings bringing more competitors, than with a strategy to secure customers through loyalty?

The solution offers protection against the downswings of the economic cycle – surely a customer relationship strategy can mitigate the worst of impending downturns. Optimists heralding the launch of the euro and the move in South America to tie currencies to the dollar, expect that these trends will bring more competition and better value for customers. Locking customers in through relationship strategies must be a valid commercial response.

Responding to social and technological change

CRM can ride the risks and opportunities of social changes, for example the increasing career opportunities and independence for women, especially in Asia, and the surging growth in the economic power of children either directly or indirectly. CRM can foresee rapid expansion in the number of retired people with energetic lifestyles funded by pensions and savings. With every competitor seeking these new categories of customer, how does a company differentiate from the range of rival suppliers? Product differences are replicable, service touches can be copied, and advertisements are neutralized by increasing marketing cynicism. Does it all come down to price, or is there an opportunity to create loyalty?

The CRM solution implies that technological advances are not so dangerous. If every change threatens the status quo for incumbent suppliers, CRM can identify the changes to behaviour patterns and lifestyles stimulated by, for example WAP phones, voicemail, laptops, PlayStation2 consoles, new drugs or therapies and new media. Armed with database analysis, expert modelling and trend projections, customer relationship management promises to provide a commercial response to these technological destabilizers.

CRM takes on the threat of a global internet market of information, goods and services. Every customer of every organization is, at a click, able to seek competitor offerings, globally. For example in consumer products, search engines like www.rusure.com will take a specification and comprehensively trawl vendor sites, simply presenting the enquirer with a supplier list in lowest price sequence. Has the economists' 'perfect market' arrived? Is price the only discriminator on the web? Or can CRM build brand relationships through customer recognition, site tailoring and personalized service to overcome web-enabled disloyalty?

Facing three types of competitor

CRM promises a response to these macro-environmental forces that are impacting on market structures. In addition, it also tackles the three trends in competitive response. First, in the face of the trend to consolidation across industries, and across countries, it protects the niche. For example in the automotive market, Ford Motor Company has acquired manufacturers like Aston Martin, Jaguar, Land Rover, Volvo, and a link with Mazda. In another camp Volkswagen has captured Lamborghini, Bentley, SEAT and Skoda. Eleven companies consolidated into two. For an automotive competitor, this feels like the arrival of two vicious sharks. Yet perhaps intelligent customer relationships based on understanding can defend against the brawn of mega-competitors.

Trend two is the arrival of piranhas: a host of tiny, very responsive, rapidly moving and dangerous competitors. None of the piranhas expect to put the major players out of business, but they will each bite a portion of market share from them. The biggest threat to McDonald's, Burger King and Pizza Hut may be the competitor on the pie chart called 'other'. Local entrepreneurial restaurateurs in every market place are their piranhas.

The third competitive trend is the category-leaping competitor. Virgin was a force in record retailing that entered the airline and financial service businesses. In the UK the trusted pharmacy chain, Boots, vaulted into a competitive position among opticians. In the USA, GE originated as a manufacturer of electrical equipment, and now threatens long-established businesses in financial and services markets. Microsoft devises software and now runs one of the busiest travel agencies (www.expedia.co.uk) on the web. These are sea hawks who swoop into a market from another dimension. How do you respond to all three types of competitor? Is the answer as simple as investing in CRM?

Time-pressured customers

The market forces and the competitive context have an impact on customers and their behaviours. Time has become a key competitive dimension, since the most valuable consumers find huge pressure on their time. Pressures come from longer working hours, more travel, more leisure temptations and the demands of fragmenting families. Thus customers expect suppliers to meet their product and service needs in a time-sensitive fashion. In a business-to- business context, delayering, downsizing, wider spans of control and reduced administrative support mean that business time is even more pressured. Here are genuine opportunities for systems that solve a genuine customer problem.

Customers expect suppliers to meet their product and service needs in a time-sensitive fashion.

The choice explosion means that a guide to selection is an emergent need in business and consumer markets. In every market from ice-cream flavours to office furniture, the variety and range of options is immense and growing. Until its closure in March 2001, Chemdex, the life-sciences marketplace, offered 1.7 million products from 2200 suppliers. The world's motor manufacturers could produce cars for 24 months without making two identical models. Customers need help. Again, this need may be met through a relationship with a supplier who knows the market and knows the customer.

So CRM has the answer

It all seems so simple. CRM appears to be the solution to new market forces, greater competitive intensity and changing customer needs. It is omnipresent: it is a favoured topic in management textbooks, MBA pro-grammes dissect it and the business pages of broadsheet newspapers make frequent references to forthcoming CRM strategies. CRM software is one of the fastest growing sectors. According to the respected research organi-zation, Meta Group, the 2000 largest companies in the world collectively will spend $10 billion per year on CRM solutions by 2003. Most business plans feature promises of enhanced customer relationships, and takeovers are justified on the basis of acquiring customer bases.

Or part of the answer?

Yet, mirage-like, now you see it now you don't. When you focus more intently and seek wider evidence across the board of effective relationship management, it is hard to prove. How much of the $1.5 billion spent on CRM software two years ago is delivering against expectation?

We saw the same promise made by relationship marketing ten years ago. There was a stark gap between the vision of relationship marketing and the reality. Customers are not gleefully extolling a sense of warmth and under-standing across their commercial relationships. Companies are not simpering complacently over the impregnable loyalty of their customers.

An alarm bell was sounded in 1998 in the *Harvard Business Review* arti-cle, 'Preventing the Premature Death of Relationship Marketing' by Susan Fournier, Susan Dobscha and David Glen Mick. The article highlighted the often exploitative use of customer data in the name of relationship market-ing. In a nutshell, they claimed that in relationships between customer and company the balance between giving and getting is skewed to the company. Companies ask for the friendship, loyalty and respect of their customers. All too often the company fails to reciprocate with friendship, loyalty and respect in return.

15

Where CRM is falling short

Friends share information openly and confide personal facts. In the name of CRM, companies are gathering ever-greater amounts of personal data on customers. Available for purchase, there are assumptions about every household's total income, its charitable-donation pattern, the age, sex, clothing sizes, occupation, leisure pursuits, alcohol consumption and media preferences of the residents. It is estimated that some details of every UK household are processed 40 times each working day. The data exchange is not mutual. Neither is it dedicated to creating relationships. Rather the individual personal data determines where and when to intrude in the consumer's life for the best probability of making a sale. And the same applies to business-to-business marketing. Knowledge of the right predictive dimensions can result in selecting one day of the week over another and so increase a company's prospects of a successful direct mailing three-fold. This is not building a relationship. Often it is screening of potential customers to exclude the worst prospects and to define the most opportune time and method of approach for the remainder.

CRM is falling short where it is technology driven, customer intrusive and, above all, company centric. Company centric means that the focus of the company activity is on the benefit of the customer relationship to the company. It asks, how can we use our knowledge of the customer to drive down company costs, to drive up company volumes and margins?

This is where relationship strategies are missing an opportunity. The essence of a true relationship is a benefit to both parties. The mutually beneficial aspects of relationship marketing are slipping out of sight. To provide a balancing mutuality, we need to address the customer-centric aspects. What does the customer want, need and expect from a relationship with a company? Only by combining an understanding of the interests of both parties can we identify the mutual meeting of needs, which epitomizes a good relationship.

Delivering value to the customer

It is the determination to provide continuous value to customers that underpins the relationship. There are of course, different approaches to giving customers value. Value to the customer can be expressed as the sum of benefits minus the price (*see* Fig. 2.2). This equation indicates alternative strategies to providing value to customers. Some organizations will focus on costs, endeavouring to lower their own costs in order to reduce prices for their customers and hence increase the perception of value. They might also look at the costs incurred by customers in the transaction and target a reduction. For example, holding inventory is a cost to the customer. If organizations are able to provide just-in-time delivery this cuts inventory and lowers the customer's cost.

An alternative scenario to build value is to focus on benefits and to enhance the perceived benefits gained by customers. This could be achieved through improved product performance, the addition of services and support, consulting, information and advice, so leading to tailored offerings.

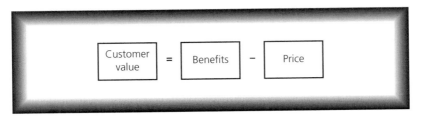

Figure 2.2 Value to the customer

Setting customer expectations

For both approaches to providing value, it is vital that customer expectations are set correctly. In the cost-driven organization, which seeks to provide the benefit of the lowest price, there may be compromises on the degree of personalization and the degree that individual information will result in tailored actions. In this instance, the organization should focus on the message of cost benefit, rather than promise a relationship it cannot deliver. Nevertheless, there are ample opportunities to apply the lessons of personal contacts to a commercial context. The organization may use the ideas and techniques selectively to give outstanding convenience at an accessible price level.

For organizations seeking to excel through offering higher benefits, there will be immediately applicable lessons across the spectrum of relationship building. It is possible to manage companies to provide value to customers. Confidence in receiving future value can result in loyalty.

What is loyalty?

Loyalty, however, is often misunderstood in organizations. Many financial institutions quote the extent of their loyal customers, confusing inertia with loyalty. There is an important distinction: inertia or the tendency to repurchase from a current supplier is not the same as loyalty. Some purchasers will continue to buy through indifference, laziness, or doubts about alternatives, but none of these patterns should be identified as loyalty. The business provided by these customers is always at risk. Given a choice, or stimulated to change, they may defect to rival suppliers. If they are locked in and somehow unable to transfer their custom, they may become negative ambassadors, warning other purchasers away. Finally, as indifferent buyers, they may deliberately withhold useful information and waste company resources.

Loyalty is an emotional bonding – a willingness to associate with and support a relationship. It is an affective influence, based on respect and trust. Where repurchase is a type of behaviour, loyalty is a state of mind. Thus, loyalty schemes such as gifts, incentives and plastic cards can act as an incentive for repeat purchasing. In themselves, they do not engender loyalty. The points awarded should rather be seen as form of 'thank you' or payment for the provision of data. WH Smith, a UK-based bookseller and stationer, uses the data obtained from its ClubCard to target future offers, minimizing customer annoyance and maximizing their own sales. A targeted mailing for a Delia Smith cookery book achieved a commendable take-up of 7 per cent.

Incentivizing repeat purchase in business to business

In the business-to-business arena, points-based reward schemes can play a part in managing change. Toshiba has a division in the UK selling air-conditioning equipment. A case study in *Marketing Direct* (October 1998) showed how Toshiba used a points-based reward scheme to support its switch from distribution to dealing directly with installers. The main thrust of its thinking was to help the installers build their businesses. To ensure the new approach was successful, Toshiba added a three-tier loyalty scheme with points being redeemable against product. This rewarded repeat business from installers.

Shaping behaviour

Since 1 May 1981, when American Airlines launched the first frequent flier card, points-based schemes have been used to influence the behaviour of customers. For example, a number of e-commerce websites use incentives to shape behaviour. One of the devices used is MyPoints. This is a US-based web reward scheme with a UK and Japanese presence, whose points are collected by over 8 million members. Numerous websites issue points for surfers browsing their site, reading e-mails and completing questionnaires. Another internet loyalty scheme is www.beenz.com. This UK-based international incentive operation sees itself as a web currency. For example, visitors to the web site of Honda UK who book a test drive on line will earn 50 'beenz' and after the drive takes place they gain another 3000 'beenz'. These may be redeemed for DVDs, sports goods, holidays and clothing. The intent of both these operations is to encourage web surfers to change their behaviour in various ways. Companies may wish customers to view certain offers, buy a product on line, commit online to subsequent meetings, or provide an e-mail addresses for future targeting.

Loyalty cards can shape short-term behaviour. Cards may be an access point to priority service or tailored requirements. They may provide a tangible link and a brand reminder of a powerful relationship. But in their own right they do not create loyalty.

What drives loyalty – dimensions of relationships

True loyalty stems from a relationship with depth and warmth. In the human model of relationships, there are four dimensions (*see* Fig. 2.3). A successful personal relationship tends to operate at the deeper end of the first scale and the warmer end of the second scale. However, as far as balance is concerned, a personal relationship can range over the entire scale – it is not necessary that both partners are equal. Similarly, a good personal relationship may be task based, social or a combination of the two.

The thesis of this book is that the nature of human relationships provides a model for creating business loyalty. Applying this theory to a business context, let us look at the four dimensions:

The nature of human relationships provide a model for creating business loyalty.

Depth	Deep	Shallow	Superficial
Warmth	Affectionate	Neutral	Competitive
Balance	Equal	Complimentary	Unequal
Basis	Task-based	Multi-functional	Social

Figure 2.3 Relationship dimensions

- **Depth**. Loyal business relationships are deep rather than shallow. Superficiality does not bring loyalty. However, where a business relationship is based on convenience and low price, this can result in long-term repurchase, provided that a lower-cost or more convenient alternative does not intrude.

- **Warmth**. Loyal business relationships operate in the neutral to affectionate spectrum. These could be characterized as informal through to professional and formal. Rivalry and competition between supplier and buyer can be damaging where mutual benefit may be disregarded.

- **Balance**. As with personal connections, even balance is not necessary. However, where there is imbalance, the outcome should not be exploitative. This is not loyalty.

- **Basis**. Loyal business relationships may be solely task based or multi-functional (if they begin to include an appropriate element of social contact).

Characteristics of personal relationships

There are consistent characteristics of effective personal relationships:

- **Knowledge**. They are based on reality and are kept current by exchanges of information, so that each party has an up-to-date knowledge of the other.

- **Application**. This knowledge is not passively held, rather it is actively used. For example, if one party knows the other has a passion for classic Ferrari sports cars, they will pass on information of events, buy copies of magazines featuring the Ferrari Testarossa and introduce them to other fast car fans.

- **Interactive**. There is a two-way dialogue, with listening as well as talking, questions and answers.

- **Long term**. Effective relationships are normally based on the assumption that they are long term and continuous. Short-term connections are often exploitative.

- **Mutually beneficial**. Each party seeks to benefit the other, as well as looking after their own interests.

Relationship reality

An organization promulgating a strategy based on customer/supplier loyalty would extend CRM to embrace the human elements of a relationship. Applying this personal model to a business context, we can say that a living customer relationship should be:

The consistent application of up-to-date knowledge of selected customers, to product and service design, which is communicated interactively, in order to develop a continuous and long-term relationship that is mutually beneficial.

This book is about how to apply the personal-relationship blueprint to a commercial context in order to build strong, durable mutual relationships in a business-to-business or consumer market, providing value to customers through goods or services or both, locally, nationally or multi-nationally.

So what do customers expect?

There are eight factors that a customer seeks in a living relationship with a supplier (*see* Fig. 2.4). Together with the product or service sought, these combine to provide superior value to the customer.

- Reliability – you keep your promises
- Trust – I have confidence in you
- Recognition – you remember my needs
- Accessibility – we can communicate
- Service/assistance – you manage my time effectively
- Education – you keep me up to date
- Preference – I get fair prices and priority
- Individuality – I like to associate myself with you

Figure 2.4 Living the relationship

1 **Reliable performance**. Dependability is a fundamental benefit sought by customers. It is the starting point of a relationship. Regardless of the exhortations in management texts to exceed expectations, most customers would willingly settle for having their expectations met, provided this occurred every time. The Swiss are one of the nations most positively disposed to public transport. It would be reasonable to assert that in general Swiss travellers feel they have a relationship with the transport provider. The seats – often unpadded wooden benches – are not luxurious. The drivers and conductors are not joke-telling entertainers. There are no free cartoon character models for children.

There are no lucky draws or surprise promotions. Simply the service can be relied on, morning and night, winter and summer, fair weather and inclement. The train scheduled to arrive for a bus or boat connection will be there on time. Dependability is critical.

Promises must be kept, including promises in advertising. The customers of an organization normally consider themselves close to the supplier and expect that this will result in truthful information. They suspect that advertising puffery may be used to attract the attention of potential new customers, but the converted should have straightforward honest communications. This truth might be expressed in delivery information, completeness of service support and balanced evidence supporting product advantages. Obviously, direct falsehoods are utterly unacceptable. But many organizations find it acceptable to use information selectively – presenting the literal truth, while omitting or concealing shortcomings.

2 **Trust**. When entering a commercial relationship with an organization, a customer feels that there should be a level of mutual trust. The supplier may provide goods on credit and the customer proves trustworthy by making the payment. The customer is trusted to provide truthful information about themselves – for example, how long they have resided at/operated from the delivery address? And how is trust manifested in return? Of course the company is trusted to make deliveries of product which is of merchantable quality. Beyond this the customer may believe that the information provided on forms headed 'confidential' will retain the expected secrecy. Yet companies sell customer data to other organizations for marketing purposes. Credit-card transaction levels by category may be bought in some countries. Data-literate customers in the USA are now deliberately choosing the anonymity of cash to make purchases like liquor, where they do not want the facts of their consumption levels to be commercially available.

3 **Recognition**. If you have a friend and meet them anew, then you recognize them and reconfirm the friendship by referring to shared memories of experience in the past. Why should a commercial relationship not echo the same characteristics? When a guest returns to a hotel the self-same form is presented to him or her for a new check-in. Could not the form be replaced by a welcome and an invitation to confirm that the information held is still current? The most damaging aspect of a commercial relationship is when an expected piece of recognition fails to happen. For example, when a bank mails a letter offering its credit card to someone already holding that particular card, a doubt is sown as to the quality of data handling. If they do not know I have an account, can I trust them to keep the account amounts

accurately? The best relationships come when previous interest is recorded – many e-commerce websites are now recalling previous browsing and creating pathways driven by customer patterns of interest.

4 **Accessibility**. The customer wants to be able to contact the supplier at all reasonable times. This may be for products or services or simply for information about products or services already obtained or which may be purchased in the future. The times that are reasonable depend on the market assumptions of the product and country context. In a good supplier relationship the customers are able to select their preferred media of communication: website, telephone, face to face, automatic or personal service and so on. They have access. In the worst examples, access is constrained into automated pre-determined times and channels. When the voice-recording on a Canadian furniture store information line tells you that your custom is appreciated and you are thirty-seventh in the queue, how accessible does the retailer feel to the enquirer?

5 **Service and assistance**. The standard and speed of service is a consistent customer issue. It is the defining moment in a relationship. The purchase has been made – there is a critical incident where help is required. If it is forthcoming then the value of the relationship has been demonstrated. A friend in need is a friend indeed. Is the speed and completeness of service in line with expectation?

6 **Education**. The customer acknowledges the expertise of the supplier and hopes to gain the benefit of this through considerate guidance and advice. A good supplier guides customers. Depending on the product or service, the best suppliers advise on how best to work together, pre-purchase preparation, recommended order sizes, selection techniques, matching opportunities, fitness for use, how to get the best out of the product, and even final disposal of the product. With the enormous flexibility of twenty-first-century printing techniques, French car manufacturers can personalize mailings, magazines and electronic communications to their potential customers. Yet they produce a single manual for each model range and expect the drivers to deduce which sections apply to the particular model they are driving.

Customers appreciate being kept informed where the communication is relevant to them and appropriately timed. And if asked they are normally well able to indicate what is or is not appropriate. Understanding a customer's business peaks and quiet times, and being aware of a private customer's lifestyle will point to reasonable communication windows. However, customers resent being treated as cannon fodder. An example of this occurs with telemarketing, where a high level of training and reward to sales staff can create a positive sales return on expenditures. But these intrusive marketing methods damage the relationship. Poor use of this communications technique jeopardizes its effectiveness.

7 **Preference**. When customers who are faced with the option of spreading their purchases between various suppliers choose to place their purchases with one supplier, they like this behaviour to be recognized and to be rewarded in some emotional or tangible manner. Likewise, when they have the possibility of moving from one supplier to another for each successive purchase, they appreciate reward for this choice. Customers often have an innate sense of fairness, and when they are aware of the significant scale of their purchases they aspire to preferential treatment based on their value. They like to see recognition extended to a real appreciation of worth compared with other customers served.

8 **Individuality and brand association**. Finally, customers may enjoy the benefits of association with particular brands that make a statement about lifestyle, position, worthiness, status or other brand values. Like friends, brands have their idiosyncrasies and these individual characteristics need to come to the fore in relationships. You would expect letters, telephone calls or publicity material to be radically different between *The Boston Globe*, *The New York Times* and *The Enquirer* – each will have its own distinctive tone of voice. Yet the sector currently spending most on CRM is financial services where many bank brands seem indistinguishable from each other.

The conclusion from this list of expectations sought by customers is that the best commercial relationships reflect the better characteristics of personal relationships. If CRM is to be meaningful to customers it must go beyond database modelling and cost-effective customer management and be based on the behaviours associated with human relationships. A supplier must behave as a 'friend'.

The best commercial relationship reflect the better characteristics of personal relationships.

Behaving like a friend

In their book *The Anatomy of Relationships*, Michael Argyle and Monika Henderson define friends as: 'people who are liked, whose company is enjoyed, who share interests and activities, who are helpful and understanding, who can be trusted, with whom one feels comfortable and who will be emotionally supportive'. The authors researched the concept of friendship extensively and derived commonly accepted assumptions about what friends do and do not do. They expressed their research conclusions as 17 rules of friendship. The first three could apply strongly to commercial relationships:

1 Volunteer help in time of need – the customer's expectations of service.

2 Respect the friend's privacy – the unacceptability of intrusive marketing.

3 Keep confidences – the concept of trust.

A person who behaves as a true friend is captivating. Companies must transform their thinking about CRM. The leap is from endeavouring to capture customers towards captivating customers with consideration. The theme of this book is that suppliers are able to captivate customers when they bring relationships to life. Focusing on living behaviours within commercial relationships, the book develops a checklist for organizations eager to implement twenty-first century relationship marketing.

Theme: Living relationships	Case example

Recreational Equipment Inc.

A company epitomizing relationships built with human characteristics is Recreational Equipment Inc. Seattle-based REI is a co-operative that sells outdoor items such as kayaks, camping gear, boots, bikes and backpacks through around 60 retail stores in the USA, plus an e-business at www.rei.com, with an additional site at www.rei-outlet.com, for 'reliable outdoor gear at rock bottom prices'. In mid-2000 REI opened a Tokyo store, followed by a fully Japanese site transacting in yen and fulfilling through a Japan-based distribution centre.

The success of REI is based on the eight key factors in living relationships:

- **Reliability.** Disappointed in the quality of a mail-order ice axe, Seattle mountaineers Lloyd and Mary Anderson believed they could provide better. In 1938 they established a co-operative, buying collectively to provide best-value camping and climbing gear. As a co-operative, REI encourages shoppers to become members for a fee of $15. Mike Foley of REI told me:

  Much of the gear we sell is field tested by employees and by a committee of REI members. Gear is also run through lab tests – many first developed by REI. Selling only great gear that will help each individual customer have the great outdoor experience they are seeking is an important part of maintaining a relationship of trust with our members.

I myself can vouch for the reliable performance. The rainwear and canvas luggage I bought in 1979 is still performing well after more than two decades of use.

- **Trust.** Gearmail is an online service to keep members up to date on new products, sales and special events. When members sign up for Gearmail online, REI promise: 'We respect your privacy. We'll never make your e-mail address available to any other company or organization.'

- **Recognition.** Members own REI, elect the Board and receive a patronage refund each July of around 10 per cent of their annual purchases. Outstanding staff retention means that regular shoppers are recognized by staff members, who take an interest in their expeditions, activities and achievements. REI may even offer grants towards costs.

- **Accessibility.** At REI the management measures customer perceptions. On the exit door of each store is a feedback questionnaire inviting customers to rate the staff on a seven-point scale. For instance: 'The staff were accessible. I felt comfortable asking questions.' Every store has a customer-services desk, and computer kiosks allow customers to check availability, specifications or obtain technical advice. The website offers an introduction to REI in French, German, Japanese and Spanish, complete with international payment and shipping advice. Internationally there is an e-mail enquiry option, and in the USA there is a 1-800 (free help-line) number.

- **Service and assistance.** Staff are enthusiastic and expert in outdoor pursuits – for example, paddling, canoes and kayak, mountaineering and hiking. In the stores, wall displays show photographs of employees in action, and after five years employees become eligible for four-to eight-week sabbaticals with most pursuing an outdoor passion. REI always scores well in 'best place to work' surveys.

- **Educating customers.** Knowledgeable staff share their expertise. Fact sheets support the merchandise. Many stores offer programmes such as cycle maintenance or basic first-aid certification.

- **Preference.** Members receive early notice of sales and special deals. They are also offered 'try before you buy' kayak demonstrations in summer months.

- **Individuality and brand association.** The original passion for the products back in 1938 shines through as strongly as ever. Three examples: the first thing you see in the Framingham store is a rock-climbing wall for customers to use. The flagship Seattle store has a mountain bike test track. Other REI stores have a rainstorm room to check the rain-proofing of their storm wear. REI members are not 'managed', rather they feel captivated by a shared enthusiasm for the outdoors. It is a living relationship.

Exercise 2			Exercises

Using this checklist, how do you rank your closest friend, your bank and your dentist?

	Close friend	Bank	Dentist
1 Reliable performance			
2 Trust			
3 Recognition			
4 Accessibility			
5 Service/assistance			
6 Education/guidance			
7 Preference			
8 Individuality/brand			

Further reading and references

Argyle, Michael and Henderson, Monika (1990) *The Anatomy of Relationships*, Penguin Books.

Cram, Tony (2000) 'CRM – The Company is King' in *Handbook of Management*, Financial Times.

Fournier, S., Dobscha, S. and Mick, D.G. (1998) 'Preventing the Premature Death of Relationship Marketing' *Harvard Business Review*, January/February.

McKenna, Regis (1999) *Real Time*, Harvard Business School Press.

Newell, Frederick and Lemon, Katherine Newell (2001) *Wireless Rules*, McGraw-Hill.

As the Chief Executive Officer greeted the Executive Committee meeting, he wondered where things were going wrong in the current 'Capturing Competitor Customers' campaign. 'Triple C' had been running for two months and yet the figures were not looking good.

The Vice-President of Sales confirmed that prospective customers had responded warmly to the range of samples provided and universally had taken them away for analysis. He himself was on the way to meet the most significant of these prospects to sign an initial order for one particular line, having cancelled his existing appointments to be there at the win. The Vice-President of Manufacturing had authorized the downtime necessary for the line change to produce the new customer's first order. Full engineering support had been provided, transferred from energy-reducing insulation and efficiency project work. The Vice-President of Logistics assured that the warehouse was entirely up to date with 'Triple C' and vehicles were on standby to make the deliveries. As for the increase in forecast costs for the month, these were simply fluctuations – an up-front deposit had been required, as commercial storage was in scarce supply in the zone. The Vice-President of Finance had brought with her the credit-rating assessment of a new customer freshly received down the line. It endorsed the customer's creditworthiness, and she was calculating the impact on working capital of the large order, just placed. Experience told that new customers could take longer to settle simply because of the set up of new systems and authorizations. She was disappointed to report that the margins on the new business were below forecast because the competitor had matched their initial prices and free stock had been needed to clinch the deal.

Gradually, it became clear that every aspect of the new customer drive had in its own way added to the operating costs of the organization either directly or indirectly by diverting resources from existing programmes of cost saving. At the point of realization, the Chief Executive Officer's private line began ringing. It was the President of their largest customer, calling to ask courteously, but firmly, why his luncheon with the Vice-President of Sales had been cancelled at short notice. He said that he had particularly wanted to understand why a promised delivery had been delayed, and whether the market rumours of price reductions were true.

New customers always seem to be attractive. The benefits they will bring are readily envisaged in terms of higher volumes and larger market share. These advantages are real, but they need to be considered alongside the associated costs and consequences. Some of these are less obvious. There are ten costs of acquiring new customers and these must be taken into account when evaluating any new business. In this chapter each cost is explored in turn. There is also a five-step technique that looks at payback on monies invested in winning new customers.

Clients are gold, prospects are silver

It was Mike Cook, Chairman of Deloitte and Touche in USA, who said that 'Clients are gold and prospects are silver', meaning that any business must understand that the value of current customers is greater than that of potential customers. This is not to suggest that businesses should not seek new customers. For example, UK-based Saga Holidays dedicates itself to serving a niche market – originally offering vacation packages for the over 60s and now extending to those over 50 years of age. True, it must satisfy and retain its 'gold' clients, but if it did not also pursue 'silver' prospects, then its business life expectancy falls into line with the life expectancy of its customers. The key issue is the understanding of the relative worth of both 'gold' and 'silver', so maintaining a balance of priorities.

Different companies, different conclusions

Priorities will differ between companies. Michael Treacy and Fred Wiersema (1997) identify three distinct value disciplines, each of which provides value to customers in different ways:

- operational excellence – provision of standardized middle-of-the-market products with a low price and hassle-free service;
- product leadership – provision of the best performing product in the market through constant innovation;
- customer intimacy – cultivating customer relationships to provide the best solutions.

Treacy and Wiersema believe that companies succeed through focusing to excel in one discipline. Choosing one discipline does not mean abandoning the other disciplines; rather, it means focusing priority efforts in one area to lead competitors on that dimension, and being content to match or follow competitors in another area.

Clearly a company focusing on customer intimacy will place a higher value on existing customers in its strategic assessment. Standardized systems and transactions in a company focusing on operational excellence may mean that the balance is less critical. However, customer retention is still vital – these companies need volume sales to provide economies of scale. Finally, the company focusing on product leadership attracts and retains customers through product performance. It needs dialogue with loyal customers in order to follow changing needs and deliver product delight. Therefore all organizations need a clear picture of the relative importance of existing and new customers.

All organizations need a clear picture of the relative importance of existing and new customers.

To establish a balance of priorities, the first task is to gain insights into the true costs of winning new customers. We will look at this and then move on to the value of existing loyal customers, before finally drawing conclusions.

What does a new customer cost?

Winning a new customer requires up-front investment across the business: (*see* Fig. 3.1).

- Research
- Analysis time
- Strategy development
- Product development
- Service and support
- Discount/samples
- Distribution
- Communications
- Sales force
- Risk of failure

Figure 3.1 What does a new customer cost?

1 **Research.** Identifying potential new customers requires research. This may be informal, involving senior executives familiar with the market, taking sales managers off the road to compile lists of prospects, or directing sales representatives to make investigative calls. All these have a direct cost in terms of employee time and an opportunity cost in terms of other productive tasks the personnel might have accomplished in the same time. Alternatively, the research may be formal with direct

invoiced costs by the research agency, plus communication costs, briefing and presentation time. Other costs might be the purchase of trade directories, mailing lists or databases. The research may extend to investigation of new markets, import/export requirements, legal aspects of foreign trade and patents.

2 **Analysis time.** Determining prospective customers from simple lists takes time and may involve seeking further data to aid the selection. For example, there may be time and budget costs for assessing customer trading history, establishing creditworthiness, evaluating commitment to the market, confirming financial stability and identifying key executives.

3 **Strategy development.** Executive time is consumed in developing and testing strategies to win new business, with policy agreements on products for focus, service support, pricing and discounting levels, plus channel plans and communications modes, staff briefing and supplier liaison. Consultants may be hired to assist and support this project work.

4 **Product development.** The existing product range may meet all the necessary requirements for appealing to new customers, though this must be checked. Alternatively new or amended products may be needed. New variants may dictate revised tooling for manufacture. Amendments may be appropriate. For example, certain ingredients and processes may be illegal in some countries or unacceptable to customers. New flavours, colours and styles may be necessary. BMW sells a 2.5-litre diesel 725 in Italy, while the minimum engine size in most other markets is 3 litres. New labelling may be needed, with translations into other languages, extra information or warnings, or the addition of international symbols.

5 **Service and support.** The service proposition may need review for new customers. New customers tend to need greater advice and support before buying, during the purchase and early in the product life until they achieve product familiarity. In addition, they may require specific installation support, training and product manuals in formats compatible with market expectations.

6 **Discount/samples.** To switch from an existing supplier, or to make a new purchase, most customers expect an incentive or inducement. This could be a trial product or samples so that they can assess the quality and consistency of the unfamiliar product. A discount might be needed. To expand its credit-card business in the UK www.egg.com, the internet bank owned by Prudential, advertised in January 2001 an offer of 0-per-cent interest for the first six months. Interest-free money is a substantial discount on the norm – after six months the rate rises to a level of 11.9 per cent. In California a new pizza take-away restaurant in its

launch strategy offered a 20-per-cent discount to diners who brought in the advertisement of a competitor torn from the Yellow Pages Directory – it was an inducement and also a competitor-disabling device. In selling new grocery lines to retailers and supermarkets, listing payments will be demanded, with extra costs attached to display at gondola ends. Negotiations may involve training levies, wastage allowances, disposal costs of non-compatible product, or buy-back of competitor stock.

7   **Distribution.** Negotiations may involve existing distributors, wholesalers or other intermediaries, who may need guidance on stock, service support and promotional strategies. Greater demands may be placed on organizations seeking distributors in new territories, and this could involve warehouse design, management secondments and profit guarantees

8   **Communications.** Advertising is a major cost, especially major media advertising intended to influence prospects. Increasingly readers and viewers are mentally or actually screening out advertising from companies in whom they have no interest. The 'commercial brake' is a video attachment that arrests recording as it detects a commercial break and resumes when the programming returns. It is also becoming more difficult to find a single treatment or message that combines reassurance for current buyers with attraction for new customers.

The difficulties faced by advertising mean that customer attraction is tending to migrate towards direct marketing with mailshot, e-mailing and telemarketing activities. The US-owned bank, Capital One, intent on growing a credit-card business in the UK, spent £27 420 000 on direct mail in the 12 months to May 2000, according to figures published by the media research organization AC Nielsen NMS. Computer databases are required to hold and – at greater cost – keep up-dated lists of prospects. In the age band 18–23 years, customers are likely to have a new address every 18 months. Brochures and other mailing content must be personalized to the targeted customer. Responses must be tracked.

In business-to-business markets, exhibitions and trade shows are important means of winning new customers. Evaluating the costs and benefits means accounting for the direct costs of space rental, facilities, electricians and other services, and also calculating the management time in design, development, manning and following up of leads.

9   **Sales force.** Clearly, sales representation is part of the customer-winning operation. To this group can be added sales-support functions who survey, deliver, install and service products and equipment. All of these will have salaries and vehicle-running costs and many will be bonused or rewarded with performance-based incentives. Customer-entertainment

expenses can be significant. A pharmaceutical company can easily invest $8000 in flying an influential individual to a convention and providing them with entertainment and mementoes.

10 **Risk of failure.** A hidden cost of customer acquisition is the danger of unwittingly mis-selling to a customer who finds the product or service is inappropriate and becomes a dissatisfied negative force. Adverse word-of-mouth is a major barrier to future customer acquisition. For example, personal computer manufacturers have discovered that people who buy underspecified PCs blame the inadequacy on the brand, rarely re-buy the same brand, and criticize it in surveys. Thus a dissatisfied buyer represents a future cost to the organization.

We don't know the investment to win a new customer!

So, the cost of customer acquisition can be both large and little understood. The costs listed above have two characteristics. First, they spread throughout the whole organization, across every department and in any cost centre. Few organizations have the systems to track every cost associated with new customer activity and thus most companies are unaware of the precise cost of this activity.

Boston Consulting Group (BCG) is a leader in loyalty research and practice. Helen Donald (2000) quotes BCG figures for the costs of acquiring a new customer for different types of retail organizations in the USA:

$11 per customer for a catalogue-based company

$31 per customer for a store-based retailer

$82 per customer for a web retailer

Each quarter, BCG, in combination with trade association Shop.org, tracks the performance of online retailers. These surveys show how web retailers are progressively reducing the costs of customer acquisition (relevant websites are www.bcg.com and www.shop.org).

And we don't know whether we are earning a return on the investment!

The second characteristic of customer-acquisition costs is that there is often no overall audit of the effectiveness of this expenditure. In contrast, a new item of plant will be subjected to the full capital expenditure procedure. Cost of equipment will be added to the installation cost. An assumption will be made about trials and bringing the machine into full production. A payback target will be established and, normally on a quarterly basis, the performance against this target will be established. There may even be an interim review to identify consequent savings to speed up the promised payback. Above all, a named individual is accountable for the return on the investment.

Five steps to understand customer return on investment

What is needed is a basic system to calculate the investment required to win a new customer and to track the return on that investment. This must:

1 Institute a system to identify all costs for winning new business.

2 Divide the total costs of acquisition by the number of new customers won in a 12-month period to determine the average cost of winning a customer.

3 Evaluate the average customer profitability.

4 Assess the number of months the business must keep a customer in order to provide a commercial payback on the investment.

5 Make all employees aware of the time period necessary to achieve payback.

Leading organizations in privatized utilities are addressing this subject full square. For example, UK-industry experts estimate that the average London householder contributes £18 per year to their electricity supplier. If installation and account-opening costs for the supplier are £50, then a new domestic electricity customer must be retained for at least two years and ten months (*see* Fig. 3.2). Similar studies in the US credit-card market show that the investment in a new cardholder is only recovered if the customer is retained longer than 18 months.

	£
Cost of new installation	(50)
Contribution in year 1	18
Cumulative profit (loss)	(32)
Contribution in year 2	18
Cumulative profit (loss)	(14)
Contribution in year 3	18
Cumulative profit (loss)	4

Figure 3.2 Customer return on investment

According to Andrew Wileman (1999), writing on customer profitability in the UK telecommunications market, Orange's subscriber acquisition costs and its share of new subscribers is the same as Vodaphone's. Yet its average annual customer profitability and retention rate has been higher, accounting for the Orange overall business value-per-subscriber being 40 per cent higher.

In commercial construction industries where business is won through the tender process, the scrutiny of all costs associated with providing the tender is routine. These organizations systematically monitor their tender costs and compare them with their strike rate. It is a discipline that could usefully be applied to other business sectors and to consumer markets.

The lesson: investment in new customers is uncertain

The high cost of acquiring new customers and the delayed and uncertain payback, means that the highest priority for most organizations should be to focus on satisfying, captivating and retaining existing customers. Only during new start-ups and rapid expansion phases should winning new customers be pre-eminent.

The highest priority for most organizations should be to focus on satisfying, captivating and retaining existing customers.

Management guru Peter Drucker has said 'the first purchase is only a trial', and thus the true role of a business is to ensure that this trial is successful and the customer is retained. The next chapter will look at the value of keeping customers.

Case example	Theme: New relationships, hidden costs, business woes

Boo.com

Customer acquisition proved too expensive for failed fashion e-tailer Boo.com. Founded in 1998 by Ernst Malmsten and former 'Elite' model, Kajsa Leander, Boo.com was intended to be a leading fashion retailer on the web. The site offered fashion brands, including Timberland and DKNY, and was launched in 18 countries and seven languages in November 1999. Funding of £74.4 million was provided by investors, including Bernard Arnault's LVMH group, the Benetton family, JP Morgan and Goldman Sachs.

To research the market, analyze the opportunity and develop the site, Boo.com recruited fashion pundits, retail buyers, marketers, copywriters and technical experts. For example, 'Miss Boo' was developed as a mannequin in three dimensions to model clothes selected by web customers. In fact the development phase overran, delaying the launch by six months.

Extravagant setting up for service support included an 80-person dedicated call centre located in trendy Carnaby Street, London. Communications were a vital investment in the start-up and here again Boo.com invested heavily. To achieve an outstanding image, Francis Ford Coppola was hired to direct Boo's television commercials and these were screened across Europe to attract web customers.

Boo.com initially had a strategy of charging premium prices. However, sales were below expectations and at the end of the first season Boo.com was compelled to cut prices by 40 per cent to clear unsold stock and win buyers.

In May 2000 the company ran out of funds and co-founder Ernst Malmsten was compelled to ask KPMG to become liquidators of the company. Mick McLoughlin, the KPMG partner heading the liquidation team, said that: 'Management spent a lot of money setting up infrastructure, but sales weren't enough to cover expenditure. It's as simple as that.' The verdict of the BBC was that Boo.com had been unable to build up customers fast enough to generate revenues to cover the high-level set-up costs.

Exercise 3

Exercises

Calibrate the costs of acquiring a new customer:

Activity (annual)   *Cost*

1 Research – proportion of budget attributable to customer acquisition

2 Analysis – employee hours @ current compensation rates

3 Strategy development – executive time on customer acquisition

4 Product development – activity dedicated to new customer design

5 Service and support – allocate with Activity Based Costing

6 Discounts/samples – discounts and financial offers to new customers

7 Distribution – new customer set-up costs

8 Communications – budget proportion for acquisition

9 Sales force – time based allocation existing/new customers

10 Other costs.

Total cost =

Divided by number of new customers gained in 12 months =

Further reading and references

Donald, Helen (2000) 'Lessons in Netiquette', *Marketing Means Business for the CEO*, Chartered Institute of Marketing, Spring.

Glick, Bryan (2000) 'boo.com's fall makes realism the fashion', *Computing*, 26 May.

Newell, Frederick (2000) *Loyalty.com*, McGraw Hill.

Treacy, Michael and Wiersema, Frederik D. (1997) *The Discipline of Market Leaders: Choose your Customers, Narrow your Focus, Dominate your Market*, Addison Wesley.

Wileman, Andrew (1999) 'What's a customer worth?' *Management Today*, June.

Existing customers – hidden value

Her feet ached and there was another whole day of the exhibition still to come. It seemed like she had been glad-handing prospects at the trade show for as long as she could remember. The air-conditioning in the hall was struggling with the number of visitors and the noise was intense. Her throat was dry and sore from making herself heard. If she had had a moment to daydream, she would have pictured herself in a luxurious spa pool but there was no time for other thoughts.

Just then, through the crowd she spied a familiar face. Her discomfort and tiredness disappeared and she smiled enthusiastically at one of her favourite people. How long had they been doing business together? She could not remember. A flood of images surged through her mind. Images of support when she had first joined the field force. Calls of congratulation when she had broken the glass ceiling and been promoted two grades. Sage advice when she had faced the government enquiry. Delightful dinners with colleagues from both companies. Humour at product launches. Patience, trust and decency when the delivery promises had fallen through, and appreciation when the problem had been solved.

She knew she was going to enjoy the next ten minutes. Thank goodness for loyal customers to help you through the day.

Continuing customers provide an anchor of certainty in a changing world. Their presence provides an intangible emotional reassurance and some tangible business benefits. Often unquantified, the commercial benefits of loyal customers are substantial. In fact there are five values that they can provide (*see* Fig. 4.1). There are ways to leverage these benefits to give even greater effect. Of course the benefits are greater with some customers than others. Pareto's 80/20 law explains that a small number of customers can provide a disproportionate value. These are the Customers that Count.

Satisfied customers buy more

The first value of loyalty is simply that satisfied customers return and provide a future profit stream. It is a principle of life that human beings seek positive experiences and avoid negative ones. A second human characteristic is to simplify complexity through pattern following. A pleasing purchasing encounter and good experience in use will encourage a return so that a pattern builds.

- Satisfied customers buy more
- You can reduce the costs of serving known customers
- Loyal customers share their market knowledge with you
- Well-served customers may pay a premium price
- Satisfied customers recommend

Figure 4.1 Value from loyal customers

In simple terms, the value of customer retention lies in the fact that returning customers tend to buy more than first-time purchasers do. Over time, the tendency is for repeat buyers to increase the value, volume and frequency of purchases. It is a tendency and there are exceptions. For instance, customers move away and there are products where needs occur only once. It is also possible to thwart this tendency with uncompetitive value, poor service, or lack of products for the consumer's next stages. For example, Honda built loyalty with small-car customers in the 1970s, but its ability to retain customers over time was inhibited by its lack of larger vehicles and estate variants. The commercial imperative is to acknowledge the tendency and to foster and encourage the factors working in favour of volume increases (*see* Fig. 4.2).

- Increasing proportion of customer's spending in the category
- Customers buying across your range
- You develop new products to satisfy customer's emerging needs
- Customers upgrade or move up the range
- Customers increase the frequency of purchase
- The scale of the customer's business grows (business to business)

Figure 4.2 Ways that satisfied customers will buy more

The first opportunity is growth in share. In many markets the customer has many sources of supply and chooses a portfolio of products from different vendors. Typically, Australian beer drinkers will have a repertoire of four brands which they find acceptable, and will split their purchases between them depending on occasion and location. The average Parisian rotates between six to eight favourite restaurants. In both cases, the growth opportunity is from a higher 'share of throat'. Relationship-building actions that captivate customers will result in a definite preference and volume will increase at the expense of competitors.

The second opportunity for growth is through customers cross-buying. Satisfied customers willingly buy other products and services from suppliers that they trust. Building on equipment sales, the power equipment division of General Electric expects to generate $17 billion revenue in 2000 from the maintenance of jet engines or medical equipment, up from $8 billion in 1995. The Swedish world leader in rock-crushing equipment for the mining industry, Svedala, is moving in the same direction. At Svedala's Annual General Meeting, 11 April 2000, Thomas Oldér, President and CEO, commented: 'Our focus on the aftermarket has meant that more than 40 per cent of Svedala's invoicing came from service, repairs and spare parts during 1999'. Service packages have been introduced, including access guarantees for spare parts, inspection agreements and preventative maintenance packages. The company estimates that the value of the market for service and parts is four times greater than the market for equipment.

Developing the concept of cross-buying, empathetic suppliers may be able to identify emerging needs of groups of their customers and develop new products and services to address these. For example, Blockbuster Video understood the feelings of young couples who rented films as a substitute for cinema visits when their children were born. Blockbuster added popcorn to its merchandise. Similarly, it observed the interests of young male renters of video thrillers and extended its rental range to 'shoot 'em up' computer games. In January 2000 the UK football club Manchester United began selling off the turf from its Old Trafford pitch over the internet through the site www.trebleturf.co.uk. Supporters of the club bought pieces of turf as a memento of the successful 1999 season (*Marketing* magazine, 20 January 2000).

Shrewd marketers can also use their customer understanding to expand volume through the displacement of substitutes.

A further opportunity is to encourage buyers to move up the range. Customers who are confident of their knowledge of a product and/or confident of their supplier will consider buying a higher specification and higher priced version. For example, quaffers of Australian red wine who have enjoyed bottles of Stockman's Bridge, will readily be tempted to buy the more expensive cabernet version. The American girl who has found Victoria's Secret to be comfortable workday underwear may well spend substantially more on special-occasion lingerie.

Greater frequency of purchasing is another way in which satisfied customers become more valuable. This is particularly evident with indulgence consumer goods such as Vermont USA-based Ben & Jerry's ice cream and the UK chain Costa Coffee.

In business-to-business sectors, growth may arise simply because the customer's own business is expanding and their requirements of you increase. UK direct stationery supplier Viking finds that the demand for office paperwork materials can grow almost as rapidly as the customer. And as customers grow their volume, the benefit can be reflected in scale economies offered to them. The consequent better value may also drive further volume.

Making the most of volume growth

Understanding the propensity of satisfied customers to buy more products, more frequently, at higher specifications creates a business potential. How do you use this knowledge to most effect? What concrete plans can be put into place to move more customers along this progression and move them more quickly?

Organizations need range-selling strategies. This begins with identifying the natural 'lead line', which tends to be the first purchase a new buyer makes. It is the order-winning product or service, or the one that most prospects see as a suitable trial. For example, the clothing retailer The Gap usually displays T-shirts near the front of the store as new customers are more likely to make a trial purchase at this price point. The Gap has enough confidence in its T-shirt designs and quality to expect customers to return to explore the wider range on another occasion. There are also natural follow-on products. For example, Volkswagen appreciates that the best prospect for a Passat is the Golf driver with a growing family. Thus a range-selling strategy researches which products or services fall into each category and creates a customer pathway. This does not preclude individual customers buying more advanced products or services; it simply makes a smooth sequential route for customers to progress up the range. A major UK do-it-yourself retailer has identified certain 'project' purchases. So when a customer buys a new bath, it is a reasonable assumption that this is the start of a project. Therefore a week after the purchase, the tile brochure is mailed to the customer with guidance on tiling and recommended adhesives. When the customer buys tiles, grout and décor, a marker ensures that after another couple of weeks a shower curtain mailer will arrive, and so on.

The key lesson is to make it easy to cross-buy. At every stage, investigate and determine the next piece of information or advice the customer might need in their progress. Booksellers could print an attractively designed receipt for every purchase that functions as a bookmark uniquely tailored to each customer. It would read: 'If you enjoy reading this novel, we think you would also enjoy xxxxx or yyyyy'. The technique is known as 'collaborative filtering' and is based on survey data from satisfied customers. Every book leads to another book; every DVD purchase leads to another DVD. And collaborative filtering can leap product categories. Boots, the UK-based international pharmaceutical retailer, analyzing purchase patterns, discovered that customers for baby products also bought photograph frames. Boots now merchandise picture frames close to the diaper zone as an aid to customers and a stimulant to sales. Growing the value of existing customers becomes a measurable business objective.

> **At every stage, investigate and determine the next price of information or advice the customer might need in their progress.**

Know your customers: drive down costs

The second golden characteristic of existing customers is that it is possible to tailor products and services to their precise needs in ways that eliminate costs and therefore increase your profitability (*see* Fig. 4.3).

There are major advantages from customer familiarity. First, there are some direct financial benefits. For example, with trusted customers, account handlers may be able to simplify accounting systems to mutual benefit. Most bad debt accumulates from new business, and the better the relationship with customers the less the occurrence of surprise payment

- Joint planning
- Less administration
- Simpler accounting systems
- Less working capital
- Less waste
- Less bad debt
- Lower manning
- Fewer errors
- Need less support
- Solve own problems
- Forecasts can result in better raw material prices

Figure 4.3 Reducing costs of serving known customers

problems. Many corporate lenders will review customer payment patterns as an indicator of certainty of income in the justification of borrowing facilities. In these circumstances loyal customers are a genuine asset in the continuing process of reducing costs.

There are also indirect financial benefits. Gradually a supplier learns the nature of the customer's business and pattern of demand. Thus over time there should be less waste, more efficient manning and fewer errors. Where errors do occur, the loyal customer will be less harsh in demanding compensation than a new buyer, because they have a vested interest in the continuity of business. A supply chain 'line of sight' or joint planning system can minimize the need for inventory in both customer and supplier, which reduces working capital needs. The certainty of demand can be used to provide guarantees to raw material suppliers and this in turn may lead to lower prices.

Over time, loyal customers require less administrative back-up where systems are understood and functioning effectively. They need less support because they understand the products. When difficulties arise, often they are able to solve their own problems. For example, a study of software help-lines shows that the users make half their calls for assistance in the first week of use of new software. Thereafter the usage declines rapidly over time. The newest customers who contribute least to margins heavily use many services.

This leads to the question which customers contribute most to profitability? Where businesses have thousands of customers, these can be clustered into appropriate segments for an evaluation of segment profitability. The key cost drivers need to be determined. Normally these are resource-based in terms of raw materials, process time and employee time. An activity-based costing approach can then be used to allocate overheads, so that the heaviest users of services and support are identified for a genuine picture of their contribution.

With an understanding of customer profitability, it is then possible to review the cost drivers and investigate scope for improving the profit for each customer. This requires a value check. Beginning with the services most expensive to provide, how well appreciated are they in the mind of the client? How important are they in the overall service equation? Which services and features save customers time, money and worry? And which do not give proportionate benefit? It may well be possible to discontinue, scale down, or charge for services that use scarce and expensive resources where the clients see little benefit. Environmental attitudes in Germany (and elsewhere) mean that Body Shop gains credibility when it provides no shopping bag for purchases – shoppers feel they are minimizing waste of the world's resources and Body Shop saves costs.

In a business-to-business context, the relationship between customer understanding and costs can be evident within the trading terms. Worldwide provider of contract staff, Manpower, has contract prices that are expected to reduce during the currency of the agreement, such that mechanisms are identified to allocate the savings between vendor and buyer.

Finally, driving down customer costs can be a valuable element in forming effective relationships. Bundy, part of TI Group, extended the principle of cost savings for the buyer to its pitch for a fuel pipeline supply to Czech carmaker, Skoda. The solution it presented displaced straight tubes, which had been moulded to shape by the car maker. Instead it provided ready-coated, pre-formed lines with connectors in place for immediate fitment. The unit cost was higher, yet allowing for wastage and labour time, the fitted cost was actually lower.

Expanding knowledge: trend spotting

The third golden benefit of customer familiarity is increased speed and quality of learning and improvement. This can take the form of observed behaviour leading to insights, or to transferred information, where the customers actively contribute to the enhancement of products or services (*see* Fig. 4.4).

The patterns of behaviour of long-term customers can indicate new and emerging trends. If customers who buy 100 per cent of their requirement from a supplier reduce their purchases of a particular item, this can illustrate a downward market trend, rather than a competitive initiative. This occurred in the Australian market for alco-pops – flavoured soft drinks with alcoholic content – where the market trend changed dramatically before comparable market data had been published. A supplier whose sales

- Trend data
- Observing usage gives insights
- Competitive information
- Ideas for new products/services
- Feedback, complaints and enquiries
- Testbed for new products
- Contribute to seminars and development

Figure 4.4 Customers share market knowledge

were declining might deduce that competitors were making inroads into their business. However, sales data showing declining purchases from those customers buying 100 per cent of their requirements could indicate an overall market decrease. And in the Russian market, where accurate market-share data is unobtainable, the information from customers buying 100 per cent of requirements is a vital market indicator.

Regular users frequently provide competitive data. They willingly pass on communications from rival suppliers on technical developments, new initiatives and forthcoming product launches. In the Austrian machine-tool and automation business, the best data on actual market prices – as opposed to official list pricing – comes from feedback from close customers.

The dialogue with loyal users carries a significant competitive advantage. The Heinz and Farley 'Baby at Home' programme claims to have contributed £11.1 million in one year in gross sales across wet and dry baby food categories, partly through the range development that stemmed directly from dialogue with 1.5 million mothers.

The dialogue with loyal users carries a significant competitive advantage.

Service offerings can be improved and refined through the interaction with loyal customers, increasing market power. Frequently, the complaints from customers can lead to major service or knowledge advances. A large UK retail bank tracked customer complaints and noted a small but concerning trend for customers to complain about selective direct mailings. In many households there are one or more account holders. Typically, one of the account holders would complain that another member of the household had received an offer aimed at 'our most credit-worthy customers' and that they themselves had not been sent this communication. Resolving this concern led to the grouping of accounts into 'households', which as a competitive by-product gave a better picture of the market dynamics.

Finally, customers can be valuable contributors to educational seminars for other customers or employees. Frequently at Ashridge Management College when we tailor development programmes for clients we include in the timetable a session from a major supplier, giving a market eye-view on the client's strengths and opportunities. These insights can be invaluable for customer understanding and priority setting.

Premium price

The fourth value of loyal customers is that they will be less price sensitive than a first-time purchaser and may pay a premium price (*see* Fig. 4.5). They are less price sensitive because price is not the only issue in their decision to do business with a supplier. Their purchasing is based around their appreciation of the overall value they obtain, including customized service, confidence in delivery, willingness to resolve problems, track record in product development, courtesy and mutual interest. The totality of the experience may result in the customer being willing to pay a price premium compared with an unfamiliar supplier. This is often called the brand premium. The brand encapsulates the advantages and values for the customer. For example, Ticketmaster UK provide a computerized web and telephone ticketing service for concerts and performances. Over 38 000 of their established customers willingly pay a premium subscription of £18 and receive early warning of forthcoming events.

- Less price sensitive than new customers
- Value of certainty to the customer
- Recognition of the benefits
- Brand value
- Opportunity to match competitor price cuts
- Switching costs

Figure 4.5 Well-served customers may pay a premium price

Where established customers are more sensitized to price, the value of the relationship is expressed in a different way. In commodity markets, for example the Italian cement industry, customers are unwilling to pay a price premium. However, where a competing supplier offers a lower price, the buyer will offer the incumbent supplier the opportunity to match this price, or narrow the gap to continue the pattern of loyalty. The dialogue is different, but the benefit is continuity in the face of competitor propositions.

The essence of the price premium is the customer's assessment of their switching costs. These can be real financial burdens of changing suppliers – time-consuming processes that represent a disincentive to change supply source. Alternatively they may be psychological costs, such as fear of the unknown. The value of the relationship lies in the understanding and appreciation of all these switching costs. (See Chapter 16, 'Building barriers to exit', for more on this topic.)

Referrals

The fifth and final benefit of a long-term relationship is the referral value, where satisfied customers become part of the attraction system for new business (*see* Fig. 4.6). Immediately and obviously, satisfied clients provide spontaneous recommendations to people or organizations they meet, that have similar requirements. In many countries Honda Cars find that one-to-one recommendations by happy owners provide a regular and effective trigger to bring potential new Honda drivers into their showrooms. This is particularly among older drivers who are least susceptible to advertising and most difficult to convert.

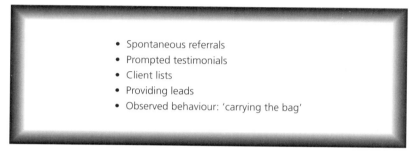

- Spontaneous referrals
- Prompted testimonials
- Client lists
- Providing leads
- Observed behaviour: 'carrying the bag'

Figure 4.6 Satisfied customers recommend

In a keynote address at the June 2000 CRM Conference and Exposition in Boston Massachusetts, organized by DCI, Ron Rose, Chief Information Officer of Priceline.com, shared current customer research findings. He reported that satisfied users of Priceline.com told an average of 18 friends about their positive experiences. Word-of-mouth recommendation is a vital aspect of expansion plans.

This process of recommendation can naturally be stimulated. Clients can be prompted to participate actively. This may be limited, for example agreeing to be included in an architect's client list. Or it may be more involving, by writing or recording testimonials endorsing a supplier, by the provision of leads or by acting as a reference site. In business-to-business marketing this can be a particularly effective way of reassuring new customers that the promised solution actually works in practice.

Prompting referrals

A major UK retailer of white goods – ovens, refrigerators, washing machines – encourages its sales people to call customers five days after the new purchase has been delivered. They ask follow-up questions, including checking delivery-crew behaviour, installation effectiveness and understanding of all the controls, to confirm that everything is in order. If there are difficulties then these are rectified. In most cases the customer response is positive throughout. The sales person closes by explaining that from time to time customers in store ask if it is possible to speak to a user of the particular appliance. Would they be willing to be contacted? Around 60 per cent decline and this is accepted with tact. The invaluable group are the 40 per cent who volunteer to be contacted. They are satisfied, confident and willing to share their expertise with new buyers. The retail group counts five benefits from asking this question:

1 Simply asking the question draws out a commitment that frequently leads these customers to buy further appliances.

2 It increases the confidence of the sales person who has a 'black book' of recent satisfied buyers. Confidence is a key determinant in sales success.

3 When a potential buyer hesitates, the sales person has a powerful piece of recommendation in their armoury – would you like to talk to a customer who bought this very appliance recently? Most buy at this stage, without taking up the recommendation.

4 If the potential customer makes the call, they will normally be convinced by the conversation, and often volunteer as new recommenders

5 If the new buyer should experience any difficulties with the installation, they tend to be more forgiving, because of the personal recommendation, and interpret the disruption as an 'unlucky day' rather than an indicator of a poor service.

This technique is most frequently associated with business-to-business transactions, but it is interesting to record the growth of this approach in consumer markets.

Finally, existing customers who will not participate in positive recommendations still provide a passive value. The well-dressed shopper striding out carrying the Nordstrom bag is a referral in her own right.

Reaping the benefits of golden customers

In conclusion, the long-term 'golden' customer brings immense benefits to suppliers fortunate enough and astute enough to create these effective relationships. The benefits accrue naturally, and many businesses thrive as a result of their loyal customers. More canny organizations go further and seek to leverage the benefits. They assiduously develop relationships and ensure the commercial benefits are managed as effectively as the customer relationships. This is summarized as follows:

Factor	Action
Cost to acquire customer	Calculate payback period necessary for customer's contribution to cover the customer acquisition costs
Increasing volume	Analyze purchase patterns, develop sales path to higher volume Make it easy to cross-buy
Lower costs	Estimate customer profitability Identify savings where no value is added
Learning benefits	Seek opportunities to observe customers for insights Share market and process learning
Price premium	Identify all switching costs and communicate them Develop barriers to exit
Referrals	Promote recommendation, provide evidence and vocabulary Create customer reference banks

An action plan to build loyalty and cement the value of relationships is a focus for profitable organizations.

Some more golden than others

Existing customers are certainly golden. However, they are certainly not all the same carat. In a portfolio of customers some will be substantially more profitable than others. In the European mobile telephone market there may be many more voucher customers, but the smaller number of contract customers use their phones far more than pre-pay customers do. A builders' merchant supplying house construction materials in the east of England analyzed its trade customers and discovered that the top 20 per cent accounted for 80.2 per cent of revenue. The tendency for a small number of people to account for the bulk of the value was first explored by the Italian sociologist and economist, Vilfredo Pareto (1843–1923). In his first work, *Cours d'Économie Politique* (1896/7), he observed that 80 per cent of the wealth of Italy was owned by 20 per cent of the population. With a complex mathematical formulation he attempted to prove that income distribution is not random and that a consistent 80/20 pattern appears throughout history.

The Customers that Count

The 80/20 law is now an established rule of thumb and a powerful tool. It is expected that in any population 20 per cent of customers will earn 80 per cent of income (*see* Fig. 4.7). Similar analysis shows that 20 per cent of customers are likely to account for 80 per cent of the service problems and support requirements. These proportions tend to be consistent across most businesses.

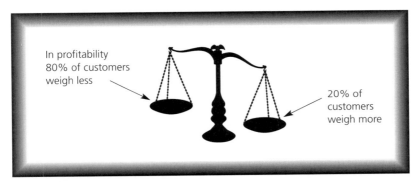

Figure 4.7 The profit balance: 20 per cent of customers provide 80 per cent of profits

The message is that a small cadre of customers delivers a disproportionately large amount of profit and they are vital. And another small collection of customers account for a disproportionate level of costs. Putting the cost and revenue aspects together produces a list of most profitable customers. This is the foundation of priority planning.

Priority to best customers

With CRM software it is readily possible to identify the number of high-profit customers and gather knowledge to seek to understand and meet their current and future requirements. Retaining these customers is vital. Peter Erskine, head of BT Wireless, was quoted in the *Financial Times* (21 September 2000): 'I am not interested in my ventures being number one in volume. There is a lot of junk out there, and we want high-value customers'.

Another important facility of CRM software is the identification of feedstock customers who will become future high-profit customers. The technology is available to identify the most valuable customers now and in future. However, building real relationships with these priority customers is much more difficult to automate.

The 80/20/80 law

The scale and complexity of business relationships demand the human skills that bring relationships to life. The eight identified aspects of natural relationships (*see* page 21) are intelligence intensive. They need the constant application of mental effort to keep them up-to-date for best customers. Your computer alone cannot make everyone feel special. The organization has insufficient human resources to provide every customer with brilliant personal service. And in fact best customers will want a combination of personal and intelligently automated service. Therefore the strategy proposal is that your organization should focus 80 per cent of effort on the 20 per cent of customers who will provide 80 per cent of future profits.

Focus 80 per cent of effort on the 20 per cent of customers who will provide 80 per cent of future profits.

Focus personal attention and human characteristics to build a living relationship with the 20 per cent of customers who make up the bulk of organizational contribution.

Case example   Theme: Existing customers, hidden value

Swissair

Swissair, now one of Europe's leading airlines (www.swissair.com), was founded in March 1931. In 1934 it was the first European airline to employ air hostesses. By 1968 it operated an all-jet fleet and by 1982 it had carried its 100 millionth passenger. However, Swissair has a focus on quality beyond quantity. In response to the demand for premium service, business class was introduced in 1984. Listening to the needs of frequent travellers, check-in was introduced in 1988 at all major Swiss railway stations with a fly/rail baggage service for passengers.

Swissair was aware that a small number of business travellers accounted for a significant portion of revenue. Sources outside Swissair estimate that 20 to 30 individual passengers represented a meaningful percentage of revenue. Swissair Directors were therefore able to invite these top customers to luxury weekend retreats to meet them and discuss their perspectives on travel. Partly as a result of this and partly through wider customer research, Swissair developed and launched a First-class product in 1999. By June 2000 First was available on virtually all Swissair long-haul flights. First featured valet parking at Zürich and Geneva (the home airports of the most regular fliers) plus washing, cleaning the car and filling the fuel tank. Swissair has an enviable reputation for punctuality, and in the rare event of departure delays, first customers are kept informed with short messages to their mobile phones. On-board television news coverage is available and on Airbus A330 flights there is hourly text-news updates on personal screens. Naturally there is gourmet catering and the seats convert into a flat bed, 201 cm in length. On arrival, First customers receive priority baggage handling. In a press release of 22 June 2000 Product Manager Bernard Ecklin said: 'We have surpassed by a considerable margin our objective of being perceived as having the best first class by 75 per cent of our top customers'.

To ensure that top customers are recognized through the process, they are provided with a 'Fast Track System'. Launched on 16 December 1999, these smart cards act as a single travel document to save passengers the time and trouble of conventional check-in and to allow Swissair to extend exemplary service at booking, check-in, in the lounge, during boarding, in-flight, and through the arrival and baggage service. Linked to this, the CLIP system contains all the significant information on the passenger and their travels. Thus both cabin and ground staff are aware of the reservation data, the frequent flier history, special requirements like bulky baggage and any interim customer feedback. Any action necessary to meet the individual's wishes can be taken in a timely and non-bureaucratic fashion.

Exercise 4	Exercises

1 List customers in revenue sequence. Divide them into two categories: high-value customers, who should account for around 80 per cent of company revenue, and the remainder, who are designated low-value customers.

2 Focus on customers' usage of service support and obtain a total value – units may be employee-hours, number of help-line calls or a monetary value.

3 List users of services and divide them into two categories: high-level users, who should account for around 80 per cent of usage, and low-level users.

4 Plot customers in one of four boxes:
- High value/high service – balanced usage.
- Low value/low service – balanced usage.

- High value/low service – probably very profitable, perhaps a retention risk?
- Low value/high service – perhaps expensive over-delivery of service?

Further reading and references

Hallberg, Garth, and Ogilvy, David (1995) *All Consumers Are Not Created Equal*, John Wiley.

Reichheld, Frederick F., and Schefter, Paul (2000) 'E-Loyalty Your Secret Weapon on the Web', *Harvard Business Review*, July–August.

Ries, Al (1997) *Focus*, HarperCollins.

Schumpter, J. (1952) *Ten Great Economists*, George Allen & Unwin, pp. 110–142 (thanks to Department of Economics, University of Melbourne for this reference).

Setting up for relationships

The company has reviewed all the benefits of long-term customer loyalty and has concluded that this is its strategic direction. What are the first steps to make the company ready for a living relationship with Customers that Count?

This section focuses on the actions taken in preparation. In normal circumstances, the preparation is a continuous updating process, conducted in parallel with the other stages of operation and interaction and the review process. The division into separate stages is artificial, but is used for the sake of explanation.

There are two types of preparatory action. First, there are internal actions designed to align the organization and its stakeholders. Alignment is essential, so that a single consistent message is received. Where different messages are signalled by the same organization, dissonance occurs and the recipient loses confidence.

The second set of actions are aimed externally, determining who are the Customers that Count: who are the most important customers of the organization, and who should they be in the future. A good relationship depends on a good fit between customer and supplier.

The relationship with the Customers that Count is important and merits thorough preparation.

You just do it straight off, like making a cup of tea.

No, you need proper preparation, like making a 'nice' cup of tea.

Oh really. So what is a 'nice' cup of tea?

Well it doesn't just happen, you need to prepare everything. Did you know there is an international standard for tea making laid down by ISO?

You are kidding!

Not at all, professional tea tasters at companies like Tetley follow a consistent procedure. They weigh exactly 6.5 g of tea, the water must be precisely at boiling point when it is added and it is allowed to brew for 6 minutes, no more, no less.

P reparation is the first stage in achieving anything important. For rela-tionships with the Customers that Count, the support of stakeholders is vital. The primary stakeholders are employees, with suppliers and distributors also contributing significantly. Long-term relationships with investors allow the strategy to be executed. Finally, it is important to signal a long-term approach to stakeholders through behaviour.

Preparation, preparation, preparation

Actors rehearse. Before a teacher approaches a class, they will prepare and practise. The golfer, Gary Player once said, 'The harder I practise, the luckier I get'. The week before its opening, the Manchester Marriott Hotel and Country Club was fully operational and welcoming employees of sister companies, business partners and supplier representatives, rehearsing in order to provide perfection for the first guests the following week. Preparation is key and this applies equally to a relationship with customers.

The company is an entity within a system, and the system provides the context of operation and the platform for building relationships. This system comprises all the stakeholders of the organization (*see* Fig. 5.1). No single element is able to deliver customer satisfaction in isolation, but each component part can in a small way diminish that satisfaction. Without the active support of every part of the system, there are risks and uncertainties for the customers that jeopardize the relationship. It is now widely recognized that it is impossible to deliver satisfaction in a service business without active commitment from all employees.

Employees	Suppliers	Distributors	Community	Investors
Permanent	Raw material	Retailers	Neighbours	Institutions
Temporary	Services	Agents	District	Individuals
Families	Their staff	Their staff	Country	Advisers

Figure 5.1 Stakeholders

Front-line staff create the customer confidence, back-office staff make the delivery possible. Distributors and suppliers are wider examples of front-liners and back-office teams. Supermarkets understand the importance of impressions: the presentation, cleanliness and driver courtesy of a Stop & Shop truck in New England USA and a Carrefour camion in France are part of the brand consistency. If their standards are below par, then consumer opinion is at risk. For the customer, the retail staff may be a personification of the brand. The reputation of the company may at a critical moment depend on the additional effort of an employee of a distributor to resolve a spare-part discrepancy.

The protests of community neighbours can damage the good name of a major brand and weaken the desire of a customer to have an association with that brand. It is said that on one occasion IBM delisted a supplier of metal computer cabinets, despite competitively priced products consistently delivered on time, in full and to specification. So why was this good performer delisted? Simply because on three occasions this supplier had been discovered allowing industrial effluent to flow into the river beside the plant, thereby killing fish stock. IBM valued its good name with its customers more highly than the products and services of this particular supplier and took pre-emptive action.

Finally, investor confidence and continuity can be significant in permitting the organization to continue operating independently. Investor understanding and trust builds over time and therefore a constant flux of investors can place a listed firm at risk of takeover. The security of long-term shareholding allows companies to invest for customer retention without the fear that its strategies will be countermanded by investors impatient for unrealistically rapid returns.

The company must align its stakeholders behind its objectives and harmonize the systems so that product and service delivery happen effectively and the building blocks of relationships may be put in place.

The company must align its stakeholders behind its objectives.

Mission – why does the company exist?

The process begins with an idea: the mission of the organization. For what reason does this company exist? What is our *raison d'être* or our cause? If we were a campaign, what would it be? If we did not exist, what would the world miss?

Many mission statements represent polysyllabic collations of mutually exclusive ambitions. They promise excellence in product quality and value, leadership in research, growth in sales and profit, 100 per cent customer satisfaction, and dedicated participation of every employee. The sentiments are worthy, but they are ineffective. Many are lengthy and unmemorable. Worse, they are indistinguishable from other mission statements and could apply to any business (*see* Fig. 5.2).

'Through total team work, we will add to our profitability with our complete commitment to all our customers and by satisfying each customer on time, every time, all the time.'

'Satisfying our customers' wishes for excellent quality of service and outstanding value. Constantly and energetically seeking to improve quality and productivity in all we do.'

Figure 5.2 Mission statements to fit any industry
Source: Marcus Child, Service Training Specialist

Credibility

Costa Coffee, one of the UK's fastest-growing chains of coffee houses, has a credible mission: 'To share our understanding and love for coffee with our guests'. Visit Costa Coffee at an airline terminal, a British high street or shopping mall and you feel some of the passion for coffee of the organization and its employees. You can envisage how people who have a real interest in coffee come to seek careers at Costa; how the company trains new staff members in the story of coffee; how it seeks suppliers who care about aroma and presentation; how the parent company shareholders will relish a cup of Costa Coffee at the Annual General Meeting.

A distinctive mission

There are exceptions to the ineffective mission statement: Procter & Gamble have a statement of purpose in their Annual Report. This distinctively reflects the company characteristics and behaviour drivers.

> We will provide products of superior quality and value that best fill the needs of the world's consumers. We will achieve that purpose through an organisation and a working environment which attracts the finest people; fully develops and challenges our individual talents; encourages our free and spirited collaboration to drive the business ahead; and maintains the Company's historic principles of integrity and doing the right thing. Through the successful pursuit of our commitment, we expect our brands to achieve leadership share and profit positions and that, as a result, our business, our people, our shareholders and the communities in which we live and work will prosper.

This statement of purpose is measurable:

- 'Products of superior quality' – a division of Procter & Gamble is able to compare its products against rival brands using a 'blind' test. It assembles a group of consumers of products in that category and asks them to assess the unidentified samples – is the Procter & Gamble brand preferred?

- 'Attracts the finest people' – Human Resources at Procter & Gamble can calibrate the organization's effectiveness in attracting the finest people by reference to benchmarks. For example, an extensive survey of students at universities specializing in business education and science in 13 European countries by Universum, a Swedish consulting firm, showed that Procter & Gamble ranked sixth most attractive employer (*The Economist*, 8 May 1999).

- 'Principles of integrity and doing the right thing' – these can be evaluated on ethical dimensions.

- 'Brands to achieve leadership share' – independent surveys can validate the actual shares achieved by Procter & Gamble brands in their markets.

Product, economic value and social responsibility

In 1998 Ben & Jerry's, the Vermont USA-based manufacturer of ice cream and frozen yoghurt products, summarized its principles of ten years of operation in a statement of mission. It is in three parts:

- **Product**: To make, distribute and sell the finest quality all-natural ice cream and related products in a wide variety of innovative flavours made from Vermont dairy products.

- **Economic**: To operate the company on a sound financial basis of profitable growth, increasing value for our shareholders, and creating career opportunities and financial rewards for our employees.

- **Social**: To operate the company in a way that actively recognizes the central role that business plays in the structure of society by initiating innovative ways to improve the life of a broad community – local, national, and international.

Ben & Jerry's can demonstrate actions stimulated by each of these interrelated parts. For example, to comply with 'all-natural ice cream', it bans the use of milk from cows artificially stimulated by reconstituted bovine growth hormone. Early in 2000 it began introducing new packaging that is unbleached by chlorine, as a way of reducing the amount of toxic water pollution. The economic aspect of the mission was proven on 12 April 2000 when the multinational consumer products company, Unilever, purchased all 8.4 million shares for a price of $43.60 per share, giving the shareholders a handsome return on original investments. The press statement issued with the takeover confirmed that the co-founders, Ben Cohen and Jerry Greenfield, will continue to be involved in Ben & Jerry's and the social mission will be encouraged and well funded.

The mission statement is a guiding beacon to management in creating strategies, to employees in executing policies, to suppliers in how best to collaborate, to customers in what to expect and to shareholders in how to judge the organization.

Customer-focused mission statements

Every company mission statement is couched in terms of the company to which it applies. A powerful concept is the customer-focused mission statement. This is like a cartoon type speech bubble. The speech inside is expressed in typical words that a customer might use. The company's mission is to behave in a way that results in customers having these views.

For example, the UK-based breakdown recovery and motorists' services organization, the AA (Automobile Association), had a customer-focused mission statement (*see* Fig. 5.3). The mission called on every person in the organization to do whatever was necessary to bring about these opinions in the minds of the customers and members of the AA.

For instance, what must happen to make every customer feel that the AA is 'easy to reach and ready to help'? This is not a check on input activities, like a requirement to answer phones within three rings, or respond to letters within 48 hours. It is about the full relationship behaviour that engenders the perception of ease of contact and willingness to solve problems. The staff behaviour is no longer rule-book driven, it becomes situation driven. It permits employees to measure themselves after each piece of customer contact.

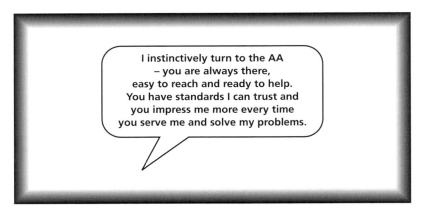

Figure 5.3 Customer-based mission statement from the Automobile Association

The vocabulary of the speech bubble is also in spoken language. This is in contrast with other mission statements that are in written language. Every language has words that feature more often in speech than in documents and vice versa. The Dutch language actually differentiates between *schrijftaal* (written Dutch) and *spreektaal* (the spoken version). With 600 000 words, the English language has the richest vocabulary of any tongue and hence more opportunity to select words for the circumstance. In written language, we refer to a 'first-choice provider', yet no individual would comment over a glass of beer that the AA was their first-choice provider. They would say: 'I automatically go to …', or 'I naturally think of …', or 'I instinctively turn to …'. A second example: the written phrase in company documents is 'rising expectations'. But no customer would use this expression to describe feelings in a personal conversation. Instead they would say: 'They impress me more every time'.

The strength of a customer-focused mission statement is in two areas. First, it focuses every employee externally on the perceptions of the customer. Second, it expresses the aspirations of the customer in conversational words that are accessible and easy to envisage and memorable.

Customer focus, employee focus, shareholder focus

The UK arm of the St Paul International Insurance Company, based in Reigate UK, has grown dramatically in the ten years since it entered the

British market. Martin Hudson, General Manager UK, has achieved a leading position for the company in most of its chosen segments. It has earned this position through a focus on customers, plus aligned objectives for employees and shareholders. In lively debates with his team, Martin has developed speech-bubble mission statements for customers, shareholders and employees that are displayed on the office wall (*see* Figs. 5.4, 5.5 and 5.6).

Visual mission statement

Ford Motor Credit of Dearborn Michigan has gone beyond words for its mission statement. Led by an inspirational Chief Executive Officer, Don

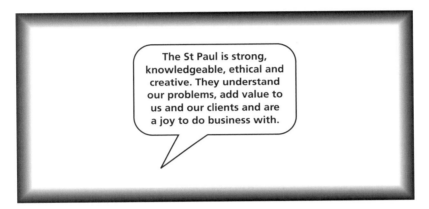

Figure 5.4 St Paul International Insurance: what we want our customers to say

Figure 5.5 St Paul International Insurance: what we want our shareholders to say

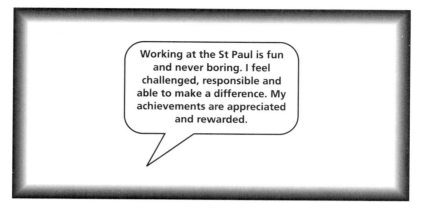

Figure 5.6 St Paul International Insurance: what we want our employees to say

Winkler, Ford Motor Credit's top 113 executives worked on a creative exercise to make a pictorial purpose statement. Winkler is dyslexic and gains more information from pictures than words. In fact, this is also true for non-dyslexics, and the Ford Motor Credit pictorial mission influences all employees. Each detail represents a company aspiration. For example, a rocket ship signifies developing new products with speed and simplicity. Crowds of people passing through a funnel are potential workers to show Ford's aim to recruit the best. A series of handshakes is a reminder of a living relationship: Ford Credit must work effectively with partners like Ford dealerships (*USA Today*, section B1, 19 July 2000).

So, the mission must reflect the company priority of creating living relationships with its customers.

Communicating the mission

Having developed a mission statement that is distinctive, realistic and externally focused, the next stage is to communicate it. Communication begins with employees.

The management mindset must be in place before all else. From India, there comes an organizational analogy: 'An organization is like a tree full of monkeys, spread over all its branches. When the ones at the top look down they see a tree full of smiling faces. When the ones below look up, what do they see?'

Cynicism can exist in any organization and a fundamental role of management is to destroy negative attitudes through consistently and reliably living the organization values. If the customers that count are truly important, then this must be evidenced by every word communicated by management and by every management act: by what they encourage, reward and penalize.

Example is stronger than exhortation and what you do is more credible than what you say. For instance, if the mission statement speaks of customers coming first, but the Board of Directors never reviews statistics on customer satisfaction, then the statement is a misnomer. Employees learn priorities from the actions of their executive role models, not their words.

What you do is more credible that what you say.

Single expansive gestures, employee conferences and high-impact launches of missions are less effective than regular and consistent reminders. Little and often is the best approach. Likewise, a single medium is less effective than a multimedia communication plan, which employs messages electronically, on paper and in person, in words, visual symbols and actions.

Cascade communications

Once the management group has determined its mission – normally with the aid of a broadly based team – there needs to be a communication exercise across the organization. This is known as a cascade (*see* Fig. 5.7). A cascade is a substantial flow of water plunging downwards, falling on the rocks below – it is very much one way, with nothing coming up, except just possibly a very determined salmon. This is the danger of organizational cascade communication – it captures little or nothing of the understanding, opinions, questions and improvements in the minds of the recipients. Dialogue is vital in confirming these and reinforcing the mission.

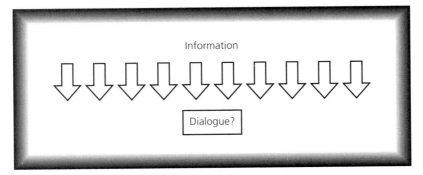

Figure 5.7 Cascade communications

Your people make relationships happen

You and your staff make relationships happen. There is no relationship with best customers without the active engagement of the people of the organization. Their interactions provide the feel and flavour of the organization. For the best customers, they personify and exemplify the relationship. Since 1996 the Carlson Marketing Group (www.cmg.carlson.com) has conducted an annual survey into customer loyalty in the UK. The 2000 survey was designed to define the drivers of loyalty and the characteristics that are most important to customers. The survey (published in *Marketing*, 14 September 2000) was based on quantitative and qualitative interviews with 3000 adults in the UK. The single highest factor of influence for these customers of supermarkets, banks and department stores was 'good staff' (49 per cent), substantially ahead of the second factor, which was 'better prices'.

Recruiting the right people

A critical moment for a new start-up is when the founder recruits the first employee. Immediately the responsibility for relationships becomes shared. Thereafter, the company depends on its people to create and cement relationships.

Honesty in recruitment is a key component in recruiting the right people for the organization. A famous advertisement was placed in London papers early in the twentieth century. The advertiser was Sir Ernest Shackleton, seeking companions on his expedition to the South Pole. The recruitment ad read:

> MEN WANTED for Hazardous Journey. Small wages, bitter cold, long months of complete darkness, constant danger, safe return doubtful. Honour and recognition, in case of success.

Shackleton's honesty shone through and he succeeded in finding men of the right calibre. An accurate description of the role is an essential part of the hiring process. Most job advertisements seem to focus on the 'honour and recognition', and omit the 'bitter cold' in their descriptions of vacant positions.

Prior experience is another aspect of selecting. The norm is to over-value similar industry experience. For example in the UK, St Paul International Insurance deliberately flout industry conventions and seek significant levels of recruitment from outside insurance and financial services. For customers in many specialist risk segments, knowledge of their own industry and its particular nuances is more important than 20 years with another insurer. Thus health professionals may be offered insurance and risk management solutions by a group of nurses and qualified medical practitioners.

The interview process is normally a core part of the selection of candidates. It has evident flaws. Being astute at answering questions in an interview room does not necessarily predict that the individual will be effective in the role envisaged. Many leading organizations are now supporting interviews with additional exercises, role plays and interactions to determine the suitability of the applicant.

For example, call-centre interviews often take place over the telephone to judge the candidate's skills, aptitudes and telephone manner. In a business where cleanliness and tidiness are essential to gaining the confidence of the best customers, one UK-based service operation deployed a practical test to check natural behaviour patterns. A scrumpled piece of paper was placed on the floor of the interview room between the door and the seat, in full view of the candidate, but apparently invisible to the interviewer. Only one in three candidates demonstrated their personal sense of order by picking up the paper.

The UK women's fashion retailer, Warehouse, had a policy of requiring a trial Saturday selling in store. Saturday is the day of the week when the best customers come to buy. Only when the manager and fellow sales people had seen the person in action with real customers and genuine merchandise would they determine their suitability for employment.

Southwest Airlines are legendary in the USA for their offbeat hiring techniques to ensure they attract extrovert individuals with a passion for service that gives the company its competitive advantage. Frederik Wiersema (1998) cites the group interview format, where 30 or more people are interviewed at the same time. One exercise requires them to make a five-minute presentation about themselves. During this the recruiters carefully scrutinize the other candidates to identify those listening, encouraging and cheering on, rather than the selfish individuals who are ignoring the other candidates and attending to their own presentations.

Frequently the best-placed people to locate and select new entrants are the current staff. They have an intuitive understanding of the company culture and the expectations of the best customers and therefore their recommendations are doubly valuable.

Keeping the right people

Taco Bell in the USA has focused on stabilizing its workforce, realizing that a stable workforce makes for better relationships internally and externally with customers and suppliers. According to Ken Irons (1998), the 20 per cent of its branches with the lowest rate of staff turnover have a profitability that is 55 per cent higher than the 20 per cent of branches with the highest turnover of employees.

Wal-Mart, with 1.1 million employees – more than the army of the People's Republic of China – have recognized the vital aspect of employee retention. In 1999 it modified its human resources philosophy from 'getting, keeping and growing' employees, to 'keeping, growing and getting' them. Coleman Petersen, Senior Vice-President of Wal-Mart's people division, states that this indicates an increased emphasis on retaining and developing talent, rather than the 'hire, hire, hire' strategy of the past. He has instituted a policy of assigning new recruits with an established employee as a mentor, plus reviews at 30 days, 60 days and 90 days to reduce attrition (*Fortune* magazine, 11 October 1999).

Motivating the right people

Motivation is a key part of staff retention. The essence of motivation is to make staff members feel important and involved. The terminology for employees can be critical in making people feel valued. Marriott speaks of 'associates', Richer Sounds employees are called 'colleagues', IKEA talks of 'co-workers'.

The essence of motivation is to make staff members feel important and involved.

For an example of involvement, IKEA, the international furniture retailer operating 135 stores, created a 'millennium thank-you' to motivate and incentivize co-workers. On Saturday 9 October 1999 in IKEA stores in 28 countries around the world, all the takings (less VAT and local taxes) were divided equally between co-workers. In addition, many stores undertook special promotions to boost turnover. Each country selected actions that would appeal to the best customers in their market. For example, Hungarian furniture buyers obviously enjoy being made to feel special, so at the two stores in Hungary, IKEA targeted customers with a birthday on 9 October and gave them presents. In Denmark the magic touch is evidently food, and Danish stores offered free breakfast. IKEA realizes the American love of a lottery and so in the USA two customers an hour received their purchases free (*Financial Times*, 8 October 1999).

Richer Sounds, the UK hi-fi retailer, has the highest sales per square foot of any retailer in the world (£5500 per square foot according to Verdict Research). It has attained this position partly through a conviction that colleagues, as it terms employees, are vital. Motivation includes incentives like free access to seven holiday homes in the UK and France, regardless of sales performance, and the use of a Bentley or Jaguar limousine for a month for the shop with the best performance. The value placed on staff is displayed to customers on the company website (www.richersounds.co.uk). In 1999 one of the Frequently Asked Questions related to Sunday openings. The answer was illuminating:

> Sunday Trading? At present we have no plans for seven-day trading (apart from our hectic Christmas period when all our competitors are open), as our staff are very anti the idea. We know a lot of employers couldn't care less about their feelings, but they really are our company's most valuable asset and we are therefore very reluctant to force the issue. As a compromise, we now open later on Thursdays and promise to keep the situation under review and in the meantime thank you again for your support.

Subsequently, after a long consultation period with staff and regular customers, Richer Sounds began opening its London West End Store for four hours on Sundays.

What really motivates?

The Gallup Organisation, widely known as an opinion polling company, has investigated how employee attitudes and involvement relate to four dimensions of business performance: productivity, turnover, profit and customer satisfaction. Research across 17 companies, 1135 business units and 41 490 employees in the USA focused on 12 statements (the 'Q12 Advantage'):

1 I know what is expected of me at work

2 I have the materials and equipment I need to do my work right

3 At work, I have the opportunity to do what I do best, every day.

4 In the last seven days I have received recognition or praise for good work

5 My supervisor or someone at work seems to care about me as a person

6 There is someone at work who encourages my development

7 In the last six months, someone at work has talked to me about my progress

8 At work, my opinions seem to count

9 The mission/purpose of my company makes me feel my job is important

10 My associates (fellow employees) are committed to doing quality work

11 I have a best friend at work

12 This last year, I have had opportunities at work to learn and grow.

Positive answers to the statements 1 to 5, 7, 9, 11 and 12 are correlated with high satisfaction levels in the customers of the surveyed organizations.

Temps matter too

Temporary staff may be crucial to the customer experience for seasonal businesses. For example, in the children's toy and game market it is estimated that 70 per cent of sales will occur in the last three months of the year. For companies like Smarterkids.com, temporary staff are needed to provide service in peak months. Human Resources Director, Donna DeRoy, recruited a team of additional Customer Services Representatives in October 1999, to respond to Christmas telephone calls and e-mails at Smarterkids' Needham headquarters. Temporary staff were delighted to discover that – just like permanent staff – they were part of the family and able to reach into the company fridges whenever they wanted a canned drink. So successful was Donna's selection that she determined to keep in contact with the temporary team throughout 2000 with a view to re-hiring the same individuals for peak 2000. Therefore she set up a Smarterkids alumni club with monthly e-mails of news, covering product and service developments as well as promotions, changes, births and marriages of company personnel.

In summary, staff, associates, co-workers and colleagues are the linchpin in building customer relationships. A key part of preparing an organization for long-term relationships with its key customers is selecting the right staff, training and developing them continuously, keeping them up-to-date and motivated and retaining their loyalty.

Keeping the right suppliers

Suppliers, too, are important contributors. Selecting and building long-term relationships with sources of supply is another part of the platform for the relationship. Long-term suppliers understand the tangible needs of the organization, and also the intangible culture or way of working. This takes time and patience.

Building understanding of the needs

As an example of building an understanding of tangible needs in its products and delivery schedules, McDonald's opened its first restaurant in China in 1991 only after years building a network of suppliers including, for example, potato growers for its fries. With around 300 restaurants in

China, 97 per cent of the food is locally produced and McDonald's is one of *Fortune* readers' most admired companies in China (*Fortune* magazine, 11 October 1999).

Building understanding of the culture

McDonald's has also built an understanding of its culture and intangible needs with its advertising agency, Leo Burnett, and is listed as one of the 13 multinational clients that have been with the agency for more than ten years. Leo Burnett emphasizes client loyalty as a way of demonstrating customer satisfaction, highlighting that Leo Burnett USA has ten clients that have been with the agency more than 25 years and eight for over 35 years (www.leoburnett.com). Green Giant, the food brand now owned by Pillsbury, itself part of Diageo, was a founding client when Leo Burnett opened in Chicago's Palmer House Hotel in 1935 and is still with the agency. Leo Burnett may actually have a closer familiarity with the organizational culture of a client than a newly appointed brand manager.

Facing change collaboratively

Long-term suppliers can also help organizations cope with change. The largest dairy company in Lithuania is Birzu Milk with 30 per cent of the national market. In the face of tougher export markets and increasing local competition, Birzu's response has been to collaborate with Lithuanian farmers to improve the quality of its milk supplies. It has supported this by guaranteeing bank loans to help farmers re-equip their dairies, and thereby has built a network of preferred suppliers (Maheshwari, 1999).

Making change collaboratively

New initiatives can emerge with supplier collaboration. The automotive company Chrysler showed a concept car in 1993 – a wild and crazy two-seat, rear-wheel drive, retro-roadster – not expecting it ever to see the light of day. Yet demand from customers and calls proffering help from suppliers brought this concept to the reality of the Prowler, launched in autumn 1997. Suppliers treated the Prowler as a testbed for lightweight body components and experimented with low-volume tooling. When they decided there was a real possibility of making the car, Chrysler collaborated with suppliers in an exercise called 'Extended Enterprise' and together they identified an affordable development budget of $75 million and divided this by the components in the car to come up with individual costings (Stallkamp, 1998). The suppliers met these and the car is an established success.

Olmsted-Kirk is a fourth-generation family company in the paper business with eight locations in Texas, USA. The company has a mission statement that includes the concept that it will deliver customer satisfaction 'through the friendliest people in the industry'.

Building up reliable patterns of behaviour to win loyalty applies to suppliers as well as customers.

It also has a guiding principle that commits it to 'earning supplier loyalty'. It believes that it takes time to achieve loyalty. Building up reliable patterns of behaviour to win loyalty applies to suppliers as well as customers.

Investor loyalty

Another stakeholder whose loyalty matters is the investor. There is a danger inherent in the trend towards automated share-buying and shorter-term holding of shares. When investors are holding a share as an anonymous commodity, hoping that it will rise and a profit can be realized, there is no loyalty. The company's fortunes are dependent on market sentiment and the actions of shareowners who have no affinity with the company, its products, services and values. The longer shares are held, the more likely the investor (individual or institution) is to understand the style, direction and values of the company. Of course, profit performance, dividends and capital appreciation are an important part of earning loyalty, but in addition a company should aim to recruit shareholders who have some sympathy for its market and its opportunities.

City communications can be devised to attract certain classes of shareholders. Many dotcoms seem to have unwisely aimed their market appeals at short-term investors wanting to 'get rich quick' rather than identifying those investors with a patient and continuing interest in their market sector. These long-term investors' needs can then be understood and met. For example, many older investors might appreciate large-print annual reports, publicized wheelchair access to annual general meetings and relevant benefits for long-term shareholding.

Institutional and individual investors may appreciate opportunities to visit businesses and to meet management and staff. Many retailers find they have durable relationships with their investors because the investors are also shoppers who patronize their stores. In the USA, Home Depot have this relationship with their investors. It also encourages staff shareownership. Although there is a legal obligation that all shareholders are placed on an equal basis as far as investment information is concerned, an action point might be to determine what kind of owners you would wish to have for your company shares in three year's time and then how you might move towards this.

Signalling to all stakeholders

Signalling is a key part of the preparation phase. It is the consistent provision of signals about the long-term values of the organization. If you are going to be serious about long-term relationships you must act the part. Every act indicates what the company is about. An accent on change – with new employees, new suppliers, new customers and new initiatives – conveys a short-term focus. The same information can be angled to stress the continuity of the organization. For example, the membership-based discount warehouse Costco recruits new people, but the organization chart on which they appear will show their peers and feature the date each joined Costco. This signals the value Costco places on long-term employment. Similarly, when announcing the appointment of a new supplier or the winning of a new customer, the words can imply that the newcomer is joining an exclusive club of committed suppliers or buyers. Advertisements and press releases can show customers who have been with the company many years, or suppliers who are celebrating an anniversary of supply.

Behaviour is the most credible indicator. When a leading organization in business services sought pitches from PR agencies, Countrywide Communications was eager to put itself forward. However, the date chosen for the presentations conflicted with a regular review meeting at an established client. Countrywide made it clear in its behaviour that it was eager to win new business, but that commitments to existing clients were paramount. Demonstrating loyalty will attract further customers or clients who value loyalty.

Stakeholders provide the power for organizations to deliver effectively for the Customers that Count over the duration. Aligning the efforts and activities of the stakeholders to the common purpose focuses this power.

Theme: Ready for customers	Case example

Weetabix

There are few examples of small local companies withstanding the onslaught of a major global corporation and thriving over a long period. A well-resourced and able adversary such as Kellogg's has proven skills in building share across the markets where it operates. Founded and headquartered in Battle Creek, Michigan USA, the Kellogg Company is the world-leading producer of ready-to-eat cereal. Products are manufactured in 20 countries on six continents and sold in 160 countries. Sales in 2000 were almost $7 billion.

There are fewer examples of companies withstanding the onslaught of two major global corporations. A major rival to Kellogg's in the UK breakfast cereal market is Cereal Partners, a joint venture between US giant General Mills, and Swiss-based global food supplier Nestlé. Cereal Partners promotes heavily strong brands such as Shredded Wheat, Shreddies and Cheerios. The combined advertising spend of these two rivals in the year ending March 1999 was close to £55 million. Logic suggests that a local company, with a market capitalization of around £400 million, should be suffering in the crossfire.

Yet Weetabix, this local company, is thriving. In 2000 the company posted results showing that UK turnover had grown for the 52 weeks to 29 July 2000 increasing by 10.6 per cent from £308.7 million to £341.4 million. The report on the Ofex exchange also indicated that the company had grown its sterling share of the UK market (www.ofex.co.uk).

How can this be? The answer is not easy to track down, as Weetabix does not court publicity. Little information is in the public domain. According to Alex Benady (1999), the answer is long-term thinking and long-term relationships: 'It shows how continuity, sound corporate governance, a long-term view and the cultivation of lasting relationships with consumers and the trade can make a small company a match for global corporations'.

There seem to be a number of factors driving the unexpected results. First, like any successful brand, Weetabix produces a consistently reliable good quality product. Invented in Australia in 1900, the Weetabix biscuit delivers a good mix of complex carbohydrates that sustain the eater for a number of hours. Easy to digest, Weetabix, softened by milk, can be eaten as a first solid food, all the way through life to old age. The advertising message has consistently focused on the product benefit of giving you strength to keep going. The product keeps its promise to consumers. After this, the quality of relationships begins to come into play.

Staff relationships seem to be excellent. The company has admirably low staff turnover. Led by Sir Richard George who joined the company in 1968, the Board exemplifies stability – five out of six directors have been in position since 1985. Clearly they have a deep knowledge of their product and its market developed over many years of focus. It is rare to see a management job advertised at Weetabix. There are no published statistics, but the local view is that stability extends to the whole workforce. Alex Benady quotes Bob Walker, a journalist on the local *Northamptonshire Evening Telegraph*, as saying, 'They pay over the odds and treat their people very well. Once you are in, you are in for good.'

Trade relationships are strong. In 1995 Weetabix was awarded a gold medal for service levels to wholesalers by the Federation of Wholesale Distributors. The range is small and it has a reputation for good product availability and high standards of sales representative. In addition, promotional merchandising is effective and all promises are kept.

There is a relationship of ten year's standing with the advertising agency, Lowe Howard-Spink, who appears to have the opportunity to produce quirkily creative adverts behind the long-term theme. Advertisements in 2000 show the trials and tribulations of a soccer referee with new words to the Bee Gee song 'Tragedy' and a similar rewording to the song 'I will survive' phrased for a harassed driving-test examiner. Weetabix sustains both. So creative are the words that a number of websites carry them. Again according to Alex Benady, the advertising to sales ratio of 8 per cent has remained consistent over a number of years.

Finally, the share-holding patterns appear to be stable. Shares are in two forms. The majority of the voting shares are in the hands of the George family and non-voting shares are listed on Ofex, a small and unregulated exchange, where most of the other companies listed are substantially smaller in scale. There is no suggestion of high levels of trading or volatility. Shareholders on the Ofex exchange expect little disclosure of information.

So, Weetabix appears to be able to grow sales against the might of Kellogg's, General Mills and Nestlé, by means of long-term relationships with employees, consumers, trade customers, suppliers and shareholders.

Exercise 5   Exercises

1 Consider your company mission. What does your company aim to deliver in terms of the customer experience? How will a customer feel about the company and the value it brings to their life, or to their organization?

2 List the key elements of customer value.

3 Rephrase them in language the customer might use.

4 Devise a speech bubble mission statement.

Further reading and references

Benady, Alex (1999) 'Unlocking the secrets of Weetabix', *Marketing*, 6 May.

Irons, K. (1998) 'Do you sincerely want to build relationships?' *Market Leader*, Winter.

Maheshwari, V. (1999) 'Sour Milk', *Business Central Europe*, October.

McDonald, M., Christopher, M., Knox, S. and Paine A. (2000) *Creating a Company for Customers*, Financial Times/Prentice Hall Chapter 3: 'Building bridges – the relationship management process'.

Stallkamp, Thomas T. (1998) 'Chrysler's Leap of Faith: Redefining the supplier relationship', *Supply Chain Management Review*, Fall.

Wiersema, Frederik D. (1998) *Customer Service: Extraordinary Results at Southwest Airlines, Charles Schwab, Lands' End, American Express, Staples, and USAA*, HarperCollins.

Customer selection

6

Your costs seem out of line with your results. Let's start at the beginning: how do you decide which potential customers are the priority?

If it moves, shoot it.

You will take any business?

Yes, if it is breathing.

What is your strike rate?

Actually, it's low.

And how about your customer retention?

We don't talk about that!

We have established that some customers are more valuable than others. Focusing attention and keeping the Customers that Count deliver profit and growth. But inevitably some customers will move, close down or see their needs change. So finding new 'best' customers is vital for continuity and growth. Not every potential customer can be a future 'best' customer. There are some potential customers you will not want to attract – bad payers, for example. To identify the best prospects, this chapter ends with a checklist of 15 questions to determine the most attractive potential customers. It also considers the benefits of loyalty from the perspective of the buyer. In a personal situation, you are unlikely to be happy marrying at random; selecting the right future customers follows the same logic.

Customer differences

All customers are not the same. Some take high volumes, some low, some need time-consuming support, some are self-sufficient, some are decisive, some vacillate, some are loyal, some buy everywhere and anywhere. There are best customers and worst customers. The same will apply to potential customers. Winning, nurturing and growing new customers is essential for future business prosperity. It is also a resource-intensive activity. Therefore focused attention needs to be given to selecting the right potential customers for recruitment.

7

Segmenting

Finding the right characteristics for selecting future best customers calls on the skill of segmentation. Consumer characteristics are a never-ending source of opportunities for segmenting markets and selecting customers. Geography is an effective form of segmentation in markets where tastes are regional – the food industry exemplifies this. For example, for Japanese consumers who use chopsticks, Nissin produce longer, less spicy noodles. By contrast, in India highly spiced, shorter vegetarian noodles are appropriate. Demographic segmentation still serves some companies well. In the pet food market, different products, prices, channels and advertising are targeted at owners of young dogs, or old dogs, or working dogs or obese dogs. Geo-demographics help define segments and provide clues to product propositions, but they do not define 'best customers'.

Occasions of use are another approach, and so tour operators to Niagara Falls provide different entertainment, facilities and accommodation for two contrasting groups. As the honeymoon destination of North America, tourist operators cater for newly weds as the second largest distinct group. The largest group are those whose lifetime ambition is to see the Falls before they die, and for many of these it is close run – they are called the 'nearly deads' (*see* Fig. 6.1). Clearly they have radically different requirements, and the guest facilities at Niagara Falls handle them in markedly different ways. This, however, is not repeat business, and this demographic segmentation scheme is not a predictor of 'best customers'.

Psychographic segmentation focuses on how consumers or customers feel and how they see themselves. It can distinguish 'outer directed' customers, who consume conspicuously, from the 'inner directed' and the 'sustenance

Segment 1	Segment 2
Newly weds	Nearly deads
Late-night dinner, flowers, candles, romantic souvenirs	Early morning calls, ground floor rooms, bright lighting

Figure 6.1 Segmentation at Niagara Falls

driven'. Often used in combination with other forms of segmentation, it provides an overview of broad type clusters. For example, when the Bluewater Shopping Mall opened south of London in 1999, marketers used the following seven shopper types to match facilities to group needs:

- budget optimists – middle-aged female, married, low incomes, traditional values, open to advertising and special promotions;
- club executives – middle-aged upmarket males;
- county classics – upmarket middle-aged females, married with affluent lifestyles;
- home comfortables – mid-market retired men and women, traditional, home and garden orientated, unadventurous;
- sporting thirties – mid-market, enjoy sports and leisure;
- young fashionables – single, image conscious, impulsive;
- young survivors – limited in interests, enjoy takeaway food.

All these are valuable approaches, but we need to go further to identify the individual customer types who are likely to be the most valuable.

Marketing theory invites us to begin with customer needs. Different customers have different relationship needs. Some customers have a higher need for consistency than variety. Others the reverse. Immediately this provides two categories, often called 'barnacles' and 'butterflies'. Customers with variety-seeking behaviour – the butterflies – constantly trawl the internet for the latest deal or the newest feature. It is unlikely that the best customers will be found amongst the butterflies.

> **Different customers have different relationship needs. Some customers have a higher need for consistency than variety.**

According to Professor Nigel Piercy (1999) of Cardiff Business School, not every customer is seeking a relationship with their suppliers. He proposes four categories of customer. The first two categories demonstrate loyalty, but differ in their desire for a relationship:

- **Relationship seekers:** wanting a close and long-term relationship with suppliers.
- **Loyal buyers:** will give long-term loyalty, but do not want a close relationship.

The second two categories show no loyalty, but again differ in the appearance of loyalty:

- **Relationship exploiters:** taking every free service or offer, but will still move their business when they feel like it.

● **Arms-length transaction buyers:** avoid close relationships and move business based on technical specification, price or innovation.

Four primary motivations

The needs of customers are the key to understanding the nature of 'best customers'. There are four primary motivations that drive behaviour in a way that leads us to best customers (*see* Fig. 6.2).

Four need types	Primary motivation	Value to company
Best deal	Lowest price	Sales volume
Novelty seekers	Something new	Research and testing
Involvement	Belonging	Referrals
Certainty	No surprises	Consistent patterns

Figure 6.2 Needs-based segmentation

In every market you will find individuals or organizations driven by an obsession to obtain the best deal. It is a competitive streak that sees buying and selling as a form of conflict with only one victor. The internal self-assessment or organizational reward system is based on whether they have achieved the lowest price. Chester L. Karrass (1994) has made a study of negotiation and analyzes the key elements in the deal making that is so important to this group. For these customers, there is no value in a relationship. They may be big-volume buyers, but they tend to provide low margins and offer little planning security.

Most markets can provide examples of innovators. Often these are few in proportion to the bulk of consumers. Their driving force is a persistent curiosity, led by a conviction that the grass is greener on the other side of the hill. They are compulsive variety seekers and novelty is more appealing to them than security. In fact they are happy to take risks. To understand the innovators' mentality read Everett M. Rogers (1995), who has made a lifetime study of innovators. For this group, too, there is little opportunity to build a long-term relationship.

Belonging is a strong emotional pull for the third group – they need to feel involved. To understand this group, read the analyses of Frederick Reichheld (1996). This group appreciates the recognition that they are important as a customer for their knowledge or influence. They follow the latest product or company announcements and welcome the opportunity to give advice or guidance. Some Customers that Count will fall into this category and they offer real opportunities to build up relationships.

Finally there is a large body of customers whose motivation is risk aversion. They want no surprises, but instead the reassurance that part of their lives is certain. They need to feel that someone is providing them with continuity if at all possible. When it is not possible, they expect long advance warning of change. To understand the importance of reassurance, look at the analysis of brand loyalty by David Aaker and Erich Joachimsthaler (2000). This group does not actively seek a relationship with a supplier, but will respond negatively if their value is not recognized. Many of the Customers that Count will fall into this category.

We will look first at the ways to approach each of these categories of customer, and then identify best customers.

Best-deal customers

For each group, there are valid strategies to handle them most appropriately. For example, each organization should identify its price-based buyers. Then there is the strategic decision – shall we seek these customers? The advantages are in volume and market share. As a brand leader it may be necessary to attract these customers to gain the benefits that being greatest in share can bring. Alternatively, these customers may detract from the position in the market you seek to adopt. Price shoppers give no security and can make businesses vulnerable by their departure.

Option one is to include best-deal customers in the portfolio of customers, but to assume no reliance on their continuity (*see* Fig. 6.3). They are exploiting their suppliers and so the supplier should exploit them in return. This means cutting off their supplies in times of shortage, in favour of more loyal custom. It means using them to clear stock surpluses in times of excess. It implies lower priority in return for lower prices, rationing of service and charging for extra support. The most able staff should be reserved for other customers.

Option one: serve them	• No reliance on continuity of demand • Use to clear surpluses • Restrict supplies in scarcity • Ration service • Low staff priority • Charge for extra services
Option two: focus on loyal custom	• Direct best-deal customers to competitors • Use price-based filters to discourage

Figure 6.3 Strategy options for best-deal customers

Option two is to decree that these customers play no part in your long-term plans. Identify and exclude them, normally through price-based filters. US corporate insurers will assess potential business against criteria that include frequency of changing previous insurers. When customer payback takes three years, why sign up a customer with a track record of moving on in less time than this?

Novelty seekers

New ideas and innovation drive the butterflies. In most markets they will represent a minority of customers, perhaps 2–5 per cent of total customer numbers. In other markets, such as high fashion and children's toys, they may represent a larger figure. They offer the advantage to a supplier that they may identify a new market trend or provide insights in usage or behaviour. They are exploratory and willing to take risks. Therefore new ideas and experimental new products or services can captivate them (*see* Fig. 6.4). They are often willing to participate in research projects and test prototypes. These customers have their value, but they are inherently disloyal.

• Identify these customers
• Consult them on trends, ideas and interests
• Experiment with them with new products services and designs
• Communication theme is 'new thinking'

Figure 6.4 Strategies for novelty seekers

Involvement customers

Create an involving communications plan for these customers (*see* Fig. 6.5). Their value is that they can act as a form of personal advertising or a secondary sales force, recommending and referring on your behalf. They will home in on prospective customers and provide information to them, which is tailored and relevant and seen as independent. This is a major asset. To capitalize on this asset a systematic information flow must be managed.

- Invite them to pilot new products
- Ask them to join a user group
- Invite them to join a project group
- Seek their advice – feedback actions taken
- Encourage directors to 'adopt a customer'
- Visit or phone after hours
- Feed their interests: business and social
- Give them information to recommend, samples
- Invite them to seminars, and bring a friend
- Exchange staff newsletters
- Feature them in advertising and brochures
- Present customer awards

Figure 6.5 Strategies for involvement customers

It is essential that these customers feel at the forefront of company information. Being the first to know of a launch, organization change or takeover will provide them with news to pass on to their contacts. In the business-to-business market, they need regular informal briefings, early warning e-mails, confidential telephone calls and copies of internal newsletters. In consumer markets, where numbers are greater, it may still be possible to make them members of user groups or friends of the brand. Volvo cars reportedly discovered that across European and American markets, the vast proportion of readers of their magazine advertising were existing Volvo drivers. Strategically they reframed their advertising copy to make it act as a script for converts to preach to non-Volvo drivers. Memorable facts and statistics were deliberately placed at the end of sentences and paragraphs to be most easily recalled for future retelling. Photographs were captioned with conversational phrases to be reused by the readers. The customers seeking involvement are like a word-of-mouth marketing department.

Certainty customers

Some customers are motivated by certainty. They may be conventional in their approach and be naturally cautious. Alternatively they may seek certainty in some aspects of their personal or commercial lives so that they can focus on other more exhilarating areas. For example, hi-tech customers – in Massachusetts known as '128 companies' after highway 128, or in California as 'Silicon Valley' companies – will seek suppliers for non-core aspects of their supply chain who are strongly consistent. They want no surprises on the office-cleaning contract!

A key value these customers offer is that they provide regular and reliable demand patterns. The danger is that their very consistency causes them to be taken for granted. Hence an important part of the relationship with these customers is to keep in contact without intruding. It is necessary to monitor potential concerns and provide solutions before they become alarmed with problems (*see* Fig. 6.6).

- Identify these customers
- Set up a monitor to track their performance (they may tolerate problems without complaining, until it is too late)
- Determine their shared characteristics
- Seek more customers with these characteristics

Figure 6.6 Strategies for certainty customers

A further benefit of these customers is that they may provide a template for identifying future 'best customers'. Analyzing their common characteristics may help identify indicators of potential customers for active recruitment who will then display the same patterns.

Objective – working towards more 'best customers'

You must be able to describe and find 'our kind of customer'.

The objective is to focus on building a business with as many 'best customers' as possible. Each organization should have a clear picture of the types of customer it is actively seeking. You must be able to describe and find 'our kind of customer'. You also must be aware of the kind of customer you would not wish to add to your customer base. It may not be possible to exclude certain customers. For example, many e-businesses will accept any order with a valid credit card. However, the more you can focus customer attraction on desirable types of customer, the better the business that will result. This focusing can be done openly by indicating in advertising and communication where specialisms lie. Racal, the telecom supplier now part of Global Crossing, used to advertise:

> Business is so varied, and organizations so different, no telecom supplier can be familiar with them all. That's why at Racal Telecom we focus on a realistic number of sectors, and give customers the very best solution from our range of voice and data services. We offer dedicated sector teams in transport, Government, retail, banking, insurance and finance and manufacturing.

Naturally, as part of the business review process you will establish where your competitive advantage most exceeds rival companies and seek to find customers whose needs match your areas of high performance.

Customers you do not want

There are some customers you do not want. Here we look at six groups you may chose to avoid in the prospect stage (*see* Fig. 6.7). It is often easier not to take on unsuitable or unprofitable custom than it is to lose the business once it has been taken on.

- Misfits
- Bad payers
- Abusers
- Non-economic users
- Price buyers
- High risks

Figure 6.7 Customers you do not want

Misfits

The first category of customers to avoid is misfits. These are people buying – in error or ignorance – an item or service that is inappropriate or unsuitable for them. For example, Mrs Fields fresh baked cookies bear on their label a statement to discourage inappropriate consumption. It reads: 'All of our products may have come in contact with nuts or nut oils. If you have an allergy to nuts we recommend that you do not consume our products.' Producers and vendors of alcohol and cigarettes work to ensure that minors do not buy their products. Where products have alternative uses and effects, such as adhesives which may deliver a hallucinogenic effect in confined spaces, manufacturers guide retailers in selling practices to prevent purchase for the wrong reasons. Reputable financial consultants will not sell sophisticated and high-risk investments to customers who have not arranged basic life insurance cover.

Bad payers

Bad payers are the next group to exclude. Establish the ability and willingness to pay in an acceptable time-scale. Here a history check is important. It is frustrating to recruit a new customer and find that initial sales invoices remain unpaid or that undue time is spent in pursuing payment. In the UK brewing industry, winning a new 'free-trade account' (as independent bars and pubs are termed) was celebrated when the first bill was paid, not when the first order was placed.

Abusers

The third category of customers you do not want are those whose customer history indicates abuse or a non-ethical relationship. Insurance companies in the UK exchange details of customers who lose an expensive camera on every holiday and these regular high-level claimants find that companies decline to provide cover for them. Hotels will blacklist and not rebook guests who behave rudely or threateningly to their staff. US food companies maintain registers of regular complainers – customers who routinely write demanding compensation for problems that appear contrived or invented. Early complaints are handled sympathetically, but ultimately it may be suggested that these customers avoid their brands in future. The engaging head of Southwest Airlines, Herb Kelleher, once had a complaint letter passed on to him. It was the seventeenth flight the lady had taken with Southwest and her seventeenth letter of complaint. His response was to write and say, 'Dear Mrs Crab-apple, We'll sure miss you.' Every company should deal fairly with customer concerns, but the rise in 'professional whingers' must be met by deflecting tactics. You cannot give full support to your best customers if resources are being abused by less-than-ethical customers.

Non-economic users

Be wary of the next group: uneconomic users. These are customers who require service levels utterly out of keeping with the scale of their business. They may hog help-lines or insist on dedicated support. They waste the time of highly paid support experts, seeking advice that is then ignored. Often they will over-order deliberately and make high-level returns. They will challenge any cost recovery procedure and seek exceptions to company policies, and in so doing, consume executive time. Another type of non-economic user is the customer of a competitor committed to them over the long term who seeks quotes simple to use when negotiating better terms with the incumbent supplier. In business-to-business transactions it is often possible to recognize the non-economic customer at the tendering stage and to price at a level that will encourage this customer to buy elsewhere.

Price-based buyers

You may wish to select out price-based buyers. Frequently these customers may be attracted to you through bargain offers. It is often impossible to persuade these customers to pay higher prices subsequently and their tenure is short-lived. Smarterkids.com, the Massachusetts-based educational toy and game e-tailer, found that this applied to the customers it gained through price promotions and it has now changed the emphasis of promotions to reward existing buyers only. Many organisations avoid price-based promotions for winning new customers.

High-risk customers

Finally, there are in many industries high-risk customers. The risk may be financial bankruptcy or threat of takeover. It may be risky through public-relations dangers by association. Or the risk may simply be volatility, where, for example, management change is so frequent that it is impossible to form a relationship with any individual in the customer's company and long-term business is unlikely. If the risk is judged unacceptable – for instance if the business would require specific investment – then it may be better to exclude this type of customer.

The kind of customers you want

In a business focused on best customers, it is important to filter out at the prospect stage potential customers who will never fall into the best customer category and may detract from provision of service to the best customers. Instead, you need to look at the seven kinds of customers you do want (*see* Fig. 6.8).

- Spend a lot, spend often
- Potential big spenders
- Different from target customers of rivals
- Customers in growth sectors
- Sources of new ideas
- Propensity to be loyal
- Similar to Customers that Count

Figure 6.8 Customers you want

In any assessment of attractive customers, volume is a key factor. The most profitable customers are not necessarily the largest, because volume users may demand best prices. However, volume still counts for a great deal. Hence many reward schemes and loyalty programmes are directly pitched to favour the highest spenders. Elite members of the Marriott Rewards program receive up-weighted points – guests staying more than 15 nights per year become silver members and are credited with 20 per cent extra points for every stay, compared with guests staying less than 15 nights.

Spend a lot, spend often

Customers you want spend a lot and spend often. Sainsbury's, the UK supermarket, conducted market analysis to understand the highest spenders and identify them. It discovered that pet-owners spend £2.5 billion per year on pet-care, and also spend more on average per shopping trip than non pet-owners. This led Sainsbury's to launch its 'Pet Club'. New members receive a welcome pack and thereafter get quarterly magazines updating them on pet issues and relevant products in the Sainsbury's stores. According to *Marketing Direct* magazine (March 2000), the average weekly spends for Pet Club members are up to £15 greater than those of non-members. Significantly, the attrition rates are well below the level of non-members, so retention provides an enduring benefit to Sainsbury's. A second approach to the same concept is provided by Sainsbury's '0–5 Club' which is aimed at customers with young children. Members receive regular magazines, prize competitions and exclusive offers, and in return Sainsbury's notes that on average the club's 330 000 members visit more frequently and spend more per visit than any other group of customers. Frequency of visit and average spend levels are straightforward and obvious criteria for reviewing best customers.

Potential big spenders

Potential business beyond today is also a factor that increases the attractiveness of some prospective customers. Examples are:

- potential for future purchases;
- part of a group of companies;
- low cost of serving: local or convenient;
- possibility of increasing margins;
- open negotiating style.

However, it should be noted that pure potential may be a distraction and may be used as a carrot for business terms that are not justified by actual turnover. Size and potential size alone are not sufficient to determine future best customers.

Size and potential size alone are not sufficient to determine future best customers.

Different from target customers of rivals

A group that may be particularly attractive is made up of customers who are unlike those your larger rivals are hunting. Admiral, a motor insurer based in Cardiff, Wales, has grown rapidly to around 500 000 customers by focusing on under-35-year-old male drivers. According to the *Financial Times* (21 December 1999), other motor insurers normally avoid younger men because of their higher risk levels.

Customers in growth sectors

Another attractive feature for future best customers is an interest in rapid growth sectors of the market. Cyprus Telecom identifies its best customers as high volume and growing in usage. In addition it values urban residences where connection costs are smaller and there is a pattern of low incidence of complaints. Finally, high internet usage is a pointer for future high-value custom.

Sources of new ideas

Customers who can aid your own organizational learning and support your preparation for future developments are also attractive. Indicators here might be:

- high-level knowledge in a burgeoning area of business;
- leading-edge techniques;
- reputation as an innovator;
- opportunity to collaborate in a growth sector;

- willingness to experiment jointly;
- openness to secondments of staff;
- possibility for mutual benchmarking.

Propensity to be loyal

A valuable characteristic of best customers is that they are loyal. Therefore it is important to analyze frequently observed qualities in a loyal customer. John Day, Aftab Ahmed Dean and Paul L. Reynolds (1998) surveyed 20 small and medium enterprises, looking at the role of relationship marketing in entrepreneurship. They uncovered a list of qualities observed in loyal customers:

- purchase at standard price;
- regularly purchase;
- do not make risky decisions;
- their business is growing;
- they deal with companies with an older managing director.

To support the first point – purchasing at standard prices – the UK-based motorists' organization the Automobile Association (AA) is conscious that the members it is most likely to lose to rival organizations, when it comes to renewing, are those who previously joined through free joint-membership deals. Thus the AA developed a specific direct marketing campaign aimed at retaining a higher proportion of this challenging category of customers. In the Direct Marketing Royal Mail Awards 2000 these results were recognized.

A further indicator of loyalty appears in the exercise at the end of the chapter (*see* page 93).

Similar to Customers that Count

Certainty has a value and finding new customers closely similar to existing customers means you are on safer ground. Nikelodeon is expanding its international reach into central Europe, negotiating deals to carry its children's TV channels on cable networks in Hungary and Poland. According to the *Financial Times* (21 December 1999), Nikelodeon's success in 28 million homes outside the USA in countries as diverse as Romania and Malaysia illustrates that it is easier for it to export children's programming in new markets and different cultures than to export TV for adults. In effect, Nikelodeon is seeking customers with characteristics and tastes common to the customers it already knows and serves.

This may be the most critical indicator of new and valuable customers. Newly won customers, most similar to your existing best customers, will fit smoothly into your organizational culture and operational systems.

Why it is good to be a loyal customer

It is often assumed that all the advantages of loyalty lie with the vendor. In fact there are 11 benefits to customers:

1 **Saves time:** no need to seek new suppliers, or to test and qualify them. Reducing supplier numbers and behaving loyally to them drives down administrative costs.

2 **Faster briefings:** on new orders and projects. Loyal suppliers readily understand your business or personal needs and your technical terms, acronyms and jargon.

3 **Reduces misunderstandings:** specifications are understood. Loyal suppliers are also familiar with your ethos, style and unspoken assumptions and constraints.

4 **Share risk:** possibility of joint developments, collaborative new product development and combined market entries.

5 **Certainty of supply:** ability to construct long-term schedules together.

6 **Priorities:** given when shortages occur.

7 **Help:** with technical problems. You know who to ask. They can provide answers to questions.

8 **Advice you can trust:** for example, information on market trends.

9 **Resource to draw on:** supplier can support you in dealing with difficult customers of your own.

10 **Recommendation:** they may refer other suppliers or services to you.

11 **Benchmarking:** loyal suppliers can be a useful benchmarking partner

Finding new Customers that Count is vital for continuity and growth. Not every potential customer can be a future best customer. A relevant strategy is to envisage the perfect mix of customers three years' hence. What steps need to be taken now to move closer to the ideal in the future?

Theme: Customer selection	Case example

Rockwell Automation

Rockwell Automation is a world leader in factory and process automation, with sales exceeding $4 billion. It trades in more than 80 countries, with over 100 000 customers. According to the 1999 Rockwell Annual Report, its customers include every major industrial company in the world. One reason may be that more than 20 per cent of its 25 000 employees are field located, working directly with customers.

Randy Freeman, Vice-President of Global Marketing for Rockwell Automation Control Systems, aims to satisfy every customer. This means meeting different needs and different expectations. Like most Rockwell Automation executives, he has an easy familiarity with the marketplace. We met in his office in the former Allen-Bradley head-quarters beneath the clock tower – a landmark in Milwaukee Wisconsin. He draws a model to illustrate Rockwell's customer profiles:

1 Global accounts:

- less than 50;
- global in scope;
- strategic in nature.

2 Named accounts:

- several thousand in number;
- national or regional in scope;
- named Rockwell Automation contact.

3 Geographic accounts:

- greater than 100 000;
- local in scope;
- handled through channel partners.

A small number of global accounts are responsible for a significant proportion of turnover. With 16 years in Rockwell, Vice-President of Global Accounts Kieran Coulton, has a clear picture of the customer characteristics he seeks in new global accounts. Customer selection means a focus on some key customer aspects. First, they must see manufacturing excellence as a differentiator. This means that Rockwell Automation is able to contribute to the customer's strength in their own marketplace. The control systems, drives, motion controls and software installed by Rockwell Automation help the customer succeed through speed to market, accuracy, lower costs or greater variety. Rockwell advertising has a theme: 'You succeed, We succeed'.

Significant scale and consistent standards are important. Customers must have a global operating framework. This means standardizing on a process worldwide so that the customer can pro-duce the same brand in the same way across the globe. For Rockwell Automation, there is an opportunity to influence standards used on a global basis via a few central facilities.

Key customers are likely to be early adopters of new ideas and technologies, and be willing and able to feed back trends and future technical requirements. They are industry leaders and show the way.

Best practices come out of the process of meeting their new needs.

Finally, they work jointly to define the value equation. They share objectives and jointly agree the focus of attention, for example, managing assets better. There is agreement on the priorities. As Kieran puts it, 'Everything is joint. You cannot force them to be intimate customers.'

Rockwell's success lies in understanding its own strengths and selecting for special attention the global accounts that value these abilities. Customer selection is a key platform of its strategy.

Exercise 6

Review customers recruited one year ago and list them in two categories:

1 The customers that now appear to be loyal.

2 Customers you have lost subsequently, or who appear likely to cease purchasing.

Compare both groups against the checklist below. Could these questions have provided an indication of future best customers at the prospect stage?

Prospecting for future Customers that Count: 15 questions to ask:

- Is the prospective customer well prepared, have they conducted their own needs analysis? Are they experienced purchasers?
- Is this customer seeking a supplier with complementary skills?
- Are they seeking full supplier qualification, references, and accreditation?
- Do they require a high level of personalization rather than buying off the shelf?
- Are they service literate, asking for details of service and support?
- Do they place a high value on time?
- Are they brand conscious and aware of the image benefits you provide?
- Do they have a stable management team?
- Do you share a common culture, with similar values?
- Is a team of buyers involved who share agreed aims?
- Are they eager for multilevel involvement?

- Are they interested in experimenting, testing and learning with you?
- Has an existing customer referred them to you?
- Are they returning to you after a period of buying from a competitor?
- Can they demonstrate a pattern of long-term relationships with other suppliers?

Further reading and references

Aaker, David A. and Joachimsthaler, Erich (2000) *Brand Leadership*, The Free Press.

Bartram, Peter (1999) 'The wrong kind of customers' *Financial Director*, October.

Day, J., Dean, A.A. and Reynolds, P.L. (1998) *Relationship Marketing: Its Key Role in Entrepreneurship, Long Range Planning*, Vol. 31, no. 6.

Karrass, Chester L. (1994) *The Negotiating Game: How to get what you want*, HarperCollins.

O'Dell, S. and Pajunen, Joan A. (2000) *The Butterfly Customer: Capturing the Loyalty of Today's Elusive Consumer*, John Wiley.

Piercy, Nigel (1999) 'Relationship Marketing Myopia' *Marketing Business*, October.

Reichheld, Frederick F. and Teal, Thomas (1996) *The Loyalty Effect: The Hidden Force Behind Growth, Profits, and Lasting Value*, Harvard Business.

Rogers, Everett M. (1995) *Diffusion of Innovations*, Free Press.

Stone, Merlin (1999) *Managing Good and Bad Customer*, Policy Publications.

Living the relationship

Relationships, whether businesses-to-individual or business-to-business, are connections between groups of people. Human values rule the judgements we make about relationships. As Mark MacCormack wrote in *What They Don't Teach You at Harvard*: 'All things being equal people will buy from a friend. All things being not quite so equal people will still buy from a friend.'

Eight values influence our perceptions of relationships between people:

- reliable performance
- trust
- recognition
- accessibility
- service and assistance
- education
- preference
- individuality and brand association.

We can learn from these values and endeavour to apply them to commercial relationships. Where it is impossible to apply them to every customer, the priority must go to best customers.

These eight values are key success factors in creating good relationships with the Customers that Count. The following chapters explore each of these values in turn. To be effective, they need to be integrated in a whole pattern of behaviour.

The fine bedside clock read 2.35 am when she heard the fire alarm. Slowly she came to and realized that she was on the thirteenth floor of the Ritz Carlton Singapore and it was a long walk downstairs. By association, she recalled false alarms in other hotels before now, but never one at this height above ground level. Roll over and hope, or run down 150 stairs? On reflection, she could not imagine Ritz Carlton allowing a false alarm, they never made mistakes. So she wrapped the luxurious towelling robe around herself and headed for the stairwell.

Sadly, this was a false alarm, and it was 30 minutes before she was able to return to her comfortable divan. It was part dream and part distant memory when she woke the next morning, but the note of apology signed by Anne Lai, the sales manager was real enough. She must have been up all night, she thought. When she returned at midday to check e-mails, there was a bowl of fresh strawberries to make up for the inconvenience.

She could think of half a dozen organizations who seemed to have limitless experience in rectifying errors, yet here was Ritz Carlton, who never made mistakes, showing how to put things right. And how on earth did they know she adored strawberries?

The Customers that Count are won by human values and the first of these, the threshold qualifier, is reliability. Delivering on expectations – keeping promises – is the starting point (*see* Fig. 7.1). There are a number of ways to secure reliable performance, for example preferring proven equipment instead of more exciting leading-edge systems. Beyond the hardware and software, consistent behaviour of staff contributes to the picture of reliability that keeps the best customers. To track performance and learn from mistakes and 'near misses', you will need monitoring systems and agreed measures. Finally, when the unlikely and unlucky coincide, you will need recovery procedures. World-class service recovery is becoming a part of competitive advantage in holding the most desirable customers.

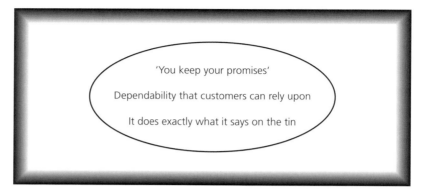

Figure 7.1 Reliability

Right first time

The paramount factor in building durable customer relationships is relia-bility. Professor Leonard Berry of Texas A & M University, leading thinker in service marketing, lists four factors, with reliability as the first. The remaining three are fairness, recovery and surprise. The quality revolution in manufacturing in the 1980s has left a legacy of customer expectations that products will work. It is a cause of surprise when a credit card fails to swipe first time. Retailers promote very profitable warranties to customers purchasing new television sets. Product reliability makes the warranties profitable because few customers ever need to make claims on the war-ranties they have bought. However, promotional efforts are often in vain because the customer's mindset is that this machine will continue to oper-ate until and beyond the date when it is overtaken by newer technology. In one survey of breakdown recovery services, a consumer-test magazine compared different roadside rescue organizations. As an aside, it made an alternative recommendation – drive a Honda and their reliability could mean you would not need a recovery service.

Building credibility

Building credibility is the first step to creating major reputations (*see* Fig. 7.2). Robust internal systems and procedures come before dazzling adver-tising. Visible and appealing advertising may recruit curious customers willing to experiment with the uncertain. Provide reliable delivery and they may return and recommend to others. Make them disappointed and they will never return, and worse they will also discourage others from trying your product or service, even after it has become dependable. Jan Carlson, the legendary leader of SAS, the Scandinavian airline, refused to sign off investment in new plane livery until his airline's on-time performance was equal to the best in class. He would not attract custom until he felt worthy of retaining it.

- Using proven systems
- Putting consistency before performance
- Testing on employees first
- Testing on experimentalist customers before extending to the majority
- Clarifying expectations to customers, employees and intermediaries
- Monitoring and reviews of 'near misses'

Figure 7.2 Building reliability

A true brand cannot have hit and miss elements. It must consistently achieve the brand promise. You would not expect the colour of Ocean Spray cranberry juice to vary, or the strength of Kronenbourg Lager. If DHL fail to answer your telephone call in three rings, you know you have misdialled and you ring again. Unsurprisingly, when Teleperformance International conducted a ten-factor mystery-shopper survey across a variety of industries in 20 countries in Europe, Asia Pacific and the USA, they ranked DHL as the best worldwide company. And consistency goes further than speed. Based in Clevedon UK, the telesales consulting firm Telecom Potential advises clients to ensure their phone agents are immersed in the customer's expectations. Maggie Evans, Head of Marketing, says in *Marketing Direct* magazine (October 1999): 'The fact that a call is answered in three rings is immaterial if you don't get the brochure out quickly'. Therefore the first step in keeping the best customers is to build fail-safe systems to deliver products and services to the expected brand standard – every time.

Making consistency happen: simple systems

Simple systems are the method for attaining reliability. When First Direct, the UK telephone bank, prepared to set up its operations in the late 1980s, it eschewed state-of-the-art relational databases, selecting instead proven software. It allowed others to pioneer internet banking, deliberately choosing to be later and more dependable. The temptation always exists to specify futuristic systems that offer novel facilities. These should not be at the expense of 24-hour, seven-day reliability.

There is a compact zoom camera from a south-east Asian manufacturer that offers more advanced specification than any of its rivals – in dimensions such as substantially greater lens flexibility, sophisticated date marking, two types of red-eye reduction and a choice of time periods for the self-timing device. The feature list on the website is impressive. But when you call up some independent websites with real customer reviews, their stories of living with the camera are not so impressive. The message is clear: reliable performance comes before all else in building long-term relationships with your best customers.

> **Reliable performance comes before all else in building long-term relationships with your best customers.**

Consistency through employee testing

Alpha testing is the first step to achieving consistent reliability (*see* Fig. 7.3). This is pre-testing by employees. Your people are the committed testers, who will explore every possible aspect of a new product or service before the customer is involved. Gillette in Boston has a shaving laboratory where staff test and experiment with new products, enhancements and variations to provide width of experience to the company.

Step 1	Alpha test	Employees try out the new version
Step 2	Beta test	Pilot with experimental customers
Step 3	Roll out	When proven, extend to all customers

Figure 7.3 Testing new products and services

Porsche put to the test new engines, suspensions and braking systems in laboratory conditions, and follow this with analysis of performance on closed racetracks and testing grounds. However, before any modification is introduced to its model range, employees will use test vehicles as their daily transportation. A local German newspaper carried the story that Porsche employees campaigned successfully to prevent the regional highway department from straightening and smoothing a particular route to the Porsche factory, in order to maintain its testing qualities.

How customers contribute

Beta testing is the involvement of willing customers – individuals who are aware of the element of risk and who are eager to try a new product or service before anyone else. Microsoft makes very effective use of students in California and elsewhere, who challenge the performance or seek limitations of new software, and so contribute to the de-bugging process. The new software can then be rolled out to all customers.

Buitoni, the Nestlé-owned pasta and Italian food brand, created Casa Buitoni as a membership club for people who appreciate Italian food. Qualification was through clipping and mailing bar codes from Buitoni packs purchased. Members received a magazine with recipes, wine recommendations, offers for cooking utensils, and similar benefits. Club members provided their telephone numbers as part of the registration process. Food-development technologists were therefore able to call and seek agreement to sending samples of new pasta variants and sauce recipes. A freephone number was provided for members to call up in the event of any questions, and to provide a post-prandial verdict on taste, appearance, ease of preparation and so on.

Clear understanding of all players

To be consistently 'good', all the people involved in the process (customers, employees and any intermediaries) must have the same understanding of what 'good' means. Brand standards must lay down a definition of the correct appearance, specification and customer experience.

When Paramount Home Entertainment, UK distributors of the *Star Trek* TV series, appointed an agency, Haygarth Group, to promote the 26 *Star Trek* videos released each year, the first step was to immerse the agency personnel in the culture, history and language of *Star Trek*. According to *Marketing Direct* (January 2000), Stuart Williams, Marketing Director, arranged a seminar for the account team on everything *Star Trek*, from alien genealogy to how warp speed works. He explained: 'We have a complex product, with a very knowledgeable customer base. If you spell a name wrong, use the wrong space ship, it undermines the whole credibility of the scheme and the videos themselves.'

Companies must help set customer expectations. For example, FedEx promises free delivery if a package does not arrive by 10.30 am, thereby clarifying the customer's expectations: 10.00 am is good, 11.00 am is bad.

Flora is a leading UK margarine brand produced by Unilever subsidiary Van den Bergh Foods. The brand values relate to caring, health and trust and the brand conveys a professional approach to healthy living. Every brand encounter confirms the same message. From the first advertising campaign in 1965 – 'Flora puts natural goodness into good eating' – to the 2000 message – 'Flora people care' – the brand has communicated a consistent core theme. Its 1996–9 sponsorship of the London marathon was consistent with the healthy identity and the way the sponsorship was executed followed the brand standards. The pack design is clean, bright and lively. The packs bear a care-line telephone number (0800 446464). Call this number and the agents taking the calls are ambassadors for the brand. They sound professional, helpful and have a high level of expert knowledge. For example, they can give you the clearest explanation of the importance and characteristics of polyunsaturated fats. Similarly, the website (www.vdbfoods.co.uk) is a valuable source of health information. To the best customers, every point of contact with the brand must be in keeping with the expectations set.

Monitors and measures

Consistency must be monitored. Nothing in life operates perfectly and so to personify reliability you must have instant measures of product performance and service delivery. This may include regular reviews of 'near misses', when a problem was averted before customer impact. Service reliability is often measured by mystery shoppers. Taylor Nelson Sofres, who have 40 000 mystery shoppers in countries across Europe, and the research organization NOP can provide routine reports and identify aberrations from the consistency sought.

Bruce Robertson is Human Resource Director of Prêt à Manger, the upscale natural food sandwich bars in London and other cities. Quoted in *The Times* (25 April 2000), he claims that staff and customers both benefit from the mystery shoppers who visit its 92 stores every week. Employees are assessed on a strict ten-point scale, and anyone who gets nine out of ten receives an extra 50 pence an hour for the rest of the week. If a shop gives 90 per cent satisfaction for a month, the whole team is sent off for weekend breaks. The measure is weekly. Whatever measures are used, it is essential that they are frequent and quickly reviewed for action aspects.

Monitoring customer complaints can also provide action points. Complaints at one supplier of building materials indicated a problem where customers placed goods into storage on receipt and only discovered variations from required sizes and dimensions weeks or months later when the materials were called off. Often the mistake was made by the customer when ordering. The action taken to prevent future problems was to call customers the day following delivery to confirm receipt and ask them specifically to check the sizes at that point. The sources of customer errors were soon traced. Better systems at customers ended blame-orientated debates and led to an improvement in relationships.

World-class recovery

When your control and monitoring indicate shortfalls in performance then powerful service recovery mechanisms must come into play. When customers complain, there is an immense opportunity to rectify or destroy the relationship. Strong recovery is another of Professor Leonard Berry's four criteria for excellent service.

Recovery after a service or product failure is important for a number of reasons. It is part of the reliability syndrome, so valued by best customers. It is a true characteristic of a good friend that they are beside you and supportive in times of difficulty.

Good recovery may even create a higher satisfaction with the organization. Leading international airline, British Airways, tracks customer opinions on every aspect of its services. It has learnt that those BA customers whose luggage has been lost and subsequently recovered, rate BA higher on luggage handling than people whose bags have always come through!

Frequent travellers, particularly those with North American experience, treat occasional baggage loss as the norm, and judge an airline by its ability to trace and return the missing luggage. Thus the objective in service is to create the customer perception: 'You can rely on them – if *ever* something does go wrong, they fix it for me fast. I'd recommend them to anyone.'

Finally, and pragmatically, when something goes wrong it is one of the few occasions when the customer has a heightened awareness of the supplier. In routine circumstances a supplier working effectively may be taken for granted. When there is a problem the customer is hypersensitive (*see* Fig. 7.4). The actions, the exchanges of information and the manner of resolution may live in the customer's memory for decades.

- Heightened sensitivity to the organization
- Emotions: puzzlement, anger, fear of consequences
- Concern for the immediate
- Challenge to the accepted pattern
- May remember for years

Figure 7.4 When something goes wrong

Five steps to recovery

When a customer realizes that something is awry, they may feel a number of emotions: puzzlement: why me? Anger may be the prevailing emotion or fear of unknown consequences. They will also have a concern for the immediate – what happens now! Therefore the first of the five steps to a world-class service recovery (*see* Fig. 7.5) is to address the immediate problem and express regret that the issue has arisen.

- Address the immediate problem and express regret
- Explain convincingly
- Prevent recurrence
- Demonstrate your calibre
- Restore confidence

Figure 7.5 Five stages in world-class recovery

Seeing it from their eyes

Seeing the problem from the customer's perspective is an important aspect of this first step. This means establishing the consequences for the customer. A Marriott Hotel associate might discover that a delay at checkout meant that the guest could not catch the planned airport shuttle service and risks missing a flight. The hall porter would show that he understood the impact on the guest and ask what would put this right. The answer might well be 'pay for a cab' and the hall porter would arrange this on his own authority.

A potent form of shaping customer opinions is asking the question: 'What can we do to put matters right?' Normally, in the heat of the moment, the suggestions are modest and practical. Whereas three days later the compensation calculator may be running differently in the customer's mind. With the Customers that Count, the offer to put things right places them back in control, when control had temporarily been lost at the moment that the original plans were thwarted.

I am truly sorry this has happened

Expressing regret is another aspect of the first stage. It is an unfortunate outcome of the litigious climate in some markets that overly cautious company lawyers forbid customer-facing staff to apologize lest this is interpreted as liability. The impact on customer opinion is dramatic. When an apology is expected and deserved it should be given. With Customers that Count a small gesture will often reinforce the apology. For example, the UK family restaurant chain Beefeater allows waiting staff to provide a free dessert if the quality or speed of service of previous courses has disappointed customers. A free dessert is also offered at the US-based dining experience, Rainforest Café, which records customer seating and service times where for instance there has been an unacceptable delay in taking a customer's order.

Clearly, the company must now make and deliver the promised solution. This must be realistic, effective and timely.

Explain convincingly

In a successful personal relationship, individuals act openly. The same model applies in relationships with customers. So when things have gone amiss, customers should be offered an honest explanation in jargon-free terms. The offer is another means of putting the customer back in control. They may accept or decline the explanation. In business-to-business transactions it is more often accepted than in business-to-consumer. Offering the opportunity to speak with a technical expert may be necessary to reassure. Likewise, subsequently telling unlucky customers what you have done to prevent recurrence may encourage confidence in future transactions, and strengthen the relationship.

Preventing recurrence

Learning from a problem or failure is an opportunity and a responsibility. Little is more damaging to a relationship with a good customer than a repeat of a problem

Learning from a problem or failure is an opportunity and a responsibility.

that you had committed to resolve. Thus detailed diagnosis must take place on why the problem arose. Was it changing circumstances, human error, systems constraints, incorrect customer expectations, product abuse or a combination of factors, which had not been foreseen? The diagnosis must extend to modelling other potential problems, which have not yet but may occur, so that these can be addressed at the same time.

Naturally the diagnosis could involve staff who work in the affected operation, internal experts and external advisors. It can be effective, honest and bonding to invite selected customers to contribute to envisaging solutions and comment on proposed revisions. When REXAM Flexible Packaging faced difficulties with rolls of plastic wrapping film for a major manufacturer of disposable medical equipment, it set up two-way exchanges of personnel to see the customer's wrapping line and for the customer to inspect the final stages of the film production. The resolution emerged from the interaction.

The solution must be destruction tested, for it must not fail in practice. The implementation phase must be closely monitored to give early confidence in its success.

This moment may live forever

The recovery operation gives the supplier the chance to demonstrate its calibre. For once the customer is providing their full attention. It is a defining moment, which may be remembered years later. The customer is seeking fairness by their standards. Stephen Tax and Stephen Brown (1998) cite three dimensions to fairness:

- the outcome should be seen to be fair;
- the procedure should be fair and not overly complex and bureaucratic;
- the personal interactions should feel fair.

Poor performance on any of these three dimensions will impact on the lasting perceptions of fairness. This can lead to damaging subversion of marketing strategy by hostile former customers in word-of-mouth criticism. Meeting the three aspects can result in decades of loyalty and a missionary zeal to recommend to potential customers.

A checklist for demonstrating your calibre includes:

- delivering on promises;
- checking subsequent transactions and any other services used by the customer for 100 per cent performance;
- explaining the complaint resolution procedure to the customer's satisfaction – seen as reasonable;

- ensuring the customer appreciates the timing and steps of the rectification – seen as speedy;
- maintaining empathy with the customer;
- communicating to all who may contact this customer so that they too can be seen as caring;
- plus something extra – 30-day call.

For Customers that Count, there is an extra technique to restore confidence. After the problem has been resolved a senior person makes a subsequent phone call (*see* Fig. 7.6). With a complex commercial issue in a banking business this may take place 30 days after the initial error. With a shopper's complaint at a boutique it might be 24 hours after resolution.

Whatever the appropriate timing the gist of the call is to say that we know you had a problem and we are calling to see that this has been resolved to your satisfaction. May we now check that there are no other concerns on your mind at this time? The effect of this is to restore confidence for the breach of faith that occurred. It goes further by seeking any other issues that may create dissatisfaction. Finally, it has the effect of drawing a line under the issue. For this top-20 per cent customer, it is a formal mark that the problem is now recognized as being over.

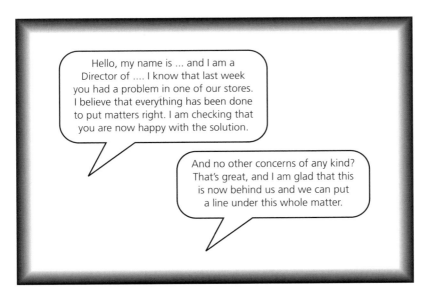

Figure 7.6 Restoring confidence

Conclusion

Customers that Count value the human characteristic of dependability. Meeting this core need requires tried and trusted techniques instead of novel and riskier systems. Comprehensive testing of products and systems, a common understanding of what is being provided, and close scrutiny of regular results provide the impression of consistency. Finally, inevitable mistakes occur, so you will need world-class recovery procedures to restore confidence. Confidence is the key dimension in retaining the best customers.

Case example   Theme: Reliable performance

Papyrus

Papyrus is a pan-European network of paper merchants and a member of the StoraEnso group, the world's second largest forest-products company with commercial roots going back to Sweden in the Middle Ages. Papyrus supplies fine paper, board and other products to printers, specifiers, designers, offices and industry in 13 European countries. Headquartered in Gothenburg, Sweden, its turnover exceeds 800 million euros.

The market is competitive: only five years ago the ten biggest merchant groups held a 65 per cent share of the European market. Today the figure is 82 per cent. End-users of printing and office paper are consolidating through mergers and acquisitions. Printers are responding by growing through acquisition or forming buying groups. Bigger, more international customers want suppliers who can promise in one market and deliver in another. To succeed in building relationships from France to Latvia, it is essential that a supplier is reliable. The print industry is pressurized. Deadlines are invariably tight, briefs change, agency clients are impatient and a finished brochure or leaflet will be subject to closer scrutiny than almost any other product. Without dependability, there is no relationship and no business.

'One word sums up our mission – reliability' is the bold statement on the Papyrus website (www.papyrus.com). 'You need to be confident that your delivery will arrive in good condition and at the promised time', says Marketing and Supply Director, Mats Nordlander. 'Whether it's a tonne of paper for a printer or a dummy for an advertising agency, Papyrus guarantees on-time deliveries.' He adds: 'Reliability means that we'll provide expert advice, great service and easy e-commerce'.

There are many examples of their efforts to achieve complete reliability. First, customers may need product information and specifications late at night or over a working weekend. No problem, they can rely on the Papyrus website 24 hours a day, 365 days a year and the content is localized by content and language for France, UK, Belgium, Netherlands, Sweden and Denmark. Having found the information required, orders can be placed electronically. Papyrus is Europe's leading e-commerce paper merchant. More than 20 per cent (over 400 million Swedish krone) of the annual turnover of Papyrus Sweden comes from online transactions (*see* Fig. 7.7), making Papyrus second only to Dell in Swedish e-commerce.

According to Mats, reliability comes from knowing what customers want. Papyrus has developed a fully integrated back-end and sales service system called CSS, embracing product administration, procurement, warehouse management and order entry. To support its aim for reliability, Papyrus has integrated these systems with the 'Saratoga' customer database. This identifies customer history, asso-

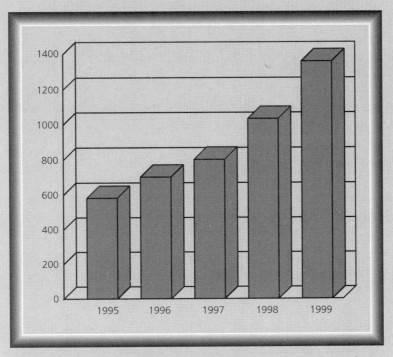

Figure 7.7 Customers buying over the net from Papyrus Sweden
Source: StoraEnso Annual Report 1999

ciated advertising agencies, patterns, preferences and buying behaviour. Accessible by virtually every employee, the information means that everyone knows what each customer expects and can therefore meet these expectations reliably.

PAPYRUS Ⓨ

The Papyrus logo also plays its part in supporting the associations of reliability. It is clear, sharp and easy to read. The primary aim of a logo is achieved: instant identification with the brand name. The letter Y is slightly stylized, different enough to be noticed, but not enough to distract from the whole word. The arms of the Y might be paper peeling away from a printing drum. It could be a papyrus plant with the paper making pith stripped from the reed. It could be an open book with its pages curving upwards. The associations of the word papyrus go further. The achievements of ancient Egypt relied on papyrus. Classical Greeks used papyrus to preserve the works of Homer, Aristotle and Plato. The Romans relied on papyrus to run their empire. The early Christians relied on papyrus to write their gospels. The fact is that papyrus – the word, the plant and the writing material – has for thousands of years been inseparable from reliability.

Finally, Mats Nordlander knows well that complete reliability is a journey, not a destination. 'We are not perfect, and of course, if ever things go wrong, our customers rely on us to put matters right. No-one is perfect, but we live for reliability every day.'

Exercises   Exercise 7

1 Review your complaints file and envisage a combination of circumstances that lets down and seriously inconveniences the most demanding of your top 20 customers.

2 Role-play the disaster-recovery response.

3 List your action points for improvement.

Further reading and references

Berry, Leonard L. (1999) *Discovering the Soul of Service*, Free Press.

Freiberg, K., Freiburg, J. and Peters, Tom (1997) *NUTS! Southwest Airlines Crazy Recipe for Business and Personal Success* Orion Business.

MacCormack, Mark (1994) *What They Don't Teach You at Harvard*, HarperCollins.

Tax, Stephen S.and Brown, Stephen W. (1998) 'Recovering and Learning from Service Failure', *Sloan Management Review*, Fall.

Hi, I'm looking for a Sports Utility Vehicle. I see you have a '99 Durango at the front of your used car lot …

Trust me, sir, it's the SUV for you.

What's the mileage and what is the condition?

Trust me, it's in real good condition, just what you need.

How come the sticker on the windshield is something over the Kelley Blue Book figure? (Thinks: if he says 'trust me' again, I'm leaving.)

Trust me … Hey, where are you going sir?

ustomers that Count seek organizations they can trust to serve them. Trust is confidence in future behaviour; it cannot be conjured creatively (*see* Fig. 8.1). Trust is earned over time, through tangible demonstrations of trustworthiness and the creation of a subjective feeling of security. There are eight recommendations for building trust, embracing multistep communication, personal contact and facing adversity together. Trust is a revocable contract and there are three specific pitfalls that can destroy trust, including abuse of privacy and broken promises. The objective must be to inculcate a resilient feeling of trusting security with best customers. To do so is not a luxury; it is becoming a prerequisite.

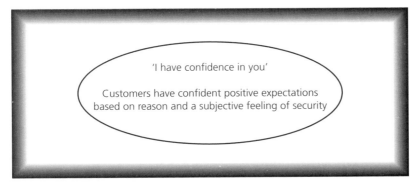

'I have confidence in you'

Customers have confident positive expectations based on reason and a subjective feeling of security

Figure 8.1 Trust

Trust is …

Trust has been defined by P. Gurvietz in a paper delivered at a special conference of the American Marketing Association in Dublin in 1997. She said: 'Trust is a state involving confident positive expectations about another's motives with respect to oneself in situations entailing risk'. Trust is an interdependent relationship when one partner has to engage without being sure of the outcome. She says the decision is based on the estimate of interest, which is a rational element, and a subjective feeling of security, which is an emotional element. Finally, she adds that 'Trust is a revocable contract'.

Customers value trustworthiness. In the twentieth century, trust in institutions, governments, politicians, lawyers, the media and organizations slipped significantly. Interestingly in the twenty-first century, customers seem more trusting of the major brands they encounter on a daily basis, than of the institutions that shape and control their lives. They have a strong desire to deal with people they trust to serve their needs. This desire is even more evident among the Customers that Count, who are conscious of their value to their suppliers and believe that this should result in mutual trust.

Trust takes time

A new brand or a dotcom start-up cannot ask for trust; trust has to be earned over a period of time though reliable behaviour and through the communication of signals of trustworthiness that are observed and believed by customers. Writing in *The Times*, Stuart Crainer (2000) quoted a survey of 200 UK internet users in summer 2000 by the advertising agency Leo Burnett. This survey revealed that for all the millions spent on marketing, consumers still trust traditional bricks-and-mortar brands more than trendy new dotcoms. Lastminute.com was recognized by 84 per cent of people, but only trusted by 17 per cent, whereas solid brands like the BBC and Prudential had substantial reserves of trust among consumers. Consumers look for patterns of behaviour and trust grows where there is consistency – consistency in messages, products and services. Time matters. American Express understands this and includes the script 'Member since …' and records the year of joining. The most trusted brands – Heinz, Kellogg's and Mercedes – have all shown reliability over many decades. On the web, Dell and Amazon are working progressively towards joining these trusted brands.

Building trust

The platform is reliability as described in the previous chapter. With this in mind, there are eight recommendations for building trust (*see* Fig. 8.2).

Counterintuitively, trust appears to build up more rapidly from a series of short interactions, rather than a single intense experience. DHL has demonstrated that regularity and frequent touch-points can build confidence in a shorter timescale. It has an enviable position in some of the smaller Asian markets where its market presence has been of more recent origin. Similarly, it is no coincidence that the most trusted retailers are those like Wal-Mart and Walgreen's in USA and Tesco and Boots in the UK, Carrefour in France and South-East Asia – all of whom are visited with the greatest frequency.

- A series of interactions has more impact than a single intense experience
- Consistent contact across different media
- Personal contact helps
- Open access to information
- Unbiased advice
- Signals consideration
- Going through adversity together
- Community commitment

Figure 8.2 Building trust

Contact variety

Varied communication channels (provided that they are all conveying the same message) can also speed the building of trust. The BBC can be experienced on radio, worldwide, on television networks, through books published by the BBC on programme themes, through magazines like *BBC Top Gear* and *BBC Gardeners' World*, and on the web at www.bbc.co.uk. Audiences may write, telephone or e-mail reactions. Little wonder the BBC exudes a sense of openness that leads to trust.

Communication is not simply through media. Vehicles can also be used to convey messages. The way a Wal-Mart truck driver handles the rig supports the brand's trust rating, and the message on the rear of the truck reads: 'We drive with our lights on for safety'. Bigger vehicles can also be used to enhance the brand's trust. According to David Magliano, Sales and Marketing Director of Go, the low-cost airline owned by British Airways, customers entrust their lives to planes. He says, in an article in *Marketing Business* (November 1999), that a lot of people are still cautious of flying:

They don't understand how planes can stay in the air. So they want to see that piece of machinery treated with reverence and respect. If you treat that piece of machinery like an advertising hoarding you are undermining customers' confidence. White is difficult to keep clean, but the passenger's perception is that clean means well maintained.

Personal contact helps

Personal contact is a huge advantage because there is human interaction face to face. Banks began leaking trust when they encouraged customers to use external automatic teller machines (ATM) to withdraw cash, instead of seeing a bank clerk face to face. The same is happening as the major petrol companies encourage customers to swipe a card at the pump instead of paying inside the filling station. Something is lost when the interpersonal connection is removed.

Careful consideration must be applied when automation is introduced, to ensure that there are still some aspects of a personal connection. For example, if you call up Virgin Atlantic and its telephone agents are busy, a recorded message from Sir Richard Branson greets the caller. He asks them to stay on the line. This is a bonus to people who recognize his voice from the media and would never expect him to be speaking directly to them, even in recorded form. The ATMs of the Hellenic Bank in Cyprus welcome cardholders by their name when a card is inserted into the ATM. At least someone knows you, thousands of miles from home.

Open access to information

Access to information contributes to a feeling of trust. Readily providing facts, advice and guidance creates the idea that nothing is hidden. The advice must not be partisan and brand-biased, but be in the consumer's best interest. For example www.garden.com, managed from 2001 by Burpee Seeds and Plants, is an e-tailer of plants, garden equipment and related products. Eager as it is to achieve sales, its buying process compares the shopper's zip code with the climate and soil type for the plant being bought. Where the plant is unsuitable a warning will flash on screen recommending against the purchase and giving the reason. In the quarter ending 31 March 2000, its recorded sales exceeded $3 million.

Readily providing facts, advice and guidance creates the idea that nothing is hidden.

Unbiased advice

Trust comes when the company provides patently unbiased advice. The telephone agents for Southwest Airlines seem to be on the traveller's side. For instance, a call asking for a flight from Dallas Love Field to Providence Rhode Island resulted in a convoluted itinerary involving two plane changes and a total fare of over $400. 'That's what the system suggests', added the lady from Southwest, 'but I'm not going to sell you that ticket. You'd be better off flying direct with another airline', and she recommended two who flew non-stop to Providence.

Signals of consideration

Potential customers do not find it easy to evaluate suppliers, particularly where they cannot judge performance quality in advance. For example, deciding between two chiropodists presents a challenge. How do you determine which solicitor or attorney will achieve the better result? In these circumstances, buyers may fall back on perceptual cues. The right gestures of interest and concern inspire confidence.

Paul Martin of Harpenden Construction, a building firm with a premier reputation located in Hertfordshire, UK, well understands how to inspire confidence. Long before the quality of the finished work is seen, the customer sees signals of consideration. He identifies sensitive issues for each project – perhaps an unreasonable neighbour – and always shows concern. At the end of each day time is dedicated to a comprehensive clean-up. Signals of consideration encourage belief in positive future outcomes. Such signals are quoted by customers in word-of-mouth recommendations. Much of Paul Martin's new work comes from personal recommendation and Harpenden Construction's customers are prepared to wait twelve months for a builder they trust.

Facing adversity

Another factor is adversity. There is an English proverb: 'A friend in need is a friend indeed', meaning that someone who stands by you when you are in need is a true friend. Trust comes from seeing the person or brand behaving consistently towards you in good times and bad. The UK-based insurance company, the Prudential, has an immensely strong level of brand trust founded on a generation of experience of the 'man from the Pru'. Come rain or shine, each week he would call, helping the family save for adversity. When they faced tough times, his advice was always there and the savings they had made on his recommendation stood them in good stead.

How brands behave when things are not going well is a more credible sign of trustworthiness than when everything is easy. Product recalls are one instance where a brand can damage or enhance its impression of trustworthiness by its early actions. Firestone, the Japanese-owned tyre company based in the USA, was seen to prevaricate in August 2000 when stories of deaths after tyre bursts on sports utility vehicles made headline news. The phased recall of tyres, state by state, left an impression of reluctance, which is likely to damage the brand's trust level. By contrast, the immediate withdrawal of all Tylenol from pharmacy shelves when a tampering incident caused a death, coupled with daily reports of progress to develop and introduce tamper-proof packs, enhanced the trust felt for the brand by American consumers.

Community commitment

Finally, the way a brand involves itself in its community as a good neighbour may also hasten the process of building trust. Ben & Jerry's, the Vermont-based ice cream business, has always made a point of supporting a social mission. Each year it gives away 7.5 per cent of pre-tax earnings to support creative and hopeful social projects relating to children and families, disadvantaged groups and the environment.

Nokia's 'Make a connection' campaign is another example, where the Finnish telecommunications company has entered a global partnership with the International Youth Foundation. As reported in the *Financial Times* (19 December 2000), Nokia provides teaching packages to children with learning difficulties and offers volunteers from its own workforce for educational projects. The programme embraces many countries, including Brazil, China, Germany, Mexico and the UK. Supporting up to 1 million children over three years demonstrates a commitment to improving life in the community. This caring approach contributes to the impression of a trustworthy company.

Trust destroyers

Companies must go beyond the actions listed that help build consumer trust. They must actively guard against the behaviours that destroy trust in the Customers that Count. These behaviours are actions that run counter to our expectations of a friend. A true friend can be trusted to keep a confidence. True friends keep promises and can be relied upon not to fall out over money. Likewise, your best customers trust you with confidences, rely on your promises and expect money matters to be handled harmoniously. Failure in any of these will destroy trust (*see* Fig. 8.3).

Respect confidences

The first way to preserve trust is to respect confidences. Companies now hold an astonishing amount of individual and personal data about their

- Respect confidences – do not sell personal data
- Keep promises – broken promises are long remembered
- Harmony over money – do not fall out over money

Figure 8.3 Avoiding trust destroyers

customers. Naturally, customers consider this confidential and they trust companies not to abuse this information. Yet personal data has a market value. When Independent Energy, the electricity and gas supplier, filed for bankruptcy in the UK in September 2000, the first asset to be sold by the administrative receivers, KPMG, was the list of 242 000 customers, bought by Innogy for £10 million.

When a relationship breaks down, the power of the information held can be considerable. It is true in divorce cases between couples, and it also applies to the severing of commercial relationships. For example, in a *Brandweek* article (28 June 1999), Jesse Kalisher told the story of a customer, who slipped on spilled food in a named supermarket and damaged his knee. When he sued the supermarket, it threatened to reveal the customer's alcohol-buying record if the case ever came to court.

Abusing personal data

Abuses of personal information from transactions and records are now becoming a significant concern in the USA. Kalisher cites instances of women who, having bought pregnancy test kits, receive unwanted mail targeting expectant mothers. He quotes an example from the American Civil Liberty Union, of a Maryland banker who accessed medical records and called in the loans of people who were diagnosed with cancer. For reasons such as this all reputable organizations in the USA are now publishing privacy policies. Good examples may be found on the Marriott and Smarterkids.com websites. They explain clearly how customer data is held and safeguarded.

In Europe the EU Privacy Directive (October 1998) limits the use that can be made of data. For example, data-flows to countries not considered to have the same levels of protection (like the USA) are prohibited. Good manners and respect for customer confidences mean that no details of Customers that Count should be passed on in any form without their express agreement through an opt-in. If companies wish to work in alliance with others, transparency is required and customers will respect being asked if they wish to take advantage of resultant offers.

Keep promises

In relationships, promises are kept. To ensure that this happens, every effort should be made to be realistic in the promises that are made. The cost of keeping a promise may be high, but the damage to relationships from weaselling out of commitments is likely to be higher. When the UK appliance brand, Hoover, launched a free-flights promotion for purchasers of vacuum cleaners in the 1980s, it never envisaged that the promotional norm of 4–5 per cent sales increase would be exceeded. To its consternation, shoppers began buying two or three cleaners they did not need solely for the flight promotion. Hoover reneged on the promise and disappointed many hopeful travellers. The marketing director and managing director both lost their jobs in the ensuing débâcle and the Hoover brand was damaged forever.

> **Every effort should be made to be realistic in the promises that are made.**

Don't fall out over money

The greatest destroyer of trust is a monetary dispute. This is difficult to prevent – especially when commercial relationships depend on money transactions. There are five clear policies to ensure that misunderstandings over money do not pollute a relationship:

1 **Respect existing customers – give no better deal to new buyers.** A telling letter was published in *The Times* (19 February 2000) from Devsiri P. Hewavidana, recounting the manner in which his car insurance company lost his trust. Just before his annual insurance cover expired, he received a renewal letter quoting an increase of £38. Having made no claims and had no accidents, he wrote to the company asking for a justification. The response referred to an 8-per-cent increase as normal for the industry. Mr Hewavidana then rang their telesales line, posing as a new customer, giving all the correct personal and vehicle information. The quotation provided as a new customer was £12 lower than he had been paying. Result: anger, loss of trust and a defecting customer.

    It is inevitable in an era of open information, data sharing, alliances, and rapid staff turnover that secret deals are unlikely to stay secret for long. Therefore ensure that promotional offers to new buyers cannot be better than terms to existing customers. Where you wish to make a time-limited introductory offer that might offend existing customers, consult them and check opinions beforehand. They will value this openness and may agree to a more competitive offer to build your business than you dared to suggest.

2 **Increase value to existing customers – continuing proposition improvement.** Tesco, a UK supermarket group with operations in

Eastern Europe and Asia, has the slogan 'Every little helps' to signify that the company strategy is continuous proposition improvement. Regularly Tesco news releases support this message:

9 June 2000	Internet cafés in Tesco stores
23 June 2000	Cashback limit at till increases to £100
9 July 2000	Examples of odd requests to van drivers, for example reset video clock
11 September 2000	£425 000 research project into organic farming
17 November 2000	Christmas gift price-cuts on perfumes and aftershave
22 December 2000	9500 extra evening staff on duty for Christmas shopping
28 January 2001	Record sales of organic products over Christmas
12 March 2001	Research results – how to stop babies crying

3 **Don't charge for what you don't need.** Standard packages suit standard customers. However, when you create propositions for best customers, they may not need every element of the standard package. Highlighting things that the specific customer does not need and deleting these items from the specification and the invoice can preserve trust.

4 **Clear explanations.** Misunderstandings can be prevented by careful briefing beforehand and through regular reviews of terms and conditions. This is particularly important when a new individual takes over from a previous contact. Any revisions in terms must be explained thoroughly and perhaps highlighted as they are first applied. Decades of trust are worth more than an unexpected 5-per-cent surcharge on weekend cover.

In some instances the cause of misunderstanding is a fluctuating product price based on a significant ingredient. For example, plastic milk bottles require a large proportion of polymers. The world price of polymers rises and falls with demand and the prevailing oil price. Given the length of the supply chain and market volatility, customers can be paying increased prices when the market is apparently slipping. To prevent sullen arguments, some manufacturers of plastic bottles provide a split invoice: a cost for the manufacture and delivery of the bottles excluding the polymer, and a separate total for polymers, quoting the actual price paid for the batch used. This form of part open-book accounting can preserve trust.

5 **Payments.** Expectations of amounts, timing and conditions of payments should be carefully set. Invoices should be a model of clarity so that there is no challenge of interpretation, or implication of

concealment. Accuracy is vital. There is an Austrian proverb: '*Strenge Rechnung, gute Freunde*', which means 'Exact bill, good friend'. In the event that payment is not forthcoming according to the expected timescale, rapid and courteous reminders should be employed.

Disputes over money can sour excellent relationships in a short space of time. Ensuring that this does not occur is an important part of maintaining long-term trust.

Trust – the objective

The objective is to be seen as absolutely trusted. A resonant example (quoted by K. Irons, 1998) is the UK holiday company for older travellers, Saga Holidays, who received some serious complaints about the facilities of a hotel featured in one of its packages. After establishing the validity of the complaint, it sent compensation cheques to the complainers and also to holidaymakers on the same package who had not complained. That is a convincing demonstration that it is an organization that can be trusted to put the interests of its customers first.

In conclusion, trust is built by carrying out all the right things over duration of time, and ensuring that none of the trust destroyers come into play. Aptly, Laura Mazur, writing in *Marketing Business* (July 1999), has said: 'Trust is not about being nice. It's going to be a basic prerequisite for survival.'

Case example	Theme: Trust

Food Inc.

Trust is personified by the relationship built by one of the USA's largest food manufacturers with a leading supermarket chain. The director I interviewed asked, for reasons of trade confidentiality for her company and the customer to be confidential. For the sake of this case example, we will call the company, 'Food Inc.' and the customer, 'Valuechain'.

Anita has been the Key Account Director for Valuechain for five months, and it is clearly a challenge she relishes. Valuechain is a cautious family-owned supermarket with around 75 stores, all located in inner-city and less prosperous neighbourhoods, and dominating market share in their catchment areas through everyday lower pricing, simple and consistent store layouts and community involvement led by family members. It is a low-tech operation, preferring hands-on management and speedy reaction to the market. For all this, it is one of the best customers of Food Inc.

Food Inc. is a sophisticated brand-led global player and an innovative leader in their industry, so I asked Anita how she handled the clear cultural differences between customer and supplier. How is trust built and maintained?

Personal contact was her answer. She may be relatively new, but she is ably supported by a team of three account managers, two of whom have been working on the Valuechain business for more than 25 years. This is deliberate and most unusual in Food Inc., who normally promotes or rotates people after two or three years in a post. At her first meeting with Valuechain, its executives were nervous that she might make rapid changes: 'We like John, take care of him', they said. She was able to reassure them about John's continuity. When she appoints a replacement for John, who is due to retire in two year's time, it will be a careful match. 'A focused non-adaptable achiever would be wrong for this account', she said.

To build trust in herself, she ensures that she has a lot of contact time with the executives of Valuechain, being in their offices at least once each week. She smiled and confided that before she goes in for a meeting, she will scan a local newspaper for the latest community issues. Where other accounts pick up food-industry trends from the internet, she gives them a personal digest of developments over a cup of coffee. She takes them to a ball game every so often, and this is where they are most receptive to new ideas.

Finally, a part of maintaining trust is about ensuring that nothing occurs to damage credibility. Anita is well aware of the pitfalls. She points out that Food Inc. is promotion orientated, with monthly new product launches. There is of course a need to support the company brands and to keep the customer up-to-date, but hard selling of a new line that does not move could damage the trust of decades. An unstated code has evolved where every promotion on the Food Inc. promotional calendar is advised, but the account managers are muted in their enthusiasm for premium lines. They only spend time on products that match the profile of the Valuechain customer. Their recommendations are accurate and their word carries a lot of weight in selecting new lines to add to the portfolio.

It is a culture in Food Inc. that senior managers spend a lot of time in the field, meeting the trade and feeling the market. Anita is very selective about who will get to her account. She is courteously effective in ensuring that IT hot-shots are steered towards other accounts and only invites executives who will appreciate the cautious value-based attitudes of Valuechain.

Trust is a revocable contract and Anita is determined that the trust between her company and Valuechain will only grow while she is Key Account Director.

Exercises   **Exercise 8**

Review instances of money disputes in the past two years with customers in your top 20 per cent of buyers. What changes could be made to reduce the likelihood of similar issues recurring?

Further reading and references

Crainer, Stuart (2000) 'Brand trust must be nurtured over time', *The Times*, 10 August.

Edwards, Paul (1998) 'The Age of the Trust Brand' *Market Leader*, Winter.

Irons, K. (1998) 'Do you sincerely want to build relationships?', *Market Leader*, Winter.

She looked at the London streets outside. It was going to be a long wait. She leant forward and opened her handbag, carefully selecting a neat black wallet from a compartment. Drawing it from the recess, she inspected it slowly. She had elected to amuse herself by counting her assets. Not money assets – this was not a wallet containing cash or even credit cards. These assets were loyalty, cards, carefully encapsulated in plastic sleeves. She looked at the first – it was her AAdvantage card as an American Airlines frequent flier; the second was an ABC card from Safeway – with this she could scan her groceries herself and walk straight past the crowded check-outs. Next came an Advantage card from Boots, giving her special deals on selected merchandise; then Air Miles for free flights; and from Argos a multi-retailer card that she used at the grocery supermarket, Somerfield. Avis offered a priority rental car card. The restaurant chain, Beefeater, had provided a card that entitled her to discounts for family dining. Bhs Choice card gave her up to 15 per cent off merchandise. Then she reached her BP Premier points card, used when she filled with fuel. She was methodical in everything and so, next to it in alpha-sequence, she touched her Clubcard from Tesco and a different Clubcard from WHSmith. Only the third letter of the alphabet and she had already covered 11 separate companies. She flicked through the whole set – it was like a 'Who's Who' of leading brands. There she was with a place on the database of dozens of major corporations, but do they know who she is? Do they really recognize her?

Knowing your customers is an elementary marketing precept. For Customers that Count it is of paramount importance, for they take it for granted that you will know and appreciate their wants. Returning customers like to be recognized (*see* Fig. 9.1). From the first impression, through growing familiarity to the full acquaintanceship, it is important to manage the process, so you understand and meet the needs of these customers. Part of this process is the careful setting of expectations to avoid disappointment and frustration from misunderstandings. Linked

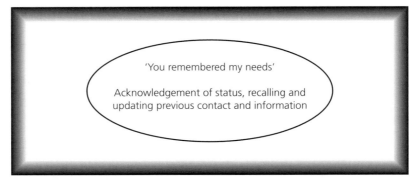

'You remembered my needs'

Acknowledgement of status, recalling and updating previous contact and information

Figure 9.1 Recognition

to this is the challenge to stay connected so that expectations are managed throughout the relationship. The objective is that each of the Customers that Count feels regularly recognized as an individual.

Beginning with first impressions

Every relationship begins with a first impression, from love at first sight to an initial stigma that must be overcome. The first contact the future customer has with the organization defines the expectation. The first impression at the Inter-Continental Hotel in Singapore is created by the porter who meets guests as they arrive in cars or taxis. As he picks up their cases he greets them and conversationally asks if they have stayed in this hotel before. When he places the bags beside the check-in table he catches the eye of the clerk and signals. If they are new guests he touches his right ear, and accordingly she will say: 'As it is your first time here let me explain the layout of the hotel and give you all the information you need to enjoy your first stay'.

It is important, then, that firms regularly assess the perceptions they are creating for first timers, through external surveys and research among new buyers. It is all too easy to see things through experienced eyes that forgive blemishes and are influenced by a halo effect. For example, where an older manager's eyes might see harmonious colours and a pleasing sense of order, the 14-year-old prospective customer will see boring, stale and samey displays.

First impressions come from varied sources (*see* Fig. 9.2). Media comment and word of mouth from older or more knowledgeable users can be the first reference a new user will come across. The South African Tourism promotion body has a word-of-mouth marketing strategy. It focuses on

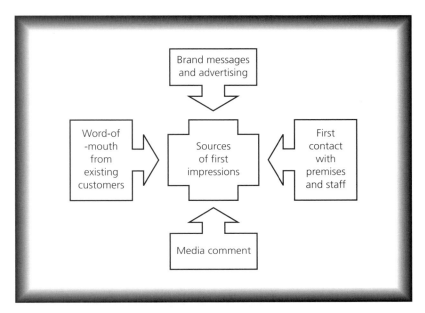

Figure 9.2 First impressions

recounting memorable anecdotes about positive aspects of holidaying in South Africa to journalists, business visitors and game park visitors for them to pass on. It is a key requirement that brands focus attention on briefing existing customers to convey the right advantages and information to prospects.

Brand advertising is another obvious and strong source of first impressions. More sophisticated targeting seemingly offers advertisers the chance to direct different messages for recruitment and retention. You should be aware that almost invariably there is spillover, in that customers from outside the target segment or market will see the message. If there are conflicting messages directed at different markets, then advertisers should envisage the consequences of the 'wrong' customers seeing the advertisements. In addition, the increasing introduction of media studies in education systems in many countries is providing an astute and cynical audience. Websites are also an obvious source. The site should accord with brand values and also be updated frequently. Seth Godin, speaking at the March 2001 Credo CRM conference in Paris, lamented that the average website is updated only after 44 days.

Other forms of advertising, such as staff recruitment, may also impact on the first brand perceptions. In addition, the style, decorative standard, cleanliness and scale of premises make a statement to curious potential customers.

The strongest first impression is given by the earliest contact with a member of staff.

The strongest first impression is given by the earliest contact with a member of staff, either face to face or over the phone. Are they well groomed and properly equipped? Are they welcoming, harassed, unhappy or enthusiastic? The initial 30 seconds will live on as a well-etched memory. The receptionist on the front desk, the telephonist on the switchboard, the exhibition stand manager knows this. However, with direct dialling now reaching most levels of management, are the skills throughout the organization as well honed to give a positive perception to the unknown caller?

Getting acquainted

The proper relationship begins with a full introduction (*see* Fig. 9.3). In high society, etiquette demanded that this be performed by the host at a party who would have given names and relevant background details and identified areas of joint interest to enable the two parties to converse. In more casual times and the business context there are still advantages to be gained from the full introduction. Nowadays the onus is on the parties to exchange information without an intermediary.

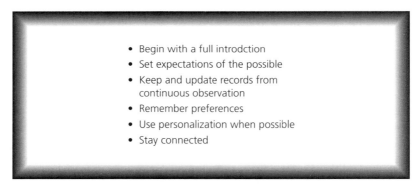

- Begin with a full introdction
- Set expectations of the possible
- Keep and update records from continuous observation
- Remember preferences
- Use personalization when possible
- Stay connected

Figure 9.3 Recognizing Customers that Count

Good relationships depend on good information (*see* Fig. 9.4). The benefit is to both vendor and buyer. The vendor needs to provide information on business credentials, goods, services, contact points, limits and opportunities. The buyer must highlight potential value to the vendor, creditworthiness and particular requirements, lest they be overwhelmed with irrelevant information and offers.

Both sides need to confirm understanding of the information received and to indicate that it has been recorded and will be taken into account in future communication.

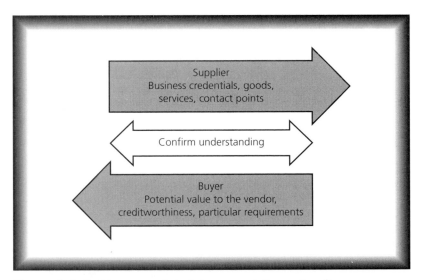

Figure 9.4 Getting acquainted: two-way information flow

Procter & Gamble ran a trial advertisement for its Pantene shampoo range of products on Cable & Wireless digital interactive television. The advertisement provides facts and guidance about the brand as part of the information exchange. Viewers are invited to click on the Pantene advertisement and answer questions about their own hair type and its specific characteristics. This enables Procter & Gamble to send a free sample of the Pantene shampoo that is most suitable for the hair type described. According to an article by Poppy Brech (2000) the trial delivered impressive results. Around 50 000 responses were generated in 5 weeks.

Ask and observe

The initial encounter may be face to face or via telephone, e-mail or website text box. For effective relationships this first meeting provides a natural chance to ask and retain data. At German trade exhibitions, industrial manufacturers diligently collect business cards from stand visitors, often scanning them into a database so that more information can be added on potential products of interest. Financial services companies in the UK are obligated under the Financial Services Act to ask customers a series of questions known as the 'fact find' and record the answers to develop appropriate financial recommendations. Stop & Shop, the New England supermarket owned by Royal Ahold BV, tempt regular customers to take out a Stop & Shop card with in-store offers accessed through a barcoded key card, which also provides a means of returning lost car keys. For this it asks for simple name, address and zip code data on the primary shopper and, if relevant, a secondary shopper. Transactions generate more customer information, though Stop & Shop's privacy policy allows customers to opt out, but they then miss mailed offers based on purchases.

When you join Blockbuster Video Club you provide information that includes age, address and telephone number. The file created might also include the genre of the first film selected, the method of payment preferred and the time of day plus day of the week when the video was taken out. This information sets up a hypothesis that this is the customer's long-term pattern. Subsequent transactions may prove, disprove or update the pattern.

What not to ask

Be aware that this information-gathering phase can set expectations in the mind of the customer. Do not ask if you cannot always deliver the differentiation. For example, if Singapore Airlines asks if you are a vegetarian, then automatically you assume that this data is recorded and henceforward a suitable meal will be available on every flight.

There are also limits to quizzing customers. Some questions are seen as needlessly intrusive. American consumers are reluctant to give information on liquor consumption. Germans and Belgians are protective of details of family members. A survey at the end of 1999 by the UK-based National Consumer Council, carried out by MORI among British adults and children, revealed that consumers are happy to provide personal information provided it is relevant, like financial information when applying for a mortgage. Said Anna Bradley, National Consumer Council Director: 'They are less comfortable when asked for details that appear unnecessary, like being asked who else they live with when applying for a loyalty card. In some cases people opt out of transactions rather than provide such data.'

Fatigue is also a factor. In shopper surveys of more than 100 questions, consumers work swiftly through the questionnaire to qualify for the prize draw, and accuracy suffers.

Who will answer, who will not

Some customers are more willing than others to provide personal data. Even the customers willing to open up may take time to build up the necessary trust. Philippe Lemoine, Co-Chairman of Galeries Lafayette in France, believes there are four different stages in customer relationships (*Financial Times*, 16 March 2000):

1 Purely anonymous customers – prefer not to be known by name and will not provide personal data.

2 Anonymous customers using personalized shopping services occasionally – selectively reveal personal preferences.

3 Customers who access and provide information – trade data for detailed and appropriate service from retailers.

4 Customers who seek an individual relationship with the retailer.

Some people will progress through all the stages and others will remain at one of the intermediate levels.

Web myths

It is often believed that web retailers are able to collect all the information they need on browsing and buying patterns. Yet it can be difficult to distinguish individuals who only browse from genuine purchasers. If customers are required to register before they can browse, they will give fictitious names in order preserve their anonymity. Later, when they buy with a credit card in their own name, there is no connection between 'Mickey Mouse' and the cardholder. Others will browse extensively on their home PCs in the evening, but delay placing the order until the following morning when they are seated at their work PC with higher bandwidth, meaning it is easier to complete the transaction.

Mismanaging data

Even when the customer willingly volunteers the data, some organizations fail to collate it meaningfully. Clive Ashbourn, Managing Director of the information handling company Data Answers, quotes an instance of a bank (*Marketing Direct*, February 2000). The bank offered three separate products and had three matching systems, each holding the data of the customers who had bought those products. Where a customer had taken all three products they would be listed separately on each of the systems. The bank originally believed it had 225 000 customers. When the data had been reviewed, it discovered only 180 000 customers. More seriously, it had calculated that the top 10 per cent of customers generated 55 per cent of the business, whereas these important customers accounted for 80 per cent of the business.

The ticketless airline Buzz, part of KLM, takes telephone bookings for its European flights. An automatic confirmation is generated and dispatched by e-mail. This is personalized with the name of the traveller. The phone agents know the preferred language of the traveller, yet Buzz prints all its disclaimers and legal niceties in five languages: English, German, Italian, French and Finnish. Most customers will print off the confirmation as a reminder of their seat reference code, so this extra page is an inconvenience that implies that Buzz does not know its customers.

You know me

Returning customers like to be recognized. The Rolls Royce Corniche costs £250 000 and typical purchasers have between six and nine other cars. One third of the buyers are female and Rolls Royce will know 75 per cent of buyers from previous contact. The recognition process is discrete and effective.

Nordstrom in the USA is another example where store staff will recognize their top shoppers through human memory, and this is welcomed. However, at another US retailer an attempt to use sophisticated video technology for the same purpose misfired. *Harvard Business Review* (July–August 1999) quoted an example of an IBM video scanner that could recognize a retailer's best customers as they entered a store. The intention was to offer them outstanding personal service, but the shoppers resented this invasion of their privacy. The model of the personal relationship holds well in a commercial context, but overt technology can damage the personal aspect.

Customers can recognize staff too. Lakeland Plastics, retailer and direct-mail seller of cooking and kitchen items based in the north-west of England, has a feedback sheet responding to customer's questions and comments. One letter read:

> On a recent holiday abroad, we met a couple (total strangers to us) who told us they had just got married. I asked them where they came from and they said the Lake District. Believe it or not my next question was 'Do you know Lakeland Plastics'. 'Oh yes', said the groom, 'I work there.'

There was a footnote saying: 'Incidentally, it was Geoff from our dispatch department'. Recognition was acknowledged.

You know what I want

The data to be collated must go beyond address, personal demographic data and product holdings. Gathering and acknowledging preferences means that you know what a customer wants. American Airlines provides a weekly e-mail letter to hundreds of thousands of club members who have registered particular interests. Thus each week an AAdvantage member can look forward to a personalized e-mail called 'Sale AAlert' which offers flight deals relevant to their future intentions. The selection is based on the user profile, including home airport and markets the member has identified. In a world overloaded with choice and variety, American Airlines saves customers time by focusing on their actual areas of interest.

Albert Hijn, the Dutch supermarket operators, identified that customers would like supermarket shopping delivered while they were out at work. Yet security was also a consideration. Working with architects and house builders it created a concept of non-return hatches, so that grocery trays could be popped safely into houses during the working day.

Increasingly the insensitive, ill-timed and irrelevant offer has the effect of damning the brand offering it. The couple celebrating their silver wedding will not only reject the seniors division of the holiday company who sent them a Singles Club 18–30 beach and booze holiday mailer. They will also sell the shares in the holding company – this group of the population spends a lot of time on personal investment to select stocks and shares. They don't back companies who show flagrant ignorance of their customers.

You remember what I have requested

Successful companies have powerful systems to record the preferences, likes and dislikes of their customers. When you stay in a Ritz Carlton Hotel and eat a banana from the fruit bowl, your choice is noted and the next day there will be two bananas for you.

It is important to know where the Customers that Count prefer the standard version and where they expect a variation. Gordon Maw, Marketing Manager of Virgin Direct, the UK financial services company founded in 1995, said in *Marketing Direct* (October 1999): 'If you want a 20-year relationship with a customer, it is no good if you can't remember what happened last week'. You know the likes and dislikes of your closest friends. Similarly, you should record the preferences of your best customers.

You know the likes and dislikes of your closest friends. Similarly, you should record the preferences of your best customers.

Peter Rosenwald, Head of Direct Marketing at Abril, a Brazilian media group, has said: 'The most dangerous word in direct marketing is *average*' (*The Economist*, 9 January 1999). There are no average customers and to treat them in a uniform manner wastes company resources and customer's time. Viking Office Products, the rapidly growing stationery supplier whose global sales now exceed 1 billion dollars, believes that 'less is more' in its tailored catalogues. Customers range from large city offices, legal partnerships and schools, to individuals working from home. Each customer receives a personalized catalogue, driven by the database that merges geodemographic information with historical sales data. Viking sees it as futile to waste money sending something that is not wanted. The more irrelevant material a customer receives the higher the annoyance factor. Thus it works to build a catalogue around each customer – if you buy a fax machine in one month, the catalogue arriving the next month will feature an offer on fax paper rolls.

Personal means successful

Knowing the customer's personal characteristics is crucial in many markets. NiQuitin CQ is a range of nicotine replacement therapy (NRT) patches from SmithKline Beecham Consumer Health Care, available in the UK, Sweden and Belgium. The special advantage this smoking cessation brand offers is a personalized behavioural support plan to work in conjunction with the NRT patch. Its website (www.nicodermcq.com) includes questions developed by Dr Karl Fagerstrom, which assess nicotine dependence. On the basis of a smoker's answers to 24 questions in a short telephone call, a personalized plan is mailed out. Over the next six weeks two further mailings are sent, and if the consumer responds, a final mailing is dispatched. The plan claims to increase the success rate of quitting by 30 per cent. Within 10 weeks of launch Niquitin CQ became brand leader in the UK nicotine patch market.

Repetition is an irritation to customers, so the answer is to gather the customer preferences at the first customer contact and then slavishly ensure that these are routinely applied in all future contacts. The British Red Cross asks regular donors for their wishes in frequency of contact and respects the answers. It establishes whether donors want full annual accounts, the shortened form, newsletter or none of these. The customer only has to ask once.

Setting expectations

Recognition is a two-way process. Customers must also recognize what the company can and cannot do. It is a characteristic of good relationships that expectations are realistic. How do companies explain their own business style in order to overcome the dangers of assumptions? Zara is an international chain of fashion clothes stores, headquartered in La Coruna, Spain. Sales from 1000 stores in 30 countries exceed £1.2 billion. Unusually for a clothing store, it does not believe in spring and summer collections. Instead it offers 'live collections', which are rapidly designed, manufactured and sold. Spanish customers understand that if they like something it must be bought there and then, as it will not still be in the shop a week later. More than this, keen fashion followers will know on which day the weekly delivery truck arrives with latest styles. José Maria Castellano, Chief Executive of Inditex, owners of Zara, commented in the *Financial Times* (26 September 2000) that when Zara opened its first UK store on London's Regent Street back in 1998, shoppers would browse and leave, telling shop assistants that they would return when the seasonal sale started. Assistants had to explain that the clothes they liked would not be in a sale because the stock changes every week. They were obliged to teach customers the shopping rules for Zara. Customers make assumptions and need training in using products and services.

Staying connected with customers

Keeping in touch with customers means that expectations are always realistic in both directions. Powerful techniques for staying in touch include spending a day in the life of the customer. It is important to check personal details with customers annually, as some data fields have a short shelf life. Dates of birth do not change, but many other facts need to be amended or confirmed. For customers in their twenties in Europe and the USA, a majority of addresses will be out of date within 36 months. Multiple listening points are important, meaning that any staff member coming into contact with a customer should have the facility to input changes on the database.

In business-to-business marketing, preferences change with the appointment of new executives, and this can happen throughout the relationship. This provides challenges in maintaining relationships with best customers. A technique first deployed by the computer firm ICL, now owned by Fujitsu, is widely used. Sometimes termed 'star-spotting', it involves a brainstorming session of key account managers, service and support staff and senior management who have contact with the client in question. The objective is to review the organizational chart of the client and identify high fliers who are likely to be promoted within two years. The company then builds an understanding of and a connection with these individuals (as well as maintaining relationships with incumbents). In the USA, star-spotting has been used to identify senior executives in General Electric capable of taking chief executive officer roles elsewhere.

Volkswagen has a plan to keep in contact directly with customers buying its cars. In the centre of Wolfsburg, Germany, where VW has its largest plant, the automotive manufacturer is creating Autostadt or a 'car town' – a 250 000-square-metre theme park dedicated to VW brands. Alongside the museum, children's playground and the Ritz Carlton Hotel are two glass towers in which newly built cars from the adjacent factories are stored. These cars are destined for new owners who have previously ordered them for collection as part of the Autostadt experience. The immaculate customer service centre has the capacity to deliver 1000 cars in a day.

Since 1997, Saturn, in the American automotive market, has had a 'Welcome Center' at Spring Hill Tennessee. You can schedule a plant tour, collect a new Saturn or simply find out more about the company whose mission is to manufacture vehicles that are world leaders in quality, cost and customer enthusiasm. The traditional Morgan Car factory in Malvern in the UK has for many years encouraged buyers to collect from the factory and even to inspect the painstakingly slow hand-building. Often the customers who choose to collect in person are repeat buyers who are staying connected.

Regularly recognized as an individual

The objective is that your customer feels regularly recognized as an individual. This comes from an effective introduction, consistently capturing preferences and purchase patterns and intelligently developing the knowledge to provide a natural relationship that respects preferences. We all like to be recognized.

Case example   Theme: Recognition

Smarterkids.com

Smarterkids.com is a successful e-business selling toys and educational software, based beside Highway 128 in Needham, Massachusetts. Competing in a fashionable and price-sensitive market dominated by the category-killer Toys R Us could be a tough call. But David Blohm, President and Chief Executive Officer, explained to me that Smarterkids has a winning value proposition. He says: 'We help parents develop their kids'. His answer to price-based rivalry is simple. If a parent buys a toy elsewhere at a deep discount, but it is never played with, the price advantage is irrelevant.

The Smarterkids website invites parents to complete a short on-screen questionnaire to profile their child. This profile identifies the child's preferences, describes the most effective learning style and makes a solid basis for recommending toys matched to these preferences. Thus the parents receive a valuable assessment of their child plus recommendations for toys and games that the child will enjoy and from which they will learn. Recommendations are age-based and range across the whole price spectrum. The first product recommendation for my eight-year-old cost $9.99.

David told me that customers who profile their children using the web questionnaire are worth 200 per cent of non-profilers. Around 14 000 customers, or 20 per cent of the total, have conducted profiles and they account for more than 40 per cent of revenue. They spend more and buy more frequently because, thanks to the recommendations, the children like the toys. Customer satisfaction is the result, and so the customers come back for more. As Blohm says: 'The more you know us, the more you love us', because the experience for parents and children is so positive.

Once parents have confidence in the suggestions, they can create a personal list of toys they would like for their child. Grandparents, uncles and aunts can click on the Gift Center, type in the child's name and see at a glance a gift list of toys and games, matched to the child's aptitudes, vetted by the parents and offering a range of price points. Buying a toy removes it from the list and therefore avoids duplication.

The slogan on the Smarterkids website is 'Learn, Discover, Grow'. Clearly this is its appeal and also its own philosophy. The company learns and discovers by staying closely connected with its customers. There are frequent focus groups and a panel of 1000 parents who are e-mailed regularly for advice and comments on new products, services or systems. To support parents, Smarterkids provides tips for school success, and invites questions on any educational topic, which are answered by seven qualified teachers employed by Smarterkids. The teachers also provide reviews of every item stocked by Smarterkids to aid selection.

Finally, I was curious about the toy war that erupts before each Christmas. What was the Smarterkids strategy? David Blohm answered proudly that its track record was excellent – last Christmas it had taken orders up until 23 December and shipped 99.8 per cent of orders before Christmas. And his strategy was simply based around looking after his best customers. Once they have bought $150-worth of goods in a calendar year, all shipping is free. Naturally, the best customers will have qualified before the Christmas spree and therefore have a strong incentive to remain loyal – buying in the knowledge that Smarterkids appreciates their business.

Exercise 9   Exercises

List the average specification of product, service, delivery timescale, technical support and other criteria of customer needs. Using this list, review the data you hold on the preferences of your top 20 customers. How close are they to the average?

Further reading and references

Brech, Poppy (2000) 'Digital television – threat or opportunity?', *Marketing Means Business for the CEO*, Chartered Institute of Marketing, Spring.

Dawson, Ross (2000) *Developing Knowledge-Based Client Relationships*, Butterworth-Heinemann.

Godin, Seth (1999) *Permission Marketing*, Simon & Schuster.

The consultants were presenting on Friday. And the Malaysian situation had changed completely. She needed to contact Rheinhard to brief him.

She found his business card clipped to the front of the file and inspected the 6-point print. His address came first – she could write to him. Her eye caught the fax number – that would be quicker. Or she might e-mail him and know that he had received the message. Then she saw the phone number of his direct line – she could leave a voicemail for him. There was the switchboard number below, so she could ring and check his whereabouts. If he were travelling, she might reach him on his mobile number. Or at least leave a text message. Oh well, if all else failed she could see his home number and he had told her the nanny was a perfect message taker. Eight different contact options, she mused, and what was the title of the report? 'Accessibility.' How appropriate!

E ffective communication is a vital factor in relationships. Like hygiene in catering, communication remains unnoticed most of the time, only coming to attention when standards fail and problems arise (*see* Fig. 10.1). Customers that Count expect to be able to contact a supplier readily, and be kept informed in return. Yet keeping customers informed demands standing

Figure 10.1 Accessibility

out from the huge volumes of advertisements, letters, calls and e-mails they see each day. How do companies guarantee accessibility? And how do they ensure that customers notice good communications? Choices are clearly important, as different people favour different media. Speed often counts. Creativity helps. But above all, interaction is vital: it is memorable and gives feedback. Interaction leaves the perception that the supplier is listening and responding, and is easy to reach.

Language and communication

Mankind has been using language for 30 000 years or more – to share information on opportunities, dangers and simply to interact socially. Language helps societies to cohere. Current estimates suggest that 2600 different languages are spoken around the world. The number is declining as communities die out and linguistic groups are amalgamated. Languages change and words are coined or imported from other tongues. The English language has absorbed words from more than 50 other languages and is now becoming the lingua franca for global communications. With more than 600 000 words in total, and 200 000 in regular use, a word or phrase exists for every nuance of meaning.

The corollary is that an extensive vocabulary also offers ample scope for misunderstanding. A German calls their mobile phone a 'handy' and expects an Englishman to understand. A well-spoken Egyptian will say 'Welcome in Egypt'. A Frenchman wears a 'smoking' to a formal gathering. An American airline seeking to increase its business-class seat sales from South America, refurbished its planes and called the new service 'Rendezvous', using an international word meaning meeting place. Resulting sales were disastrous, because of the reluctance of secretaries in Brazil to make a booking. In Rio 'Rendezvous' is a particular type of meeting place, where men pick up prostitutes, and the thought of booking their boss into brothel class was out of the question.

In meetings, when a Londoner suggests 'tabling a subject for discussion', they mean 'let us put it on the table and talk about it'. When a New Yorker says the same thing, they mean, 'let us put it to the side of the table and not talk about it'. Same phrase, opposite meaning. Feedback is essential to ensure comprehension.

Comprehension

The sheer volume of distracting messages and communications clutter may also affect comprehension. The competing quantity of letters, brochures and advertisements mean that poor communication can be swamped and not be noticed at all. Nowhere is this more evident than with e-mails. Any subscriber has the facility to create a verbose message, attach several files and, with a few clicks, wing it to an enormous circulation list and thereby jam the system with irrelevance. The Customers that Count will judge you by your worst piece of communication, and it will proba-

The Customers that Count will judge you by your worst piece of communication.

bly be an e-mail message. The answer is a descriptive heading, a succinct message and a restricted circulation (*see* Fig. 10.2). Yet few companies provide training and guidance for their staff in e-mail manners.

Today the e-mail box is more cluttered than the traditional mail box. According to *eMarketer* (January 2000), IMT Strategies claims that 59 per cent of consumers ignore e-mails from unfamiliar sources. However, where permission is sought – known as an 'e-mail handshake', responses are higher and it is five times more cost effective than direct mail. E-mail, like other communication methods, presents an opportunity and a threat to relationships with the Customers that Count.

- A heading that describes the contents, indicates urgency and action required – don't write 'message'; write 'Benson rang – meet earlier flight'
- Succinct phrasing – aim to use 100 words or less, single screen
- Restricted circulation – who really needs to know this?

Figure 10.2 The perfect e-mail

Media preferences

Comprehension is the objective and this requires knowledge of the media preferences of the best customers. Some will be orientated towards the written word and enjoy correspondence. Others will prefer verbal communication on the telephone or face to face. Visual approaches may suit others better. There are at least 20 means of communicating with customers and all have their role (*see* Fig. 10.3). Some customers wish for brevity, and others expect the full version. Circumstances impact on methods, and urgency can be taken into account. Understanding all these factors enables the company to create and follow a preferred media pattern for Customers that Count. In this way communication matches customers and their perceptions of the quality of communications improves.

Routine choices	Creative choices
• Face to face	• Printed on a T-shirt
• Letters	• Pigeon post
• Telephone	• Flowers in company colours
• Fax	• Sky-writing/plane banner
• E-mail	• Special advert on early-morning TV
• Videotape	• Poster on road to office
• Audiotape	• Message in classified ads
• Brochure	• Message in a bottle
• Media advertising	• Captioned photograph
• Via a third party	• Singing telegram

Figure 10.3 Twenty ways to communicate

Creativity in communications

Creativity can also capture attention and set up the perception that the communication is worthwhile, and interesting. A start-up London advertising agency, desperate to stand out in the creative rivalry of the media world, identified ten prospect customers. Knowing that typically a marketing director in a fast-moving consumer-goods company receives two brochures from agencies each day, it sought to differentiate itself by delivering a carrier pigeon in a cage to each prospect. The cage was tagged with a message: 'If you would like us to present our ideas for advertising your business, take this cage to an open window, release the pigeon and it will fly swiftly to us. We will respond with a presentation. If you do not want our ideas, eat the pigeon!' Happily all the pigeons survived and the reward for creativity was three invitations to pitch, resulting in two client wins that became good long-term business.

All the senses can be deployed to develop memorable communications. Mrs Fields' Cookies can arrange for packs to be sent to a client as an edible message. Radion, a discontinued detergent brand aimed at removing the smell of sweat from working clothes, once advertised its brand on the back of bus tickets. The tickets bore the logo and were impregnated with the highly distinctive perfume of the washing powder. Any one who had ever used the product had instant recall through the aromatic connection.

Longstanding relationships need sparkle. A consulting firm in Sydney scans the American press for coverage of the industries of its client customers. When a relevant snippet is discovered, this is roughly torn from the page and immediately faxed to the client with a brief and apt message. The impression is fostered of immediacy and client interest.

Perceptions good = wonderful, poor = disastrous

Perception counts. Customers talk readily about communications and are quick to judge. Oddly, there appears to be no middle ground or average in customer judgements. Any factor is amplified so that a good missive is described as wonderful and an error results in castigation. Therefore it is all the more important to get communications right.

To create the perception that a company is accessible, customers need to be able to see how easy it is to get in contact. The Ford Customer Assistance Center in USA has defined standards to sustain a customer impression that it is accessible. This means that correspondence must be turned around in five days, while for telephone calls there must be at least 95 per cent accessibility, with a maximum hold time of 30 seconds.

Customers need to be able to see how easy it is to get in contact.

Easy to enquire or complain

Make it easy to complain or enquire. Offer a freephone number: 1-800 in the USA, 0800 in the UK, a numero vert in France or a ligne verde in Italy. Analysis by General Electric in the USA shows that, on average, in their lifetime customers buy 15 major appliances like washing machines, dish-washers, refrigerators, ovens and tumble dryers. Therefore the company has invested heavily in the GE Answer Center to manage customer relationships and make sure problems are addressed swiftly and effectively. More than 3 million calls a year are handled. The GE Answer Center can be located by calling 1-800 626 2000 in the USA or via the website (www.geappliances.com). The Answer Center website offers answers to frequently asked questions and a 'repair or replace' calculator for appliances.

Make available pre-addressed cards for comment. A phone conversation is better for conveying empathy and can also be used to solicit further comments or advice. However, for some the act of writing out a note of complaint is cathartic and speeds the process of returning to normality.

Encourage staff members to seek comments and draw out concerns from customers. Multiple listening points can multiply feedback. The more varied the feedback mechanisms, the better and more representative the responses. Often the most loyal customers are forgiving of errors and reluctant to complain. Inviting them to contribute to product improve-ment will capture their ideas. It also builds the feeling that you are accessible and willing to listen.

Interactive communication

Wherever possible encourage two-way communication. Dialogue is supe-rior to monologue. Even when it is not taken up, the option of dialogue is important. The Customers that Count feel that they have the option and you were willing to listen. If they made no comment, that was their choice. Interaction also provides a measure of customer understanding.

There is a critical proviso. When you encourage interaction, an expecta-tion is set up of a response. When a customer completes a feedback card with a tick against the box 'response required', they imagine they will have a letter within ten days. If a customer telephones then they would like an immediate answer, but will bear with a return call in 24 hours. E-mail implies a response time within a couple of hours (*see* Fig. 10.4).

This is not happening across American and European companies. Many surveys have shown that e-mail answers are taking anything up to eight days. Customers are disappointed and frustrated by the performance so far below expectation. There are some positive exceptions. The customer serv-ice operation of the Spacepen company was able to provide an e-mail response for a school project in less than three hours, including file photo-graphs and comprehensive company and product data.

Means of communication	Expectation for reply
Letter	Seven to ten days
Telephone message	The next day
E-mail message	The same day

Figure 10.4 When does the customer expect a reply?

Like a trusted friend

The objective is to build with best customers a sensation of accessibility. They must believe that you are like a trusted friend: it is easy to reach you, you welcome hearing from them, messages are understood and action is taken, and it is always interesting to hear from you.

Theme: Accessibility	Case example

Southwest Airlines

Southwest Airlines is one of the most successful airlines in the USA. Based at Love Field in Texas, it flies point to point to 54 US cities. It has a radically different style – a no-frills airline with a sense of humour – which is apparent anywhere you touch the airline. You expect a no-frills operation to imply a short wait for a telephone agent to become available when you call 1-800 I FLY SWA, but the creative and entertaining recorded message makes the time race by.

Interaction is encouraged by ground and air staff who willingly engage in repartee and note comments and suggestions with candid enthusiasm. The recruitment process has carefully selected people who are sociable and demonstrably interested in those around them. On board, the inside back page of the flight magazine '*Southwest Airlines Spirit*' amuses with 'facts of life' about life in the USA. Fliers may contribute letters via post or e-mail.

The in-flight messages from the pilots are short, efficient and often amusing. On a flight from Baltimore Maryland, I heard this announcement:

Federal Law forbids smoking in the lavatories of this aeroplane. There are smoke detectors in the lavatories and it also an offence to tamper with these devices. It may occur to you that if you find yourself tampering with the smoke detectors on a one-hour flight, you could have a serious tobacco problem.

The website (www.southwest.com) is pleasingly uncluttered. Flights can be booked by mail, phone or e-mail. The website invites prospective employees to submit a resumé on line. The Southwest message to potential employees is: 'You can't help but smile when you work for a company that knows how to play as hard as they work'.

It is easy to reach Southwest Airlines, it relishes communication from customers and it is certainly fun to hear from. Yes, it feels like a trusted friend.

Exercises

Draw a relationship map for each Customer that Counts, following the example in Fig. 10.5.

1 Identify every person in the customer's organization with whom you have contact.

2 Place their name or their role at the head of a column in a spreadsheet.

3 Identify all the people in your organization who have contact with customers.

4 List them in the left hand column, as the first cell of a row in the spreadsheet.

5 Mark where relationships exist and evaluate the quality of the connection: in the customer's perception, how frequent is the communication and how effective?

6 Establish action points for improvement.

7 Investigate opportunities for creating useful connections in cells where none currently exist. For example, the advertising agency

	Customer contact 1, e.g. Chief Executive	Customer contact 2, e.g. Purchasing Manager	Customer contact 3, e.g. Production Manager	Customer contact 4
Company contact 1, e.g. Chief Executive				
Company contact 2, e.g. Sales				
Company contact 3, e.g. Technical Advisor				
Company contact 4				

Figure 10.5 Relationship mapping

JWT identified an opportunity for finance directors of agencies and top clients to lunch once every 12 months as a means to build another connection with their Customers that Count.

Further reading and references

Gronstedt, Anders (2000) *The Customer Century: Lessons from World Class Companies in Integrated Communications*, Routledge.

Underhill, Paco (2000) Why we Buy, TEXERE .

There was a line waiting for service at the rental car desk. The clerks seemed oblivious to the anxieties of the travellers and proceeded in a slow and deliberate fashion. One of the clerks paused to light a cigarette. This incensed one of the travellers who burst out angrily: 'You are stealing my time! I need a car and I need it *now*. I've been waiting in line for 10 minutes. That's my time and you have stolen it!'

S ervice and support are part of the product offer in almost every transaction, personal or commercial. And routinely, one benefit provided by this service is the more effective use of time for the Customers that Count (*see* Fig. 11.1). In affluent societies money is in greater supply than time for busy working people. Where companies can justify financial investment, their lean structures mean they have little time to invest. For these customers, time is their scarcest resource and the most valuable. There are focused ways to handle these cash-rich/time-poor customers.

There are other Customers that Count who have more time and they require different approaches. Understanding the function of time for customers means that you can meet their time needs. Value for money was the theme of the twentieth century. In the twenty-first century customers are seeking value for time as well. You can refund their money, but you cannot give time back.

'You manage my time effectively'

Service and support that gives customers good value for time

Figure 11.1 Service

Time and money matrix

To provide good value for time, it is necessary to understand customer groupings by time type. There are four such groups (*see* Fig. 11.2). Each requires different handling for best effect. We will look first at the group who are well resourced financially but face real time pressure. How can we serve their needs?

Different customers have different time expectations. A winning strategy is to categorize and recognize customers so that their varied wishes are delivered. This is relatively easy to implement in a key-account management operation where the organization has dedicated support for its major customers. For example, a raw-materials supplier to Procter & Gamble will have a key account manager who will well understand its expectations of urgency and time certainty. They will convey this in specific terms to all involved in business support to the Procter & Gamble relationship. Behaviours will be reviewed at annual supplier evaluations and will be communicated in measured dimensions against targets.

For larger-scale operations handling hundreds or thousands of customers, it is possible to categorize customers by value to the organization and their own real or perceived need for speed. Airport fast-track lanes and phone-number recognition systems allow more rapid access for Customers that Count. Points-based schemes can create priority levels. The higher the number of points, the higher the priority accorded. For example, points might be awarded for volume of orders, profitability of lines ordered, con-

Time category	Consumer example	Corporate example
Time poor/ cash rich	Company executive	Telecomms, media technology
Time poor/ cash poor	Small-scale farmer	Public sector organization
Time rich/ cash rich	Ladies who lunch	Protected monopoly
Time rich/ cash poor	Retired manual worker	Protected public sector

Figure 11.2 Time/money matrix

sistency and regularity of orders, patterns of usage that fall outside the peak times, influence with other customers, low levels of product returns and infrequent need for support. Where complaints have been made and service failures have occurred, these customers can be placed on a higher priority level while confidence is restored.

Retailers may need additional systems to help recognize customers by their time sensitivity. One simple and effective model used by a UK retailer of liquor taught store staff to put customers into different typologies. These were made more memorable by association with animal characteristics. Three examples of higher spending types were:

- **Hawks:** Determined and confident customers who swoop into the store and know exactly what they want to buy and where it is located. They expect rapid and competent service at the till. Staff were taught not to engage hawks in conversation, but simply to swipe their payment cards swiftly and let them fly out of the store as rapidly as they had entered. They take very little time, but spend significantly

- **Elephants:** Slow and deliberate customers who want to walk slowly around the store and examine the merchandise carefully. They want advice only when they ask for it and then they expect full and accurate answers. They like to talk at the till and to receive confirmation of the wisdom of their choice. They take a long time, but can also spend significantly.

- **Rabbits:** Nervous and insecure customers who are unsure of their purchases and need to be approached calmly and quietly and offered advice. Left alone and they may hop out of the store without buying anything. They should not be surprised lest they bolt. Handled in the right way, they will spend heavily.

The retailer noticed improved ratings in customer-satisfaction surveys among their higher spending Customers that Count – both the time-poor and the time-rich.

The time-poor/cash-rich customers

The time-poor and cash-rich have fascinating needs (see Fig. 11.3). First, they have an obvious requirement for speed that must be met by their suppliers. Second, there is a powerful desire not to waste time, which means comprehensive and unhurried advice in order to preclude reworking and revising. Finally, where they choose to allocate a significant piece of time, this represents an important investment and they expect a memorable and positive return.

Mindset 1	Fast is best
Mindset 2	Time-wasting is a crime
Mindset 3	Looking for a return on time invested

Figure 11.3 Handling time-poor/cash-rich customers

Fast is good

For time-poor/cash-rich customers speed and convenience are vital. For routine and low-involvement activities they seek rapid convenience. In other words, they have low patience thresholds. Supermarkets have monitored the average buyer of yoghurts – typically they spend 11 seconds in front of the fixture, and in this period they need to be able to grasp the brand, category and flavour selection. Thus grocery brands need bold and simple designs with pictorial graphics that are instantly recognizable. Stores need to deploy category management to bracket similar types of yoghurt together to be easy to choose in this time band. Leading suppliers vie for the position of 'category captain' or merchandising adviser to a retailer. For example, one category captain recommends that a refrigerated fixture be split into four sections: children's yoghurts, the diet range, the standard assortments and luxury-indulgent desserts.

Time-poor customers need real speed in service and also ample evidence of efforts being made to achieve speed for them.

These time-poor customers need real speed in service and also ample evidence of efforts being made to achieve speed for them. It is the actual and the perceptual (*see* Fig. 11.4).

Actual speed of service can be delivered through automatic systems, like Amazon's Page You Made (described in *The Economist*, 13 October 2000). This facility analyzes your click-stream to identify interests, allows you to refine the record and produces rapid suggestions. Another automated facility is the conference-venue selection system offered on the website of the Florida Marriott Hotels (www.floridamarriotts.com).

In the business-to-business sector, Graniterock, based in Watson California, speeds the service of supplying construction materials. At the commodity end of the scale it is hard initially to believe that there are factors other than price involved in customer decisions. However, Graniterock knew that customers pay more than a dollar a minute to rent the trucks that they use to transport materials to construction sites. So the company embarked on a time shrinking strategy. Loading faster reduces truck-rental costs for customers. It launched a card and reader system called GraniteXpress in 1988 for faster loading. Customers found that average loading time shrank from 24 minutes to 8 minutes. In 1999 Graniterock gathered together representatives of their 40 most valuable customers and announced a new scheme using radio frequencies, which further speeded the process by a couple of minutes. It provided faster service to the Customers that Count.

- Automate to speed the process
- Think ahead to save customers time
- Carry out actions in parallel
- Give priority to Customers that Count
- Manage time perceptions
- Provide time certainty
- Let customers invest time for the future

Figure 11.4 Make it faster (or seem faster)

Thinking ahead to save customers time

Much effort is being invested in thinking ahead to save the customer time. Otis, the Connecticut-based manufacturer of elevators, incorporates intelligent devices in new installations. The remote elevator monitor (REM) devices are programmed to detect wear indicators. In effect they spot future failures before they happen. Otis technicians receive automatic notification and are able to rectify these emerging faults before they impact on customers. Otis extended the concept by taking REM online, permitting customers to monitor the condition of their elevators remotely through the web.

A world leader in time saving for customers is Entek, which designs and manufactures failure prediction systems. Its website (www.entekird.com) describes time-saving systems that provided concrete financial benefits to customers. For example, Adelaide Brighton Cement, a significant Australian cement manufacturer, whose product is exported to numerous markets in the Pacific and South-East Asia, gained the following benefits:

- a 15 per cent improvement in plant availability, worth $5 million;
- avoided six to ten kiln shut-downs per year;
- reduced the cost of out-sourced maintenance contractors, worth $30 000 per year;
- saved $125 000 by reducing time-based maintenance schedules;
- a lower inventory of maintenance items.

Abu Dhabi Duty Free pre-select goods for its customers. Its 'Treasure Chest' offers 14 sets of pre-selected items from Lancôme, Continental, Barbie and others, for those who have little time for gift buying.

Thinking parallel

Simultaneous activities can accomplish tasks in a timely fashion. Gillette understands the twin concerns of the male in the morning: a shave to last the whole day accomplished in the minimum time. How does it meet this? By thinking in parallel. Initially it launched the twin-track razor with two blades, and in 1998 it launched the Mach 3, with three blades. A single hand movement and three blades cover the facial area. The Venus, launched in 2001, offers the same three-blade benefit to female users.

Texas-based Dallas Airmotive knows that its major airline customers need maximum hours in the sky to operate profitably. Thus, when an air engine needs servicing, it is removed from the wing and a replacement unit is provided so that the plane can turn about and continue flying while its original engine is overhauled.

Fast is an expectation

Customers appreciate an advance in time saving for a very short period. Soon it becomes the norm, taken for granted, and so dissatisfaction arises for organizations that are not abreast with time developments. Once a UK customer has experienced the joy of just giving their postcode for the whole address to be known, they begrudge the minutes explaining and spelling the street name to another service provider. When Viking stationery prompt your order requirements, it feels like wasting time to buy from a supplier who expects you to remember your own recurring needs.

What is 'fast'?

Perceptions of time are critical. A supplier of leather to manufacturers received a call from a customer seeking a complex piece of information. The response was to agree to call right back with the answer. The help-desk attendant was pleased to discover the full answer within two hours and called the customer before the end of the morning. This met his personal standard of quick response. He was dismayed when the customer complained that she had been waiting beside the phone for an immediate ring back. One phrase created different expectations in the mind of customer and service provider.

Making it fast for the Customers that Count

Technology now permits real speed to be delivered to the Customers that Count, at the expense of others. According to *Business Week* (23 October 2000), Charles Schwab Corporation's top-rated Signature clients (minimum assets of $100 000 or trading more often than 12 times per year) never wait more than 15 seconds for a call to be answered. Other customers, lower down the value sequence, may wait 10 minutes or longer. Big spenders on the Sears Roebuck company credit card can expect time slots of two hours for repairs to be carried out. Lesser spenders receive four-hour time slots.

The computer tomography (CT) division of Siemens in Germany is planning to install TV cameras in selected clinics and hospitals where its hardware is due to be installed. Through the internet, technicians at Siemens CT Division will be able to see when the facility is ready for the installation in order to arrange correct shipping dates; too early and the equipment hampers the building operation, too late and the customer is delayed.

Making it seem fast

To meet perceptions of speed, wise service providers seek a little insight into the way in which customers make judgements on rapidity. For example, the UK savings bank, TSB Bank, before its takeover by Lloyds Bank, developed a strategy to address customer concern about lunchtime queues at teller windows. Part of the plan was to attack the actual task and roster as many staff as were needed to fill each teller position. An equally effective aspect was to attack the perceptions of waiting time. Large mirrors were located around the banking hall, positioned to be parallel with the line of the queue. Observation showed that customers fell into two types: the narcissists who distracted themselves by looking at their own reflections, and the voyeurs who seized the opportunity to look at the images of others undetected. Research showed that the combined approach delivered a perception of shorter waiting time (*see* Fig. 11.5).

Music is an alternative distraction element, most effective where customers have similar musical tastes and least effective in telephone queueing. Euro-Disney has raised sound-based distraction of queues to a fine art. As a line winds its way forward and back along the guide rails, visitors are able to anticipate the thrill of the forthcoming ride, spurred on by the roar of the carriages and the shrieks of the riders.

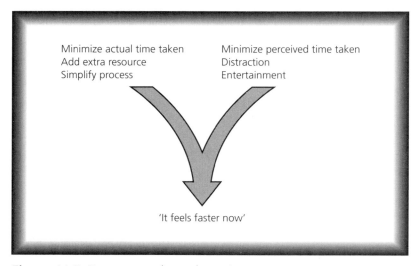

Figure 11.5 Two-pronged attack on time

Lufthansa makes boarding seem faster by a priority system that sends window passengers to the aircraft in the first wave, middle-seat passengers next and finally aisle passengers. The customer perception of waiting is minimized by diminishing the time they are standing with hand luggage in a confined space. Sitting at the departure gate until their turn arrives is preferable.

In the business-to-business arena, accurate information creates perceptions of time efficiency. A wholesaler discovered an enhancement during the UK fuel blockades of September 2000. Drivers were equipped with mobile phones to enable them to call customers an hour before the delivery took place. This was designed to reassure and to avoid problems of customers not expecting deliveries in time of fuel shortage. The impact was so positive that this practice is being continued for the most significant customers, who now rate this service operation as their most time-efficient. Time certainty has a real value. In other businesses, practice has shown that delivering service with a sense of urgency, using pace, enthusiasm and cues indicating an awareness of speed, can have a powerful effect on perceptions.

Delivering service with a sense of urgency, can have a powerful effect on perceptions.

Invest today, save later

Customers are willing to invest time initially when they are confident that it will subsequently save time later. On a trip to Costco to bulk-buy cereal, detergent, toothpaste and toilet rolls, the consumer is spending money today to save money over the following period. Similarly, the customer will put in bulk time to provide information on preferences, previous experience and expectations for the future, in order to save time over the following period.

Time saving is available to people who take initial time out to sign up with Peapod. Peapod is a web-based shopping service (www.peapod.com) owned by Dutch-based supermarkets group, Ahold. Peapod is designed to save time in supermarket shopping. Peapod receives orders from members electronically and then Peapod's personal shoppers will select the items from supermarkets within the Ahold group, like Giant Food and Stop & Shop. Peapod will even honour saver cards and the discount coupons that households receive with their Sunday newspaper. Peapod delivers within agreed time windows. The Peapod slogan is 'We know you have better things to do with your time'. One shopper is quoted in the promotional brochure as saying, 'Saturday in the park with the kids is a lot more fun than Saturday in the supermarket with the kids'.

The next time-saving stage beyond out-sourcing grocery shopping is to out-source many other activities. Personal out-sourcing can include dog walking, hiring a gardener, or finding and supervising a builder for repair work. The Time Energy Network (TenUK) is a UK-based out-source service found at www.tenuk.com. A potential customer commits to a lengthy discussion that enables TenUK to profile their likes, dislikes, lifestyle and priorities. As result of this, an understanding is developed so that time wasting is avoided. For example, if they were estranged from their parents, TenUK would not provide a reminder for a Mother's day card.

Profiling commercial customers demands a substantial investment in time from both parties. For example, in corporate assurance the first 12 months is a period of learning about the business context, culture and practices, risks and opportunities. For this reason some major commercial insurers will be reluctant to take on accounts that appear unlikely to remain for the duration. The time-driven switching costs are a disincentive to change on both sides.

Setting up electronic data interchange and facilitating electronic ordering takes time, and this time represents an investment for subsequent time saving. Demonstrating the time saved each quarter is an effective reminder of the value of an incumbent supplier. It can be a discouragement to seek alternatives.

Making time spent feel worthwhile

Where time investment is a necessary part of the process, it is important that this is made as pleasant as possible. If you cannot save time, then make the time worthwhile (*see* Fig. 11.6).

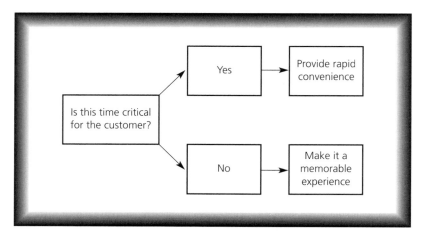

Figure 11.6 Decision tree for time

When the London-based Selfridges department store made the significant decision to open a second store at Manchester's Trafford Park retail centre, it had no control over the journeys of customers to its door. What it was able to offer was an experience inside the door that made travelling an hour seem worth the effort. Thus the brief to designers and merchandisers demanded that the result would justify such a journey. This set challenging standards and the result was a range of goods that could not be bought in the local stores habitually patronized by customers.

Avoiding bad time experiences

Avoiding the negative is another aspect of delivering a positive experience (*see* Fig 11.7). Disneyland discovered from a post-visit survey that a small proportion of visitors had their day at the Disney Park ruined when their car refused to start for the homeward journey. With a view to managing the whole experience, Disney introduced breakdown trucks to fix car problems for free in their parking lot. They wanted the whole day to be worthwhile.

- Ensure the travelling time is worthwhile
- Ensure the exit experience is positive
- Add enjoyment to essential activities
- Enrich with something new
- Souvenirs, photographs, mementoes
- Unhurried support
- Relaxed entertainment

Figure 11.7 Make it memorable

A new strategy in time management for customers is to take essential but unenjoyable time slots and recast them with new benefits. Of necessity, many people must wait in hotel receptions for taxis, for colleagues or visitors. Setting up television screens with CNN broadcasts allows them to keep abreast with news headlines. Car drivers see filling their car with gasoline or diesel as a distress purchase with nothing but a utility payback. In response, filling stations are extending their pleasure, offering music, confectionery and lottery tickets, as well as becoming local collection points for internet purchases. Order from your PC or WAP phone and have your purchases delivered to your personal locker at a neighbourhood filling station. It brings a new perspective to the chore of refuelling.

Enrich time with something new

In Japan the 22-store discount chain Don Quijote sees its role as entertainment. According to the *Financial Times* (21 December 1999), President Takao Yasuda says that the company does not see itself as a retailer, but as an imaginative provider of space where young people can amuse themselves, especially at night. He adds that a lot of customers are tired of karaoke clubs and bars. Don Quijote keeps changing product line-ups and moves merchandise around so there is always something new to see.

The UK chocolate-assortment brand, Celebrations, has also sought to provide a sense of something new. To make their website (www.celebrations365.com) worth visiting they add a reason to celebrate every day, with an anniversary or an occasion that merits buying chocolate. They take this further by inviting consumers to log the birthdays of friends and relations with Celebrations, so that they can be reminded by e-mail to get them a present. It takes time to set this up, but there is, naturally, a social pay-back. Finally, they suggest that you advise them of your own birthday and the e-mail addresses of people who might need a reminder of this important date.

Pleasant and memorable business contacts

In the commercial arena, time is also necessarily spent in routine activities with customers. Where these cannot be short-circuited, the challenge is to make them as pleasant and memorable as possible. Clear information on the time needed is a start here. Good directions and accurate travel information also help. Ensuring comfort and providing learning for customers help to make a day feel beneficial. Amusement is useful and souvenirs, mementoes or reminders can add to the positive aura of the review, demonstration, project appraisal, or whatever. A strong message is that any occasion you take time from your customer, it should feel worthwhile for them.

All resources should be deployed to make customers feel their time has been worthwhile. For example, trade shows demand a considerable time commitment from customers. A trend identified in the magazine *Sales and Marketing Management* (June 2000) is for more attendance at trade shows by chief executive officers. With a celebrity CEO, customers will remember a meeting for years. IBM customers may well meet CEO Louis Gerstner at an exhibition. Likewise, Caterpillar customers could retell to many people how they chatted with Glen Barton at October 2000's Mine Expo. Steve Jobs, Apple Computer's chief, gave keynote addresses at seven major technology events in 1999.

Where your most valuable customers come to you for service or advice, the sensation they should gain is that your support is unhurried. They will already be aware that you value their time. Now, the task is to illustrate that your time is at their disposal. This is another perceptual issue.

In its marketing of four-wheel luxury vehicles, Range Rover has always acknowledged two tenets. First, that time is needed for prospective owners to appreciate the true qualities of the vehicle. Second that you must value the time of someone who is in the market for a vehicle costing £50 000 ($70 000). The concept of 'A Country Affair' is built on this. It is a series of one-day events at UK stately homes and castles, to which customers and highly qualified prospects are invited to enjoy a range of country pursuits, which includes putting Range Rovers through their paces. Other pastimes are archery, abseiling, shooting, hawk-flying and croquet – all designed to make sure the customers feel their time is well spent.

Value for the time-rich

We have focused on the time-poor customers, since so many of the most valuable customers fall into this category. There are, of course, other valuable customers who are time-rich. Identifying these customers and meeting their different needs is another skill (*see* Fig 11.8).

The time-rich may be persuaded, through pricing or convenience, to pass through constrained systems at quiet times, thus leaving the crowded hours more clear for those compelled to slot into them. For example, telephone banks in Germany, the UK and the USA have encouraged some of their best customers to conduct banking business late at night, when there is less pressure on the system. Transport systems from the Boston U to the Paris Metro incentivize time-rich travellers to use off-peak services. Sainsbury's, the UK supermarket, provides a bus service to its stores from outlying villages for those without their own cars – typically senior citizens. Services are often timed to run mid-morning on Tuesdays, which is a quiet time for a food store. The time-rich help to spread the load and achieve better system utilization. The benefit to the customer is to have unhurried access to facilities with high levels of staff support.

Business-to-business markets can be segmented by time sensitivity and by the times they wish to access the system or need deliveries or service support. This exercise can result in better service to pressured customers, as well as to those whose time is less constrained.

Giving value to the time-rich	Gaining value from the time-rich
• Advice on when to access the system • Higher level support at off-peak times • Incentives to use quiet times	• Off-peak throughput • Testing and research • Word-of-mouth recommendation

Figure 11.8 The time-rich

Value from the time-rich

The time-rich can add more value than simply representing throughput in off-peak hours. With their willingness or ability to invest more time than other customers, they can be a valuable source of testing and research. They are often interested to try out a new facility of operation, and able to take the time to give a customer perspective. They will complete surveys and questionnaires (although it is essential that their comparability to other busier customers is checked).

It is possible to create peer-group sales support from customers who are interested in the product and who have time available. They may be delighted to join user groups that assist fellow customers and feedback conclusions to companies. It may be possible to give them the vocabulary to recommend products to other customers. The car manufacturer Volvo is well aware of the asset that well-briefed existing owners represent, and they provide a regular magazine that highlights strong sales features for them to use in car conversations with friends and neighbours.

According to *The Economist* (13 October 2000), the San Francisco-based cosmetics company Kibu.com (now no longer trading) used peer marketing to promote its site to teenage girls. It recruited time-rich schoolgirls to go to the malls, sports facilities and clubs that other girls their own age patronize, where they handed out free samples of products like lip-gloss. In effect these girls were promoting the website and creating the perception that the face of the brand is the face of a friend your own age.

Handling the time-poor and cash-poor

Where the time-poor customers are also cash-poor then the appropriate response is to simplify products and procedures and use automation to handle the issues cost-effectively. Banks and insurance companies in South Africa have used this to good effect to provide services to low-income groups who had not previously been served by the financial services industry.

Value for time

The objective is to create the perception that the customer receives a fair return on time invested. An enterprising Californian appliance repairs company charges a minimum of one hour even when the repair is accomplished in minutes. This is a standard arrangement, but it discovered through feedback that this created a poor feeling of value for time among customers. Creatively, it now has a new approach. Where a task is finished well within the hour, the representative explains the minimum charging policy, and then asks if there is anything else they can do in the remaining time. Only occasionally are they called on to put this offer into practice, but universally the customer has a better perception of the value for time provided.

Create the perception that the customer receives a fair return on time invested.

Professors Mittal and Sawhney (of the JL Kellogg Graduate School of Management) have explored the concept of 'return on time invested'. Their hypothesis is that retention of best customers will increasingly derive from the extent of their return on time invested. Where the return is high, success will result. For example, Microsoft required users to invest significant time in understanding the processes involved in Word. Subsequent products like PowerPoint, Access and FrontPage use the same processes. These were now familiar and hence users gained a positive return on time invested across the product range.

Teaching customers how to get best value out of time

Teaching the customer how to get better value from their time is therefore a critical consideration. Overloaded peak-time phone lines offer suggestions of quieter times to call. Customers are taught to have key data available before initiating contact so that they receive more time-effective service. Hewlett-Packard printers come with self-help advice, providing checklists of actions to try before calling the help-line. Websites provide instructional elements for first-time or infrequent users. Similarly, advertising agency J. Walter Thompson teaches new clients how to brief advertising most effectively to ensure all the considerations are covered in a way that will obviate rework.

Helping customers budget their time

Setting realistic time expectations at the first encounter is another technique to achieve positive customer attitudes to time. Disney set up A–boards advising the queue waiting time at high-demand rides in their amusement parks. Disney realizes that a wait of unknown duration seems much longer than a defined period of waiting. It therefore allows guests to budget their time in the same way as financial quotations allow people to budget their money.

Conclusion

Understanding the function of time for customers means that you can manage their time needs most effectively. Where possible you can speed the best customers through the process by streamlining operations and prioritizing the most valuable users. Time-rich customers may be diverted to off-peak time slots to enhance their time and improve rapidity for the time-poor. Negative time experiences can be avoided or transformed to increase value for time. Where it is not possible or effective to take time out of a process, an alternate stance is chosen: make the time invested as enjoyable and productive as it can be. Value for money was the theme of the twentieth century. In the twenty-first century, customers are seeking value for time as well.

Marriott International

Marriott International is a leading worldwide hospitality company. Its heritage can be traced to a small root-beer stand opened in Washington DC in 1927. Today Marriott International has more than 2000 lodging properties located in 58 countries. Truly a large global brand, it still carries the feel of a family organization to its guests – at Marriott, customers are always known as guests. This family feeling pervades guests who are members of the frequent-stay program, 'Marriott Rewards'. For instance, a member may recognize Bill Marriott, Chairman and Chief Executive Officer, in the elevator and pass him a new business card as a way to advise a change of address. There are more than 12 million members of the Marriott Rewards program and Marriott International dedicates significant resources to meeting the special needs of this group of high-value guests. The team responsible for this is led by Lynne Roach-Hildebrand, Senior Vice-President of Loyalty Marketing. I met Lynne at the Marriott World Headquarters just outside Washington DC.

Lynne is ever aware that a guest's time has a value. She explains that Marriott Rewards members are time-conscious and like to see this recognized. Time consciousness may be about doing things quickly, but on other occasions it means allowing the guest to take their time over an enjoyable experience. For example, Marriott notice that the same guest will love to linger and interact with the concierge in the evening, but the following morning, it is 'grab and go' for breakfast.

As far as speed is concerned, Marriott aims to save its guests time whenever possible. It is an important part of training for Marriott Associates to recognize the human cues that indicate 'I'm in a hurry', and respond accordingly. This thought process begins even before the guest arrives at the hotel. Eager that no time is wasted trying to find the hotel, guests are encouraged to print hotel location maps directly from the Marriott website (www.marriott.com). It is a well used website – in 1999 it took well over $100 million in reservations. High-frequency guests may be invoiced monthly to eradicate the minutes for payment at the end of a stay. Conference organizers appreciate the time-saving in identifying and selecting potential locations for conventions. They can use a dedicated Marriott website, which illustrates features, facilities and facts like room sizes of available hotels.

Lynne Roach-Hildebrand is proud of the way the Marriott Resort experience makes the most of guests' vacation time. She tells me: 'We value guests' time, so we want to make sure they have the maximum amount of time devoted to enjoying themselves'. Consequently, when guests book a vacation at a Marriott Resort, Marriott will send advance details of the facilities of the resort. Marriott's Personal Planning Service gives them the opportunity to consider how they wish to spend their time. Some day's later Marriott will contact them, take details and, ahead of the vacation, schedule golf tee times or spa treatments. This means that guests are vacationing from the moment they arrive. Lynne adds, 'If we did not do that, they would take the first 24 hours figuring out what is available, and that could be one fourth of their vacation time'. Vacations are precious and guests value this help in making the most of the time available.

Good service is timely service.

Exercise 11   Exercises

Survey your customers about your time sensitivity: compare yourself with their other suppliers across a range of products and services, including some from outside the products/services that you are providing.

Further reading and references

Borrus, Amy (2000) 'How Marriott never forgets a guest' *Business Week*, 21 February.

Brady, Diane (2000) 'Why service stinks' *Business Week*, 23 October.

Mittal, Vikas and Sawhney, Mohanbir (1998) 'Managing Learning to Lock in Customers' *Financial Times* Mastering Marketing Supplement, Part 6, 19 October.

Seiders, Kathleen, Berry, Leonard L., Gresham, Larry G. (2000) 'Attention retailers! How convenient is your convenience strategy?' *Sloan Management Review*, spring.

Yeh, R.T., Pearlson, K. and Kozmetsky, G. (2000) *Zero Time: Providing Instant Customer Value*, John Wiley.

Hi. I am calling you from Helsinki. I'm at ForestProdFest and I am look-ing at a fascinating new device and I thought of you.

> You thought of me ... I don't follow you. You sell us yeast improvers and we bake bread, so what are you doing at a forest products exhibition?

Hear me out, you'll love this technology! It cuts more planks from a trunk with less sawdust than you can imagine.

> I cannot imagine sawdust. We don't put sawdust in our bread either, what are you talking about?

I'm talking about the conversation we had last month. What were you saying to me about the mechanical slicer?

> Don't mention that thing to me – waste, sensors jammed with crumbs, cleaning downtime, what can you do about that?

There's a flight to Helsinki in the morning...

T he pace of change is an evident business challenge to all. Yet the Customers that Count have an advantage others never see. Their suppli-ers provide insights into the future, they challenge existing assumptions and thereby provide a value beyond the worth of the products and services they supply. In effect, the Customers that Count have the benefit of external anten-nae that protect them against the uncertainties of the future. Leading businesses use a variety of anticipatory techniques to gather new questions and possible answers for themselves and they share these insights with their most important customers, keeping these customers up to date (*see* Fig. 12.1).

'You keep me up to date'

Offering expertise and insights to customers
to help them spot opportunities
and threats posed by the future

Figure 12.1 Education

Pace of change

The pace of business change is an ever-present discomfort. Every time a company identifies a trend it can exploit, along comes a counter-movement. Ford's research showed huge demand for the vehicle that became known as the Explorer, the largest sports utility vehicle available. But it was to face environmental pressure for its gas-guzzling performance and social pressure from other road users for its threatening bulk. Years of patient commercial development in the Middle East clothes-washing market were arrested by a bizarre coincidence. Sales of Ariel detergent plummeted unexpectedly in the Arab world at the time of the Israeli and Palestinian conflict, November 2000. It occurred because the controversial leader of Israel is named Ariel Sharon and, by association, sympathizers of the Palestinians could not bring themselves to purchase the brand bearing his name.

Customers sense the huge rate of change and have weekly reminders. Compare the changes in the first 70 years of the twentieth century with the last 30 years. And in high-change industries like the technology media, entertainment and telecommunications, the perception is stronger than the reality. Will cigarettes really be displaced by mobile phones as the manual plaything for image-conscious teens? In the third generation (known as 3G) of mobile telephony, will these teen users book cinema tickets on WAP phones? Or will they stay at home battling with Lara Croft on freely downloaded software? Will there be real battles over scarce resources like water? And what is happening to the humble water closet? *The Economist* magazine (29 August 1998) warns that Japanese sanitary-ware supplier, Toto, is launching the toilet designed for diabetics which analyzes the urine and displays on a screen the amount of sugar in the blood. The company is now working on a liver-condition check that analyzes protein and blood in the urine. Whatever next, wonder customers, competitors and bemused bystanders – who may all be caught up in the maelstrom without realizing it.

Who can help in changing times?

Change is the opportunity for many businesses, yet in reality their priority is to contain any threat that change may pose to them. Keeping up with change is the entrancing combination of inspiration and perspiration. When you find yourself in uncertain circumstances, you look for a guide to help you find your way around. For example Pampers, the diaper brand of Procter & Gamble, recognizes the enormity of the move from childlessness to parenthood and offers guidance to new mothers and fathers on a website (www.pampers.com) that offers answers to questions you had not even thought to frame. Through the experience Pampers has collated, it is able to offer norms, trends and answers. Furthermore, such is its knowledge that it can make predictions about the future as your new babe develops. This is a good pattern for other markets and industries.

Outsiders often have insights

An important ability is to see more clearly for others. 'Oh wad some pow'r the giftie gie us' sang Scottish poet Robbie Burns in the poem 'To a Louse', 'to see oursels as others see us'. It is a facility you are able to offer to the Customers that Count: with your insight and perspective, you can protect these customers from implications as yet unseen to them. Your knowledge can reassure them in times of threatening change.

The twin benefits of focusing on potential change are that you will be ready before your competitors and also you will be able to provide some psychological security to best customers. Purchasing executives of Procter & Gamble reportedly set out the expectation to new contractors that their ideal suppliers keep them abreast of market changes, *before they ask*. In other words, it is seen as part of the ongoing relationship to advise of any change that may have an impact on the customer.

Examples of market developments that various suppliers have foreseen and communicated in recent years are:

- the impact of the European Union Working Time Directive on customers' employment practices;
- expected currency movements in Latin America;
- trends in PIN number replacement by iris and other body-part scanning techniques;
- changes in the personal taxation regime for expatriates working in Russia.

This becomes a joint trend-seeking exercise when conclusions are shared and the mutual implications are explored. It is not a chargeable extra, rather a built-in extra whose costs are recovered through the profitability of the relationship with the leading customer.

Techniques for anticipation

In order to protect their own futures and those of the Customers that Count, organizations are using five different techniques to anticipate trends in markets (*see* Fig. 12.2). In turn we focus on each of the five.

- Customer based
- Market based
- Supplier based
- External sources
- Internal sources

Figure 12.2 Techniques to anticipate trends

Customer-based techniques

Marketers always begin with the customer and therefore the first area for focus is on the customer. For example, Kraft Foods uses its website (www.kraft.com) to encourage consumers to share their ideas in a 'Wisdom of Moms Exchange'. These suggestions for using Kraft products are posted ostensibly for the benefit of other users – it is certainly a well-visited section of the Kraft site. However, it is also a valuable source of information on new trends, new food practices and new opportunities for promoting or extending the use of Kraft foodstuffs.

Focus on lead users

Asking the majority of customers their views on the future is often ineffective, as the majority of customers are unable to envisage radical developments. With this in mind, many firms focus on specific groups of customers known as the lead users. In any market there are always experimenters who set new trends and others who identify and follow these new directions before the majority. Everett M. Rogers (1995) identifies this advance group as the 'innovators' and the fast followers as 'early adopters' and presents a strong case for understanding the adoption process.

To understand emerging trends it is important to know who are the early adopters, for it is they who determine which of the experiments will make it to the mainstream. In some markets, for example in stylish drinks or youth clothing, there are certain cities, districts or bars where early adopters are known to gather. Dutch-style lager, Grolsch, focused on sampling in these leading bars and this was part of an effective entry strategy into the UK market in the late 1980s. UK clothing retailer, Next, understands that the early adopters are heavy users of the Next catalogue and reportedly have identified a body of buyers with a track record of buying products that go on to become fashion successes. Hence when a threshold number of these buyers select a new line from the catalogue, this flags up a need to order large stocks for the retail stores. Similarly, pharmaceutical companies in the USA list medical practitioners most likely to support new therapies and provide feedback and referral. Advance users of a drug with the side effect of drowsiness highlighted this not as a problem, but an opportunity for meeting the needs of allergy sufferers for whom the side effect provided a night-time benefit. The lead users had spotted a trend.

Don't ask customers, just observe them

Alternatively, suppliers watch rather than ask. They choose to observe and video customers, searching for unmet problems and usage difficulties. The customers simply accept the present situation and are themselves not aware of the difficulties. Yet a medical-products company recorded on video surgeons conducting microsurgery. It was able to identify inefficient movements that current equipment forced on the doctors. Unasked, it improved the ergonomic efficiency of its products. Customers had shown them the way.

Simulating the customer's challenges

In another example, a major food retailer noticed a significant piece of behaviour on video film of aisles in their stores. Elderly customers – frequently female and typically around 30 cm shorter than the average shopper – would reach unsuccessfully for products such as the bedtime-drink mix, Horlicks, and then leave the store without having bought the item and without asking for assistance. Spurred by this insight, the retailer investigated the routine purchase items of older customers with the help of a UK charity focusing on the elderly. Encouraged by the charity, the store executives underwent an artificial ageing process. This entailed donning visors smeared with Vaseline to simulate poor sight, neck braces to restrict movement, heavy rucksacks to bring about a stooped posture, gauntlets to replicate arthritic hands, and diving boots weighted with lead to restrict walking speed. In this attire, they took the shopping list around the store to experience the challenges of buying. As a result of this exercise the supermarket now shelves items at a more suitable height, provides large print labelling and makes locations obviously convenient.

Living the life of your customer

Close to the customer means understanding how they live their lives. As a practical instance of living the life of your customer, London-based advertising agency Hicklin

Close to the customer means understanding how they live their lives.

Slade and Partners took empathy with youth culture to a new level in summer 2000, when they arranged for a group of their clients to see Europe's hippest youth market first-hand. They flew their clients into Ibiza at midnight on a Wednesday for a non-stop party, before returning them at 7 am on Friday.

A further technique is to collate and study the media consumed by your customers and end-users. This includes magazines for their industries, websites identified by key words used by customers, and attending trade shows of customers. All these locations can provide insights into trends in customer needs, thinking and behaviours.

Market-based techniques

The second source for identifying trends is market based (*see* Fig. 12.3). Obviously there are published market trends that can be extrapolated, such as moves to miniaturization, cross-manufacturer compatibility, open systems and so forth. Beyond the obvious are techniques such as identifying markets that are more advanced or more competitive than your own.

Advanced markets are a source of ideas. If you are in the paper business and concerned that the 30-year threat of the paperless office may actually occur courtesy of e-mail brochures and internet newspapers, then you would seek early signs in Finland, which has the highest internet penetration. A credit card company, interested in the cashless society, would

Customer based	Market based	Supplier based	External sources	Internal sources
Observing users	Identifying market influencers	Most innovative suppliers	Alliance with companies in related areas	Cross-function brainstorming
Identifying lead users	Countries where market competitive	Studying supply industry media	Benchmarking world-class industries	Scenario planning
Studying customer's consumers	Indicator markets	Exhibitions of supplier industry	Business schools, agencies	Champion to receive ideas from staff
Studying customer's media	Role-playing market entrants		Planned legislation	Talking to the next generation

Figure 12.3 Anticipatory techniques in detail

investigate Iceland with the highest penetration of plastic cards. Only 14 per cent of transactions use coins or notes, compared with 80 per cent in other European countries – you can buy an apple, a newspaper or a hot dog with plastic, and even pay for childcare with a card.

Intensely competitive markets have their own value. Rivalry forces innovation. Therefore if you want insights, seek out the most competitive marketplace. For example, in the hotel business, great attention is paid to developments in Dubai, United Arab Emirates. There are 269 hotels in Dubai, so how will a new hotel like the Burj Al Arab Hotel stand out? First, at 1053 feet, it is taller than the Eiffel Tower in Paris. Its high staff ratio provides sumptuous service, whilst in technology it is currently showing the way for the world hotel industry. Suites offer DVD players, 42-inch flat screen televisions with internet access and a facility to view on-screen any caller at the door. Press the wrong button on any elevator and you can countermand the instruction with a double tap of the button, so you will not be annoyed by a stop at the wrong floor.

Pre-payment stimulated an enormous surge in mobile telephony by permitting phones to be bought and operated by people unwilling or unable to commit to a credit-based arrangement. With pre-payment, teenagers were suddenly welcomed to the market for 'handies'. Where did this trend first manifest itself? It began in Portugal, Europe's toughest market, where consumers had real concerns and constraints on their expenditure. Mobile-phone operations began in Portugal in 1989, when TMN, a subsidiary of Portugal Telecom, was launched. In 1995 TMN, endeavouring to move mobile phones beyond the luxury category, arranged for pre-payment of calling packages for mobile phones. Portugal has a unique ATM network called Multibanco, jointly owned by 30 shareholders who represent Portugal's retail banking operations. This combined ATM network has developed facilities that include bill payment at any ATM in the network. Fines and charity donations can also be made. TMN was able to use this system for pre-payments, thereby giving customers control over their costs. The result was an explosion of demand. Telecom companies from other countries noted the success and rapidly followed in their own markets. When you are seeking new trends, the lesson is to look for the market under the greatest pressure for innovation.

Who shapes the market?

Another way to uncover likely market trends is to understand the influences on the market. Who sets the standards? Which organizations or bodies set the direction? A perfect illustration of a company in sympathy with influencers is the toy company, Mattel Inc. Since her appearance in

1958, Barbie has been the leading toy for girls. Barbie sales amount to more than $2 billion annually. Achieving this in the fickle, fashion-conscious toy market is a substantial accomplishment. The solution is a model for other businesses. Mattel has groups of spotters, who are employed to follow late teenage girls in malls, sports stadia, clubs and gyms, to observe and report on their clothing, accessories, interests and occupations. Do they carry mobile phones and laptops? Do they have tattoos on their shoulders? In the mind of the six-to-eight-year-old owner of the doll, Barbie is 17 or 18 years old and therefore she wants her to be doing the kind of things she sees girls of that age doing. Older teenagers influence her and therefore Mattel observe the influencers.

In commercial markets one customer or a leading competitor may be the main influencer and hence merit special monitoring. Patent registers should be assessed for new developments or the registration of new product names. Elsewhere it may be an institute or government body. Often the designers and service providers are the influencers, such as architects in the construction industry. Certain music idols were the influential adopters of scooters and created a worldwide craze that was unshaped by advertising. Identify the influencers, and follow their patterns.

Do other markets show the way?

For some categories, there are markets that lead the way. In tractor cab design, features follow patterns in passenger car cabins with a four-year lag time. Carpet designers keep abreast of the curtain colours in vogue. Clothing fashions were originally established for adults and reinterpreted for children's outfits. Now both children's and adult styles are led by youth culture. As 20-year-olds assume wider-leg trousers and looser clothing, so the business suit is cut more generously.

Supplier-based techniques

The third view on trends that may affect your leading customers is supplier based. There is a natural tendency to look downstream to customers for inspiration. Sometimes the new developments come from higher up the stream. There is much valuable information to gain from your own supply chain, and the resulting thoughts can be highly interesting to your customers.

An obvious starting point is to attend trade shows of suppliers and read the appropriate industry journals. Specialist journalists enthusiastically report new approaches. Increasingly you will see their e-mail address at the foot of the column, and practice shows that sector journalists welcome questions from industry outsiders to stimulate their own investigative thinking.

Probably the most powerful technique is to audit your supplier network and identify the two or three most innovative suppliers, based on their contribution to new developments over the past three years. Getting close to these companies pays handsome dividends. Innovation is not evenly allocated – Pareto's law implies that a small number of firms are responsible for a large number of the changes in an industry. Find these among your suppliers.

> **A small number of firms are responsible for a large number of the changes in an industry.**

For many European grocery and food industry executives, RHM Technolgy in High Wycombe, UK, is the groundbreaker in developments in its sector, and on the shortlist of innovators. Two examples of its thought leadership will suffice. The first is its response to concern among European consumers about genetically modified ingredients in food. RHM Technology developed, ahead of demand, a system to detect the presence of genetically modified ingredients. Using DNA extraction and purification, polymerase chain reaction and TaqMan™ chemistry it is able to identify the presence of genetic modification in soya oils at one part per billion. Related detection techniques enables it to identify species and even the sex of fish and meat products from processed product samples. For a second example we can look at the 'impossible' project that RHM Technology took on in 1997: the 'bakery-produced crusty loaf'. The challenge was to combine the crusty characteristics of home baked bread with the keeping qualities of plant baking. The result was the breakthrough development of the Hovis Crusty Loaf.

For your industry, who are the thought leaders among your suppliers, and how closely are you working with them?

External sources

External stimuli are the fourth source to identify impending trends. These are less easily categorized, and yet often provide greater advantage in the opportunities they present. Immediately accessible contributions can come from consulting firms, advertising agencies, research institutes and business schools. All these bodies have the enviable benefit of being able to view at close quarters the changes and developments across industries. In a single month a programme director at Ashridge Management College, one of Europe's leading business schools, can be working in four different countries with clients in financial services, computers, construction, brewing and retailing. The potential to see openings in one industry, using ideas borrowed from another business in another continent, is honed over time.

Benchmarking another industry

As well as using sources of cross-industry insight, curious managers can engage in benchmarking with world-class companies in other industries. A bank trying to manage availability and cost effectiveness for the cash replenishment of ATM machines benchmarked with a supplier of quick-drying cement. Both needed to forecast accurately, minimize stock and to respond rapidly to change. The banker gained interesting dimensions and comparisons from a different industry facing a comparable challenge.

Alliances

Alliances can bring an awareness of other ways of doing business that will add value to your largest customers. Identifying leading companies in related areas – companies with which you are not in competition – can be very beneficial. For example, in the UK the Jigsaw consortium is a collaboration between Unilever, Cadbury-Schweppes and Kimberly-Clark launched in 1997. Together these companies pool their consumer databases for effective targeting of direct mailing of customer magazines and offers. They are able to learn from the shared data which households are potential best customers for individual brands, drawing conclusions from patterns of consumption of other brands within the consortium. On a European scale, a brand working on collaboration across 13 countries is Procter & Gamble's Pampers. To promote the Pampers Playtime brand of diapers, in 1999 it formed an alliance with Mattel's Fisher-Price. Together under the theme 'Let's Play Together' the two brands have created joint point-of-sale material and are investigating creating joint in-store baby-care sections. There is another dimension to this co-operation. According to *Marketing Magazine* (11 February 1999), the intention is for Fisher-Price to learn from Proctor & Gamble's strength in brand development and raise its advertising profile. In return, Pampers will gain access to the Fisher-Price pool of child development data to improve its understanding of its best customers.

PEST analysis

The consequences of political, legal and economic change for major customers can also be a stimulant to explore and create new trends. Likewise, considering how they might adapt to social and technological developments can produce helpful ideas and suggestions. A PEST analysis (*see* Fig. 12.4) summarizes the four macro-factors into a usable template, to help to focus on critical issues.

Political/Legal	Economic
EU directives, taxation policy, ecology regulations, government stability, planning controls	Growth in the economy, inflation rates, interest rates, euro exchange rates, energy costs
Socio-cultural	**Technological**
Population demographics, lifestyle, work–life balance diversity, social mobility, education, consumerism	Internet, computer-aided design, production, communications, life cycle of inventions

Figure 12.4 Macro-environmental PEST factors

Sci-fi

A final suggestion for an external source of ideas that may change the dynamics of your customers' businesses comes from a German business school student: read science fiction and imagine the consequences in your market. Reflection is an important part of the process. Intelligent behaviour can only occur if the individual has developed the power not to respond immediately to stimuli. Creative innovation depends in part on prolonging the interval between stimulus and response.

Internal sources

The final approach to spotting potential trends for your customers, ahead of your competitors, is through internal sources. In an interview with the *Financial Times* (1 December 1999), Anders Knutsen, Chief Executive of Danish hi-fi and television manufacturer Bang & Olufsen, had an interesting angle on customer dialogue. One of the aims of Bang & Olufsen is to surprise consumers when they encounter its products, so Knutsen commented: 'We never ask our customers what they might want from future products, because they don't really know. Our designers plant ideas and values in the marketplace, not the other way around.' So how might companies proceed with internal techniques?

Problem-solution cocktail

A strong asset that companies have is the combined insight of market and supplier. Hence a powerful vision of what could be possible comes from inter-functional brainstorming that deliberately forces together sales teams and those with supplier contact. This delivers a cocktail of intuitive sympathy for customer problems and knowledge of forthcoming product possibilities. Frequently, problem and solution meet each other in debate.

Scenario planning and diversity

Another exercise is to create a set of three different scenarios of possible futures of the company, and charge three independent teams to populate the scenario with more detail, implications and conclusions for product and service development, to counter the possible consequences of their particular scenario. The UK energy provider, National Grid, developed a series of scenarios for the impact of events on electricity demand, and expressed some of these in an appealing advertisement:

- Is it the wettest month since records began?
- Will Grandad go to bed early?
- Will the footy go to extra time?
- Is that a low over Iceland?
- When did the clocks change?
- Is the night shift on?
- Is it really a dull evening on telly?

When assembling teams, it is important to consider variety of background and provide teams with youth and experience, qualitative and quantitative backgrounds, male and female, local and international, positive and cynical representatives. Diversity produces better responses than uniformity. The disastrous launch of the space shuttle 'Challenger' on 28 January 1986 can be blamed partly on the uniformity of the male engineers from similar graduate schools who shared a common set of values. There was no maverick to champion the safety concerns of the outside contractors like Rockwell Avionics, who feared the ice on the launch pad, and Morton Thiokol, who warned of the effect of cold temperatures on the rubber O rings. Minimize the danger of 'group think' by insisting on diversity in brainstorming and scenario planning teams (*source*: Cranfield School of Management).

Escalating employee suggestions

Appoint a champion to receive employee suggestions, so that innovative ideas go to a known individual, who has an obligation to respond. BBC Worldwide UK appointed Marie Oldham to be its trendspotter in 1997. Her role was to identify emerging threats or opportunities for the commercial arm of the UK broadcaster in its selling of books, magazines and videos. She welcomed ideas and information from any source in order to help her predict the next wave.

Sometimes the best source of inspiration about the future can be new recruits or newly promoted individuals who have not learnt the hidden assumptions about the business and can challenge – with naïve questions – the well-trodden path of their predecessors. Young engineers and new graduates can be an asset if encouraged to reveal their first thoughts in their new role. Bill Gates, Chief Executive Officer of Microsoft, attributes his best ideas to the many visits that he makes to schools. It was a fourth-grade student who asked him his most challenging question: 'Mr Gates, what will computers look like in 100 years' time?'

However you seek the internal ideas to foresee the future of the business for you and your best customers, ensure the challenging concepts are documented. Both Unilever and 3M have effective GroupWare systems, allowing qualified individuals in their organizations to access latest creative thinking, research and concepts.

Educating customers

Having captured all the insights into the shape of the future world, there is a translation process. How will these factors impact on your best customers? Good friends find numerous ways to influence, suggest and protect each other, when they contemplate future threats and opportunities. There is no single approach. Clearly, a combination of formal and informal channels has the greatest impact.

> **Good friends find numerous ways to influence, suggest and protect each other, when they comtemplate future threats and opportunities.**

Customers may welcome formal input to their business or personal plans. This could take the form of a presentation or a document on market changes and impacts of trends. Across the world, the advertising agency, J. Walter Thompson will advise on the multimedia climate in presentations for major clients. In the UK, Lloyds TSB Bank sends retail customers a summary of the envisaged economic impact of the Chancellor's fiscal budget changes each year. *The Economist* magazine each December publishes its views on trends for the following year in a special supplement.

At the other extreme are spontaneous conversations and off-the-cuff discussions with clients and customers. These can occur at any time and their effectiveness is often linked to the memorability of the encounter. A follow-up e-mail or telephone call can reinforce the conclusions drawn from the discussion. The most effective model appears to be the coaching style. This requires the supplier to think through the context and issues beforehand. It is necessary to find a suitable time and place when the customer or client is receptive. The debate will be structured. A typical framework might have four steps:

1   What are your aims and goals for the next three years?

2   As a reality check, what might work against achievement of these aims? Are there other issues to be considered?

3   Are there other opportunities that could be progressed?

4   What can we do to support each other in moving forward?

It is more effective to pose questions and seek to explore issues together, rather than to provide packaged answers. The result is normally a set of actions, such as agreement to provide further information, or jointly to investigate trends as they materialize.

Future-proofing your customers

The purpose of education is to prepare for the future with knowledge, skills and confidence. This applies to the educational relationship you have with your customers. You are a support system in an uncertain world. Your objective is to future-proof the Customers that Count. First, there is an obvious tangible element of economic interest. The more certain you can make your customer's business, the more certain are your own prospects. Second, you are adding another value to the relationship. This intangible element of peace of mind reinforces allegiance and sets the tone of a co-operative support.

Case example   Theme: Keeping the customer up-to-date

Rockwell Automation

Milwaukee-based Rockwell Automation is a world leader in factory and process automation. With sales exceeding $4 billion and trading in more than 80 countries, it offers a range of over 500 000 components and items. However, Vice-President of Global Marketing, Randy Freeman, explained to me that global accounts are in effect buying the knowledge of how to be more productive. Global accounts come to Rockwell for the understanding, guidance, advice and integration that keeps them at the forefront of manufacturing technology.

Keeping the customer up-to-date means a combination of historical understanding and future-orientated thinking. When the average global account manager is seven years in position, compared with two or three years for the automation engineer in some leading manufacturers, a number of Rockwell Automation's customers can depend on them for company or market experience and future insights. The Rockwell impact may be significant. When a new global account manager was appointed, one key customer commented: 'The guy you put in will affect my career'.

Randy Freeman provided an example of the Rockwell impact. Customers have been faced with wider and wider ranges of products. The future is finding a cost-effective pathway through complexity. To minimize life-cycle costs, Rockwell engineers will agree standardized design constraints to narrow the standard range for a particular customer. There may be five different input cards for 120-volt input, each with its own performance characteristics. Rockwell Automation specifies a single card that does the job of all five. Although in unit terms this may cost $10 more, the customer benefits through lower life-cycle costs: with lower inventory, better spare-part availability and transferability of engineers across any plant worldwide.

Future-proofing customers increasingly implies integrating different systems. Vice-President of Global Accounts, Kieran Coulton, described how when working closely with Daimler-Chrysler (the global automotive manufacturer based in Auburn Hills, Michigan), Rockwell Automation discovered that new vehicle launches were being delayed through integration bottlenecks on the plant floor. This was critical – being first to market is a vital factor in the automotive industry. According to Chantal Polsonetti of ARC Strategies, 80 per cent of 1998 Daimler-Chrysler revenues were generated from products introduced in the last five years. Each piece of production equipment needs to interface with other equipment and the overall production system. So Rockwell investigated and assumed responsibility for integration management, setting requirements and processes for multiple suppliers. This responsibility extends to covering the costs of rectification if the connectivity fails. The past was selling products; the future is guaranteeing a production system.

To track the leading edge of technology, Rockwell carries out pure research. At the Rockwell Science Center in Thousand Oaks, California, over 300 scientists and engineers study scientific challenges facing customers. They have links with 113 universities and invite major customers to explore knowledge frontiers. Rockwell Automation also has research and development centres in locations that include Moscow, Prague and Düsseldorf. Scientists focus on advanced material processing, surface chemistry and intelligent control techniques. The lessons are applied to customers' challenges. Rockwell Automation may propose a solution before the customer asks.

Finally, Rockwell Automation is showing the future for supplier assessment. Kieran Coulton and Randy Freeman highlighted their move to providing customers with a 'return on the relationship'. Global account managers calculate the hard factors and estimate the soft factors to provide a value statement that shows how much in dollars the relationship has delivered. It is difficult to quantify, but can run to tens of millions of dollars. For example, there is a financial value of 4 per cent extra capacity from the same production. You can estimate the market share advantage of being three months earlier into the market. They even include a notional charge for consulting services, had these been bought on the open market.

Whether it is in technology, complexity theory or supplier assessment, Rockwell Automation is collaborating with its most valuable customers and offering them the safeguard of another eye on the future.

Exercises   Exercise 12

Conduct a PEST exercise on your largest customer:

1 What are the political and legal, economic, social and technological factors shaping the business for the customer over the next three years?

2 Assessing the impact of this, where are the most significant threats and opportunities?

3 How can you mitigate the threats and help the customer capture the opportunities?

4 How, where and when could you communicate the conclusions to the customer?

Further Reading and references

Newell, Frederick (2000) *Loyalty.com*, McGraw Hill.

Paul, Lauren Gibbons (2000) 'The New Relationships', *Managing Automation*, July.

Polsonetti, Chantal (1999) 'Rockwell Automation Services Fuel DaimlerChrylser Speed-to-Market', *ARC Strategies*, December.

Rogers, Everett M. (1995) *Diffusion of Innovations*, Free Press.

Warburton, John and Cardoza, Nick (2001) 'Ford and the Sport Utility Vehicle – a True Ethical Dilemma?' *Directions*, Ashridge Management College, Spring.

www.foundation.no/scenarios – for information and examples of scenario planning.

www.gbn.org/scenThink.htm – for examples of country scenarios.

Tony Hadjianniadjis – Director of Hear and Know Consultants Ltd – heard the ringing of his mobile phone. It was one of his most valued customers, who had over the years booked hundreds of places for company executives on his development seminars. It was not good news. Regrettably one of three managers booked on tomorrow's seminar was not available and they were offering to pay the cancellation fee. 'No, no', said Tony. 'I cannot charge a cancellation fee, you are one of my original customers. I cannot think of it.' Embarrassed at the short notice, the Human Resources Director began to insist, but Tony was adamant.

Loyalty works both ways. At 8.00 am the next morning the seminar opened and every place was taken. The Human Resources Director had made huge efforts to find a last-minute substitute for the absentee, rather than be disloyal. Rewarding loyalty brings its own rewards.

It is important that Customers that Count feel appreciated. To be able to do this, it may be necessary to have recognition systems that identify best customers for preferential treatment. Providing preference will reinforce their loyalty (*see* Fig. 13.1). Nothing is more certain to destroy their loyalty than the sense that they are being taken for granted. Customers that Count expect and deserve to see their importance reflected in extra privileges, priority service and special recognition. There are many practical ways to

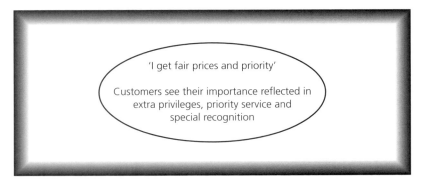

Figure 13.1 Preference

demonstrate this preference. You must also ensure that they are reminded of the special benefits that they receive so the advantages are appreciated.

Do you think I am important?

Customers that Count are normally aware of their scale and importance. They expect that their level of purchases and/or the duration of the relationship deserves some preference. They need to see confirmation that the supplier also appreciates their worth. And they react badly to the feeling that they are being taken for granted. For example, this may arise if they discover that new customers are tempted with better terms than they themselves receive. Given the scale of data openness and the speed of employee movement between organizations, it is proving impossible to keep prices concealed. There are no secret deals in the twenty-first century. Therefore, a manufacturer of electronic components in Asia first clears with major customers any promotional discounts that it wishes to offer to achieve customer acquisition. Interestingly the best customers, who were previously highly critical of special new-customer deals, emerged as very understanding when involved in the strategic decision making. Consultation therefore is the first technique of appreciation.

Cards trigger preference

To show preference, it is essential that best customers can be identified. For industrial concerns with a small number of very large business partners, the normal key-account management system addresses this. In phone-based businesses, automatic caller identification allows telephone agents to be aware of the caller before answering and data can be displayed on-screen as the greeting is given. In retail and consumer businesses, card-based identification may be used. For example, airlines may ask that Frequent Flier cards be shown at lounge entrances to confirm eligibility for preferential treatment.

There are limits to the effectiveness of loyalty cards. In mid 2000 the second National Consumer Survey of Plastic Card Usage in the USA showed that while 43 per cent of US consumers shopped with greater frequency at stores whose loyalty cards they held, only 29 per cent of US consumers in the survey actually carried a loyalty card. In the UK certain high-profile retailers have abandoned card-based reward schemes. The supermarket Safeway dropped its ABC card scheme in May 2000 and Wal-Mart-owned Asda has also decided loyalty schemes are no longer part of its strategy. Other retailers, including pharmacist Boots and bookseller WHSmith, continue to invest in the data gathering and cleansing that is essential for valid operation of loyalty schemes.

A limitation of loyalty-card schemes is that the card is not scanned until the retail experience is in its final moments and therefore little can be done at that stage other than to thank customers for their continued patronage. Reward schemes are a piece of the sales mix and have a part to play in thanking customers and influencing them to change their behaviour, but are not an effective appreciation system for Customers that Count.

Reward Customers that Count with privileged speed and information.

How to show appreciation

There are many ways other ways of acknowledging Customers that Count (*see* Fig. 13.2). These need to be matched to the type of business and to the characteristics of the customers. These include privileged speed or information, special services, gifts and celebrations.

- Early warning, advance information
- Ability to operate at last minute
- Private access
- Priority information services
- Customized services
- Simpler systems
- Additional personal services
- Support in difficult times
- Celebration in good times
- Recognition of landmarks
- Pleasant surprises
- Certain prices
- Better prices

Figure 13.2 Ways to show preference

Early warning

Customers that Count appreciate being given advance warning or a preview of new lines. Low-mileage Hondas that have been used by the company's executives are highly sought after in the UK used-car market. Therefore Honda dealers write to invite their most valued customers to a preview day to see and buy these vehicles ahead of the general public.

In July 2000 members of British Airways Travel Services received e-mails advising them of a time-limited offer on flights to Sydney, which was to be promoted in press advertisements two days later. In effect, they had first bite of the cherry.

Last minute

In other circumstances, customers may want to be able to operate at the last moment. Frequent travellers on the Eurostar train service between London and Paris or Brussels are able to check-in later than non-members.

Recently, Europe's paper mills have been operating at capacity. This has lead to long lead times for orders. A creative form of priority to Customers that Count from companies like Helsinki-based StoraEnso is to dedicate production capacity on a given day to a top customer, allowing them to specify the product very shortly beforehand. This permits the customer to respond to their own market dynamics at short notice, overcoming the lead-time problem.

Private access

Cruise company Cunard has commissioned the construction in France of a new 3100 passenger cruise ship. The *Queen Mary 2* will make its maiden voyage from Southampton on 4 January 2004. At a cost of £538 million, this will be the largest, longest, widest and tallest ship ever built. For example, with 17 decks, it will tower 200 feet above the waterline, equivalent to the height of a 23-storey building. The ship's whistle will be an exact replica of the one on the original *Queen Mary*, so that her famous predecessor's voice will once more be heard on the ocean. Cunard expects the *Queen Mary 2* will be the most famous ship in the world. To show loyalty to current customers, Cunard has launched 'Patron's Preview'. This is a scheme of first priority to those travelling on its existing ships for bookings in the season of inaugural sailings.

Richard Guy's Real Meat Company is a UK purveyor of foods using natural farming methods. At important times, taste counts, and its business is hectic in December, with many occasional customers wanting the best-quality poultry for the Christmas table. Its outlet in Wheathamstead, Hertfordshire gives preference to regular customers by offering a last-moment collection service for Christmas orders, after the butcher's shop is officially closed.

Priority information services

British Airways strives to keep its best customers ahead of the game. Executive Club Members at Silver and Gold level have access to the

Terminal 1 lounge at Heathrow, where they can view a live link to the London Stock Exchange and see share price movements as they occur.

Similarly, Toshiba Air Conditioning division offers access to its projects department to UK installers who spend more than £50 000 worth of equipment per year.

Customized Services

Some of BMW's best customers in the USA lease their vehicles. By using its customer database, BMW is able to contact its most valued customers as their lease nears its conclusion. These customers are offered a privileged facility to order a new BMW, customized to their precise specification, including perhaps the omission of the trunk badge that indicates engine size for those drivers who wish to keep their horse power confidential. The ordering and delivery time-scale is managed so that the customized vehicle is available at the end of the lease.

The cleaning products supplier, ChemStation of Dayton Ohio, provides another example of tailoring. According to its website, (www.chemstation. com), its system is one-part science and two-parts organization. The company analyzes the items its customers want cleaned. It has expertise in cleaning for catering outlets, industries such as meat and poultry processing, vehicle cleaning, odour control, cleaning of manufactured component parts and many others. It custom blends a formula that is bulk-delivered to the customer's premises. Containers are placed where needed and the company will monitor quantities of cleanser at regular intervals and top up stocks when required. ChemStation eliminates receiving, storing, handling, disposing and reordering chores for its customers.

Simpler systems

Best customers are the most trusted customers and – in recognition of this – they may benefit from simplified systems. These might include ordering procedures, or practices for warranty returns.

Additional personal services

DSM Polypropylene, a division of the Dutch chemical and life-science company, has provided opportunities for employees of customers in other countries to spend time working in their German plants, as a personal-development assignment. Similarly, free haircutting is one of the special services that the airline Virgin Atlantic provides to its best customers in its pre-flight airport lounges.

Warnings and support in difficult times

Customers that Count may gain advance information of disruption or interruption to services. This will enable them to make contingency plans. Priority in time of scarcity is another special indication of the importance of best customers. Costco frequently obtains special buys in limited quantities to offer to its customers on a first-come first-served basis. Yet staff get to know their regulars who cannot always reach the store before the stock is exhausted and it is not unknown for a private reservation to be made.

Celebration in good times

In 2000 the Hellenic Bank of Cyprus sponsored its country's Olympic team, making a donation every time a credit card was used. To the customers that showed the highest increase in usage between February and April 2000, the bank sent a letter of thanks for the support for the promotion and included an Olympic-themed T-shirt.

Account-card customers of the UK department store John Lewis and its supermarket subsidiary Waitrose are eligible for substantial discounts off the entrance charges to events sponsored by the partnership. At most events there are clearly signed areas sponsored by Waitrose where account customers and a guest receive complimentary light refreshments. The Solheim cup is held every two years, pitting the 12 best European lady golfers against their American counterparts. Best customers of Waitrose were invited to attend the October 2000 event held at Loch Lomond Golf Club in Scotland.

Recognition of relationship landmarks

Time passes rapidly in dynamic businesses and it can be easy to be unaware of the duration or extent of a particular relationship. In marriage, anniversaries are marked and celebrated. After five or ten years of a business relationship with Customers that Count, there is an opportunity to celebrate and create an occasion that draws attention to the strength of the relationship. In 1998 the UK home-improvement retailer, Homebase, wrote to customers of five years' standing with a simple thank-you card, enclosing four discount vouchers and a straightforward and friendly message that recognized the long relationship. It was well regarded and some of those receiving the mailing telephoned to say how much they appreciated the gesture.

A creative dealer of agricultural machinery in the Midwest of the USA recorded purchases over the years. When he delivered his tenth tractor to a local farmer, it was decorated with a huge red bow, and a huge cardboard cut-out figure 'ten' filled the cab.

Pleasant surprises

Professor Leonard Berry of Texas A & M University suggests that the occasional surprise can provide delight in a service relationship. The essence of a pleasant surprise is thoughtfulness and appropriateness. The action should seem individual and spontaneous rather than carefully calibrated. Stewards on Aerolineas Argentinas observe first-class passengers. When they appear to have enjoyed a particular wine, a further bottle will be presented just as the passenger is preparing to leave the plane.

The luxury brand of food for cats, Sheba, aims to provide its cat-loving customers with surprise and delight by drawing their attention to its website: www.sheba.com. A characteristic of cat owners who choose Sheba is that they have a higher-than-average access to the internet and a strong relationship with their cat. Thus the website enables owners to post photographs of their pet and share stories of how their cat got its name, their kitten's favourite hiding place and extreme examples of feline mischievousness. Strictly speaking, this is an open-access website, yet in practice it acts as a club for Sheba's best customers.

Certain prices

The German-based construction company Hochtief has an international reputation for designing and building bridges, airports, tunnels and dams. These projects can have a time-scale extending to five years or more. The governments, civic bodies and institutions commissioning such ventures fear price escalation. In response to this need, Hochtief will provide in some circumstances a guaranteed maximum price. This GMP is the highest amount that the customer could expect to pay. By design, efficiency and cost saving through the project life, Hochtief can also hold out the possibility that the actual price may be lower than the GMP. Customers that Count appreciate certainty.

Better prices

It is a frustration to many borrowers that banks and other lenders are aware of the difficulties and barriers to switching institution in mid-loan. Often borrowers find themselves involuntarily subsidizing the discounted terms to new borrowers. This breeds resentment and leads to disloyalty regarding subsequent loans. The Coventry Economic Building Society offers another approach. It progressively reduces the interest rate for customers after a five-year period, subject only to a good payment history.

Being taken for granted

It is clearly important to acknowledge the importance of top customers through preferential treatment. There is one danger, however. It can happen that in the hurly-burly of competitive existence Customers that Count receive benefits without realizing that they are gaining something special. If the benefits are unnoticed, they are unappreciated. Shrewd suppliers find opportunities to draw advantages to the attention of their most valuable customers. When you waive a charge because of the customer's volume of business, ensure they realize the exceptional nature of the circumstances. Reminders of value need to be effective, albeit often subtle. The annual value statement provided by Rockwell Automation (*see* page 180) is a strong example.

> **It is important to acknowledge the importance of top customers through preferential treatment.**

Conclusion

Customers that Count should be able to count on some external signs of appreciation. The phrase 'thank you for your business' is more powerful in gaining future custom than the word 'please'. Some of these thank yous should be tangible in terms of time and money benefits. Others should be personal, emotional and intangible. The perception of the customer should be: 'I am glad that they think I am worth it'.

Case example   Theme: Preference

Marriott International

Marriott International, a leading worldwide hospitality company with more than 2000 lodging properties in 58 countries, has a long-standing commitment to earning customer loyalty. The company led the 1985 *Business Travel News* survey of business travellers, and dominated in subsequent years. *The Service Edge* by Ron Zemke (1989) featured Marriott as a leading example of customer care. Marriott's 1999 Annual Report lists 14 examples of recognition received, including the Malcolm Baldrige National Quality Award, won for the second time by the Marriott subsidiary, The Ritz Carlton Hotel Company. In August 2000, for the second consecutive year, Marriott International was selected as a CIO-100 honoree by *CIO*, the magazine for information executives. The CIO-100 award program recognizes organizations that have mastered the 'customer connection' by establishing a strong customer relationship management strategy enabled by modern-day technology.

Talking to Stephan Chase, Director of Customer and Competitive Strategy, Full Service Lodging, I learn about the strength of this loyalty. For some guests, Marriott is their hospitality solution. They use Marriott for business and leisure stays, they carry the Marriott Rewards Platinum Visa card and are Elite members of the Rewards Program. Members may progress to owning a Marriott time-share unit and even come to Marriott to arrange a daughter's wedding.

I ask for a quantification of this loyalty. Stephan Chase replies with research among members of the Reward program: 'Some members, when asked, are willing to drive as much as 17 minutes out of their way'. There may be a rival hotel closer, but they are willing to be inconvenienced on location, simply to stay with the brand they trust.

This loyalty deserves preference in return, and Marriott matches this with its Rewards Program. Guests who are members of Marriott Rewards are in tiers: Silver, Gold and rising to Platinum. Tiers and benefits are well understood throughout the organization.

Silver-level benefits include priority room selection, late check-out, check-cashing privileges and gift-shop discounts. Gold adds access to the Concierge Lounge, free continental breakfast, free local calls and faxes in the USA and room upgrades whenever possible.

The biggest benefit and the most valued is reserved for Platinum members. Guests who stay 75 or more nights in the calendar year are provided guaranteed availability at Marriott Hotels, up to 48 hours ahead. Guaranteed availability is not, to my knowledge, offered by rival hoteliers. Lynne Roach-Hildebrand, Senior Vice-President of Loyalty Marketing, explains that high-frequency travellers often face many changes in their itineraries. 'This guarantee wildly simplifies their lives. It restores convenience and control', she adds. Guaranteed availability is a powerful piece of preference – provided only to the very best customers.

Exercise 13	Exercises

1 List the extra benefits provided to your top 20 customers
– would a medium-sized customer find these attractive enough to be aspirational?

2 Ask a sample group of top customers to list the extra benefits they believe they receive – how close is their list to yours?

Further reading and references

Sconfeld, Erick (1998) 'The customized digitized have-it-your-way economy', *Fortune*, 28 September.

www.cmg.carlson.com – the Carlson Marketing Group website, which includes loyalty case studies from a variety of industries such as manufacturing, agriculture, aviation, hotels and restaurants.

Zemke, Ron (1989) *The Service Edge*, New American Library.

Who's your friend?

Personality is vital. We like to associate with people who have definable personalities and who reveal their emotions and opinions. So too, the Customers that Count, like to associate with supplying companies and brands whose position they know and understand (*see* Fig. 14.1). This respect can override some price considerations. Therefore companies aiming to garner the long-term loyalty of top customers must build their brand respect. This means making choices about what the brand name stands for. Then the choice must be made real by living and delivering a promised benefit. It also requires espousing a set of values. Both promise and values must be demonstrated in actions and behaviours, and here consistency is important. With this consistent approach, brands create the opportunity to extend the relationship with top customers to other fields.

Friends we like to associate with

Personality is important. We look for distinguishing characteristics in our friends. In our social circle we will mix with some friends who are studious and others who are fun-loving. We will like people whose lives are planned and others who act spontaneously. We also expect to see and to experience

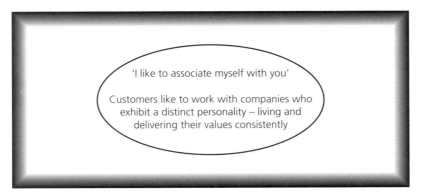

Figure 14.1 Individuality

consistency over time. If people act out of character we need an explanation. There is not a right or a wrong style. But what we find uncomfortable
is someone that we cannot place on the spectrum.

We see emotional signs of happiness, worry and grief. We relate to a
variety of emotions in our friends. But, in western society, an absence of
emotion is seen as concealment and lack of openness. This presents us with
a social challenge. We admire and like to associate with certain people, recognizing their positive characteristics and forgiving their shortcomings. We
want the same in our commercial relationships. We want to discover and
see the signs of personality.

World's most respected companies

In 2000 leading management-consulting firm PricewaterhouseCoopers conducted for the third year running a survey to identify the world's most
respected companies. Across more than 70 countries, 720 chief executives of
publicly-quoted companies, state-owned enterprises, large subsidiaries and
private companies had their views taken. The conclusions were weighted
according to the GDP of the country of origin of the respondent. The
results were published in the *Financial Times* (15 December 2000). The top
four companies were General Electric, Microsoft, Sony and Coca-Cola. This
wide-scale respect helps to explain their continued success. Customers like
to deal with respected organizations with which they can be proud to associate. Respect gives these companies credibility that is like a licence to thrive.

However, it is the business-sector leaders that are even more interesting.
In intensely competitive industries, widely held respect is part of the competitive advantage that helps to retain the loyalty of best customers. For
example, US-based Pfizer is signalled as the world's most respected healthcare company. This gives its name a value that encourages medical
practitioners to continue prescribing their
pharmaceutical products. The utility company
sector is led by Duke Energy in USA, and
French-based Vivendi – a lead that reinforces
their relationships with consumers in the countries where they operate.
Wide respect will help them to keep the loyalty of their best customers as
the water and electricity markets become increasingly competitive. We like
others to respect our choice in relationships.

Peer-group respect is another benchmark. For 11 years the magazine
Management Today has published a survey of the UK's most admired companies. Companies in each industry sector are asked for an assessment of
their rivals. An improving position is a mark of rising respect. The survey
published in December 2000 showed companies like Pearson, the media

We like others to respect our choice in relationships.

group, and BBA Group, a leading enterprise in aviation services and materials technology, entering the overall top 20 most-admired companies and dominating their industry sectors.

Building respect

Based in Mlada Boleslav in the Czech Republic, Skoda Auto – a motor car 'power brand' of the 1930s – lost its way in the communist period. Reputation and the image of quality were lost. In some markets the Skoda became the butt of comedians. However, by 2000, under Volkswagen majority ownership, Skoda was well on track to be a brand that customers are proud to associate themselves with. The raising of the brand image was achieved through a combination of real product improvements and perceptual cues. Product improvements included using Volkswagen platforms and durable designs. The perceptual cues included the fitment of chunkier indicator stalks and tuning the sound of the door closing to a reassuring 'clunk' – such are the subconscious ways buyers judge car quality. An accolade was the award of Car of the Year 2000 for the Skoda Fabia by German car magazine *AutoBild*.

Branding and what it means

Respect comes from a combination of familiarity and confidence, and this is captured in brand identities. Brands are recognizable, supporting the growth of familiarity. Brands are also a guarantee of consistency, encouraging the growth of confidence among customers. Brands, like individuals, also stand for a set of values (*see* Fig. 14.2).

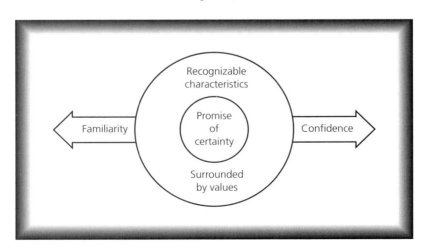

Figure 14.2 Individuality = brand identity

A brand is a promise of certainty, surrounded by values. Caterpillar makes a promise of effective earthmoving around the world. When customers think of Caterpillar, they have a picture of a product and some values: yellow, tough, anywhere, any weather, changing the landscape. Caterpillar has taken over a corner of the customer's mind with images of its values. So strong are these values that this industrial brand has now leapt into the consumer arena through the London fashion company, Overland, with a range of tough clothing, boots and even schoolbags that can go anywhere and survive any weather. In this instance, the values transcend the market sector.

A promise and some values

In successful brands, customers trust the certainty and also recognize the values. For example, when regular diners approach one of the outlets of Minnesota-based Rainforest Café, they have a certainty about the food offer. It will be more exotic than McDonald's, but it will not be served as quickly. The décor will also be exotic, with a jungle theme that is distinct and consistent whether you are in Opry Mills Nashville Tennessee or Manchester England. The values espoused by Rainforest Café will be clear: the Rainforest Café Friends of the Future Foundation is dedicated to supporting environmental causes. It is likely that customers will share some of the core beliefs of the Rainforest brand about the importance of preserving primary forests. If the prices are higher, the customers will understand what they are receiving in return in terms of tangible products and emotional associations (*see* Fig. 14.3).

An emerging trend is for regions, cities and countries to use the branding approach to make themselves distinctive in concrete terms and also in intangible ways. Freeport in Maine is on the map as an outlet centre for

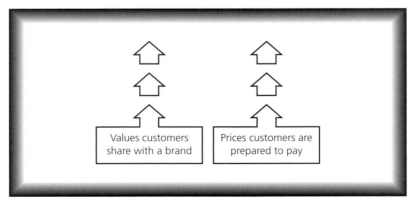

Figure 14.3 Brand values

bargains of all types. Intangibly it has associations of the great outdoors, partly linked to the state of Maine and partly through the presence of LL Bean, renowned mail-order retailer of hiking, fishing and outdoor equipment. Similarly, Wales ran a media campaign in 2000 themed: 'Two hours and a million miles away'. Pictures of deserted beaches and scenery appeal to people living in the crowded south-east of England. Wales identified its targets as affluent couples who take short breaks and professional couples with young children who take a second holiday in the year. As well as attracting new visitors, the Welsh Tourist body is reinforcing the behaviour of its highest-spending holiday visitors. Wales offers values and stands for something that regular visitors can see and believe in.

Making choices

Brands stand for something and this means making choices. A brand cannot own *all* the virtues; it has to select a group of values that are deliverable, distinct and meaningful to customers (*see* Fig. 14.4). For example, Wonderbra rarely if ever mentions comfort or sensuality, which might be assumed to be important aspects in selecting a brassière. Its focus is all about confidence and power. If you try and be everything to everyone, you appear as nothing in particular to any special group. The Rainforest Café cannot beat Kentucky Fried Chicken on prices. Freeport cannot rival New Orleans in its cuisine. Wales cannot offer Ibiza's sunshine and nightlife.

It is important to loyal long-term customers that they know where the brand stands. Is it easy to use like Apple or are the processes more challenging? Is there a single global offer like UPS, whose familiar brown trucks appear the same everywhere? Are we to expect the excitement of ground-breaking advanced technology or more considered developments that prove compatible with previous generations of technology? You may buy Caterpillar boots, but you would not fit a Caterpillar engine in your speed-

- You cannot be fastest, cheapest *and* best quality
- Branding is about making choices

Figure 14.4 A brand cannot own all the virtues

boat. But another brand making earthmoving equipment – Volvo – convincingly supplies Penta marine engines. Brands must make choices and communicate what they are and what they are not.

Consistency

Having established the brand's values and position, it is critical that these are communicated consistently. Doug Hamilton, Creative Director of London-based branding company Wolff Olins, says in the *Financial Times* (7 June 2000) that:

> Too many internet advertising campaigns are like the *Titanic*. We have the launch and then they disappear. To build a brand you need a consistent message and a sustained campaign. Your brand needs to be the same everywhere, whether you are advertising on line or off line.

The vodka brand, Absolut, understands the importance of consistency in communications. A good media buyer could reduce costs of magazine advertising by specifying 'run of paper', so that the advertisements could appear anywhere through the magazine at the journal's choice. Instead, Absolut vodka sacrifices a discount for a consistent position on the outside back cover of magazines. It is as if it was saying we are the last word in vodka. In contrast to the 15-second hustle that characterizes television advertisements for American cars, Saturn always uses 60-second showings. This conveys its openness and the fact that it has time for its customers. The consistency of these messages is critical for credibility with the Customers that Count. It is often the case (despite the replies they may provide to researchers) that they are the most conscientious audiences of advertising for the brands that they patronize.

Expected behaviour

The nature of the brand creates certain expectations and it is important that these expectations are met for Customers that Count. These may be actual or perceptual considerations. For example, an American candy store damaged the perceptions of its most regular customers by the way that the sweets were weighed. The sweet-toothed eight-year-olds were keen to have the most candies for their money. Instead of weighing under and then adding more candies to achieve the desired balance, the shopkeeper poured generously and then removed items to get down to the correct weight. The removal was at odds with the image of generosity and the shop lost some of its most valuable customers.

Some brands, like the internet currency beenz, are expected to be informal and will use your first name in communication. Other brands, like Lloyds TSB, will be more formal and will communicate with appropriate titles: Mr, Mrs, Ms or Miss. Some other brands will logically involve themselves with you in other ways; for example Sheba will refer to the name of your cat in correspondence.

Consistent delivery is an important part of keeping the brand promise. This consistency must be apparent in changing times. Thus branding is a continuous process and changes are needed to maintain salience (*see* Fig. 14.5). Without these tweaks, brands can be left behind – technically or psychologically. Montgomery Ward, the US department store and catalogue group, filed for bankruptcy in 2000, after 128 years. During its illustrious history the brand had provided quality goods at competitive prices: 'Satisfaction guaranteed or your money back' was originally its slogan. The brand had kept its personality alive with ingenuity over the years. For example, according to *The Times* (30 December 2000), in the 1939 Christmas season it offered a Christmas give-away for children – an illustrated poem by an employee, Robert May, about a reindeer with a shiny red nose. In the first draft, the reindeer's name was 'Reginald', replaced by the name 'Rudolph' at publication. But a brand has to be kept alive with distinctiveness and it appears that the company was unable to sustain this.

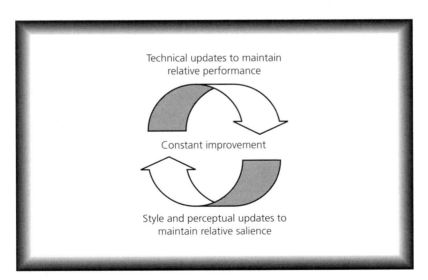

Figure 14.5 Branding – a continuous process

Yet it is easily possible for a brand to make changes to formulation, packaging, information or the service in a way that affects the brand promise. When the Unilever brand, Persil, launched Persil Power, the new formulation was so strong that it washed holes in underwear from Lubeck to Liverpool. But the brand promise was maintained. Unilever's swift response and replacement of the new brand variant recreated the brand promise.

Friends are allowed to make mistakes, as long as they admit them and make amends.

Friends are allowed to make mistakes, as long as they admit them and make amends. Customers that Count see brands in the same light. We can forgive them both.

Extending the relationship

A further benefit of branding for customer and brand owner is that a brand can be extended to cover a wider range of items. The customer gains the reassurance that they can buy the new item with the same confidence as they buy their normal purchase. Or they can achieve the same peace of mind in a new category. The brand owner has the responsibility to ensure that the quality expectations are carried over to the new product. The brand then gains additional sales and profit – mostly from existing satisfied customers.

Unilever is using the provenance of Cif and Persil cleaners as a form of brand endorsement to help launch a home service operation called 'MyHome'. This is a laundry, home-cleaning and dry-cleaning service for time-pressured consumers. The service staff use proven Unilever cleaning brands as part of the brand promise.

Friendship characteristics

There is a German proverb: '*Alte Freundschaft, gute Freundschaft*' which means a long-established friendship is a good friendship. Brands are like friends, and to a brand's longstanding customers the brand is like a good friend to them. The most successful brands develop a form of character with human virtues. They then work hard and consistently to keep up the good name of the brand. They want customers to be proud to associate themselves with the brand.

Horlicks India

Horlicks, the malted milk brand, now owned by SmithKline Beecham, was first patented in 1883, originally manufactured in Racine USA and subsequently in Slough UK. The brand has powerful credentials as a nutritious drink. The malting of barley through the natural process of germination releases enzymes. These enzymes break down complex carbohydrates to simple sugars that are easily assimilated by the body, making Horlicks easily digestible. As well as tangible promises, Horlicks also delivers strong emotional values, from the Poles to the equator.

As an example of the tangible benefits, Horlicks has been an essential provision for expeditions to Mount Everest and both North and South Poles since the early years of the twentieth century. In fact, so impressed was the American explorer of Antartica, Rear Admiral Richard Byrd, that in 1935 he gave a 3000-metre mountain the name Horlick Mountain after the brand (as described on the Horlicks website, www.horlicks.com).

Around the same time, the brand's emotional credentials were being laid with an advertising theme in the UK that was to continue for decades. Horlicks was presented as a solution to 'night starvation'. Advertising dramatized the benefits of sound, refreshing sleep resulting from regular bedtime consumption of Horlicks. This was a strong combination of a recognizable brand, a product promise and a set of values and associations.

The brand values have been further developed in India, which is now the largest market for Horlicks anywhere in the world. In its earlier days Horlicks was imported from the UK. Tariff costs and diminishing import permits led to manufacture in India by 1960. Calcium was added to the Indian product in 1988 as a nutritional enhancement. In 1994 Horlicks was relaunched with the addition of vitamins and minerals and positioned firmly as a health drink. Building on this position, the recipe was enhanced in 1998: 'Incorporating vital micronutrients that are known to have a proven direct co-relation with mental sharpness and physical activeness', as the company stated in its press release of the time. Akhil Chandra, General Manager, Marketing, SmithKline Beecham Consumer Healthcare, said: 'The new formulation addresses widespread critical nutritional deficiencies in India. These deficiencies are common even in well-to-do, middle-class homes because some of these micronutrients are not consumed in adequate amounts on a daily basis.' New Horlicks with Smart Nutrients was subtly encouraging parental aspirations. The implication was that feeding children Horlicks might help make them brainier and better able to play a part in India's successful software industry.

The strength of the Horlicks brand in India has enabled the company to extend to related product areas, with product versions available for nursing mothers and young children. There are even Horlicks biscuits (a wide selection of Horlicks products can be viewed on www.indiangrocery.com/ groc_beverages).

Around the world, over more than 120 years, Horlicks has confirmed itself as a trusted brand. The *Economic Times* of India conducted a survey in 2000 of India's most admired brands. Horlicks ranked third. Indeed a brand the customer is proud to associate with.

Exercises   Exercise 14

What are your brand values? What choices are you making?

1 List four positive human characteristics that you want your brand to possess.

2 List four other positive characteristics that your brand does not possess.

Further reading and references

Aaker, David A. and Joachimsthaler, Erich (2000) *Brand Leadership*, The Free Press.

Clifton, Rita and Maughan, Esther (eds) (1999) *The Future of Brands*, Palgrave.

Gordon, William and Pringle, Hamish (2001) *Brand Manners*, John Wiley & Sons.

Morgan, Adam (1999) *Eating the Big Fish*, John Wiley & Sons.

Reviewing the relationship IV

At stages in any relationship, personal or commercial, it is wise to take stock of the situation. This entails standing back and reviewing the trend of the relationship – on balance are things improving or deteriorating? The review will look at the positive aspects of the relationship and how these might be enhanced. It will also focus on the negative parts of the relationship to identify those that may be turned around. The evaluation may suggest no change is needed, or, at the other extreme, that the relationship should be terminated.

This section looks at relationship review in four areas:

- measurement of relationships – what are the dimensions of successful relationships?
- barriers to exit and how to discourage good customers from leaving;
- failing relationships – lessons and how to ease the exit of unprofitable customers;
- mutual interest and how to increase the two-way benefits.

How are things with your friends at Schenectady?

What do you mean, boss?

They don't seem to have placed an order this month.

No, but things are just great with those guys.

Well, their moving annual total of purchases has been sliding for six months now.

Oh sure, things must be a little hard for them right now, but we'll be fine.

You know, I never saw those guys at our Golf Day.

They couldn't make it this year. That's how it goes sometimes.

When was Service Support last over there?

I'll check with Fleischmann.

Yes check it all and come back with our score. I'd really like the measure of how we're doing with them.

K eeping track of the relationships with the Customers that Count is vital. First, it conveys to the employees, distributors and others that the relationship is important to the business. Second, it identifies opportunities and threats for the future of the connection and permits relationship management. There are some best practices in relationship tracking. These include identifying what are the most important factors to be measured and comparing performance with indicators.

The two functions of measurement

The measurement chain is a crucial part of organization review. The chain begins with developing measures, which convey corporate commitment; actions follow, which are rewarded; and results are the final outcome (*see* Fig. 15.1). What gets measured, gets recognized and rewarded.

Measurement has two functions:

1 **Showing commitment.** The first function is to flag-up that the company sees its customer relationships as important. This message is conveyed to

all who become aware of the measures. This means certainly employees, distributors and their staff, retailers, service suppliers and possibly shareholders. The best customers will also receive the message in the measurement process. As an example, the UK building society, the Birmingham and Midshires, a former winner of the *Management Today*/Unisys Service Excellence Award, regularly surveys its valuable customers. The survey communicates a number of messages. The fact that it has only five questions shows that there is due regard for the time of the customers. The free space for comment shows that customers are able to set the agenda. The last line, bearing the home telephone number of the chief executive, demonstrates commitment.

2 **Basis for decisions.** The second function is to form the factual basis for policies, decisions and actions. If you track the performance of on-time, in-full deliveries to Customers that Count, then it is possible to compare it with the average delivery performance to all customers, and to take actions that improve service to give top customers a priority reflecting their status.

Customer response measures are the basis for action at Xerox. Company divisions check customer satisfaction three months after equipment installation. They use the resultant scores to award commission to sales staff: 70-per-cent customer satisfaction could result in 70 per cent of the notional bonus being paid out to the sales person. Logically, the company pays incentives only for those sales where the customer is satisfied. This rewards sales people who truly meet the customer's needs.

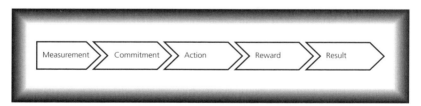

Figure 15.1 Measurement

Reward

Dell, the leading direct-selling computer company with operations in 34 countries, defines the ideal customer experience in terms of three key drivers of loyalty. For each driver, there is a summary statistic that best reflects that driver. These statistics have quarterly targets set for them. Management bonuses are tied to fulfilment of targets (Reichheld, 2000).

Measurement leads to action

Focusing, like Dell, on key ratios will lead to management action on the issues that impact on the retention of all customers, and especially of major buyers. This is responsive relationship management. The international car rental company Avis understands the importance of the telephone manner when drivers call its 1-800 number. It therefore measures ratings of the effectiveness and warmth of its operators. The data is used to focus management attention, financial resources and training priorities to raise the scores.

What areas should be measured?

Measures should cover every angle on the relationship. For business health, Kaplan and Norton (1996) recommend that measures should extend beyond financial dimensions. Similarly for relationship health, measures should go beyond the opinions of the customers themselves. What are the behind-the-scenes factors that permit good performance for best customers? What are the internal drivers that lead to improvement over time? How do good relationships link to financial results? To answer all these issues a focused balance of representative measures is needed, covering staff performance, customer intimacy, learning measures, efficiency of the relationship and financial performance.

This will yield a raft of possible statistics. Focus on those vital few factors that drive growth in good relationships. This may mean contrasting the service provided to a group of customers who have grown dramatically against a comparitor that has remained stable in purchases. Exclude the external factors in the customer's market and isolate the performance drivers in the service to the customer that enabled growth or restricted it. Measure what grows relationships. In one instance this came down to 'people with a passion for the business'. Bob Lutz, one-time Vice-Chairman of Chrysler, highlighted this factor in his question: 'If you had a choice of eating in two restaurants, one driven by profit maximization and the other by love of food, where would you go?' Measuring the motivation of front-line employees is not as easy as recording financial expenditure or sales, but it can be the better indicator for future relationships with Customers that Count.

Focus on those vital few factors that drive growth in good relationships.

John Deere, the manufacturers of green and yellow tractors, with operations in more than 160 countries and global sales of more than $11 billion, has a four-part scorecard to measure how each of its business units delivers 'genuine value' for John Deere's stakeholders. Their scorecard includes:

- human resources – employee satisfaction, training;
- customer focus – loyalty, market leadership;
- business processes – productivity, quality, cost, environment;
- business results – return on assets, sales growth.

The final outcome is a basket of indicators that combines a record of today's relationship with best customers with the internal factors that best promise continuity and improvement. Thus John Deere measures employee motivation and training levels in order to make the company irresistible to its best customers.

Employee measures

From the ideas in Chapter 5, we can recognize the importance of measuring employee motivation, skills and their confidence in senior management (*see* Fig. 15.2). A single statistic that can serve as an approximate measure for all three of these factors is staff turnover. A low level of staff leaving the business can indicate that employees feel positive about their work, have built up a level of skill and ability through training and experience and are happy to be led by the company executives. Improving staff retention is a measure that can impact directly on the satisfaction of best customers. Long-term staff support long-term relationships with Customers that Count.

Another employee measure that can pay wider dividends is to check that everyone understands the mission and vision of the organization. This serves the customer well, as it indicates that priorities are clear and that everyone is 'singing from the same hymn sheet'. It may be a better calibration of effective communications than asking the direct question of staff.

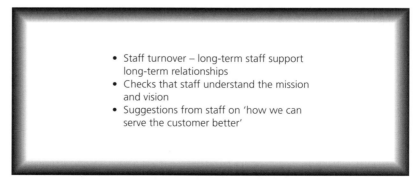

- Staff turnover – long-term staff support long-term relationships
- Checks that staff understand the mission and vision
- Suggestions from staff on 'how we can serve the customer better'

Figure 15.2 Employee measures

A third suggestion for a powerful employee measure is to capture ideas from staff on 'how we can serve the customer better' and record the number of ideas and the quantity implemented. The objective is to achieve and maintain a high number of business-improvement suggestions. A continuous flow of implemented ideas also creates the motivational feeling that 'things are always getting better around here' and that 'there is always some news for customers'. Both of these are strong forces for growth with best customers.

Customer measures

For effective customer measures, whom do you survey? Northern Electric and Gas, the utility company based in Newcastle-upon-Tyne, UK, surveys representative customers receiving its services and also specifically those who have made a complaint. Complainants are a valuable body of customers, because they have identified themselves as being aware of standards and willing to communicate perceived shortfalls. Best customers who have complained often accept invitations to sit on customer panels. These bodies can provide fuller and more timely information to companies eager to boost satisfaction scores of Customers that Count. Surveys may encompass distributors, consumers, market influencers (for example journalists) as well as customers themselves.

Customer satisfaction surveys are clearly crucial. Yet directly asking customers if they are satisfied provides an average measure across customers with different standards. A more effective way to assess customer satisfaction is to ask two more probing questions:

- Will they definitely repurchase?
- Would they recommend the service/product to a colleague in the same position as themselves?

Committing to re-buying is a stronger indicator of genuine satisfaction, than ticking the 'satisfied' box on the questionnaire. Similarly, the confirmation that they would recommend is in effect a public testimony. According to Anita van de Vliet (1997), 3M, in their European customer surveys, ask three questions:

- Are you completely satisfied?
- Would you definitely recommend?
- Would you definitely repurchase?

These responses are known as the 'top box' and the company target is to have 50 per cent of customers in the top box.

Surveys too, have their limitations. In the mass market, many companies have little choice but to administer wide-scale surveys to gain customer feedback. However, when a company focuses on its best customers, the numbers involved mean that it may be possible to conduct in-depth interviews instead. Every two years 3M sends managers to talk to 40 or 50 individuals working for a particular major customer. The 90-minute conversation is an on-the-record encounter. Much more is revealed and more possible action points can emerge. Subsequently the managers will report back to each individual with an action plan and also report back to the company as a whole.

Recording and rewarding on the strength of customer-retention levels is a powerful incentive to focus on best customers. The statistic is simply the percentage of business deriving from customers with whom the company was trading in the previous year. Normally a band is provided, for example 60–75 per cent of revenue should be from existing customers. This allows for and encourages newer smaller accounts coming on stream, and penalizes loss of major existing business.

A third calibration (*see* Fig. 15.3) is the share of business with a major customer. In other words, where a customer is splitting purchases between two or more suppliers, the valid measure is the place within the portfolio. Is the proportion of business increasing or decreasing? Boeing continuously monitors the fleet mix of the world's leading airlines to establish the proportion of its planes and the trend in each airline. For many industries, this type of data has been difficult to obtain historically, but with the expansion of e-procurement, this measure will be a valuable source of comparison.

Business processes

This is a measure of how efficiently your internal processes deliver service to customers. Understanding the detailed requirements of major customers

- Satisfaction surveys
  - 'Would you recommend us?'
- Percentage of last year's customers buying this year
  - target a percentage band
- Percentage share of customer's purchases
  - position within customer's portfolio

Figure 15.3 Customer/distributor measures

enables the company to focus on certain internal processes that provide the necessary standards and results.

As an example, in healthcare products, delivery reliability is particularly critical. According to information on the 3M company website (www.3M.com), 3M's Japanese healthcare operations established closer links with manufacturing facilities in the USA. Promise-date reliability to customers in Japan was increased to 98 per cent. In addition, inventories of healthcare products in Japan were reduced by about 25 per cent.

Financial measures

Financial measures are also valid measures of relationships with the Customers that Count. There are two particular measures that seem to indicate the strength of relationship:

- increasing level of purchases;
- premium price or resistance to discount offers from rivals.

As we have seen in Chapter 4, one of the benefits of a strong relationship with a best customer is that purchases increase over time. This derives from several factors:

- customer confidence in the supplier, leading to purchase of other products in the range;
- trading up by customers who become happy to buy more expensive and higher-margin products;
- growth in the business of the customer (applies to business-to-business market only).

It is therefore reasonable to measure the scale of business over a period of time. Where there are a small number of Customers that Count, their sales may be graphed individually, and many sales management software packages permit this. Where there are more customers, or the pattern is confused, it is possible to average all the purchases made by customers in their first year of trading and to compare this with the average of all two-year customers, three-year customers and so on. It can be instructive to see at what point purchases tend to level off (*see* Fig. 15.4).

A company in the life-science industry with customers in agri-chemicals and pharmaceuticals discovered that the patterns in the two industries were different, and also that the analysis functioned only for major customers – for smaller accounts, the year-to-year fluctuation was too great to draw conclusions. It is statistically true that larger volumes tend to fluctuate more than smaller volumes. In addition, if best customers are receiving truly world-class service, and gaining value, then they may be prepared to reflect this in the prices that they pay. In certain fast-moving consumer goods businesses, a number of marketing directors receive bonuses on the premium that their brand is able to command over own brand lines.

In other businesses this loyalty may be expressed differently in terms of customers' reluctance to move their business to a discounting rival. Quest, owned by ICI, is one of the world's leading fragrance, flavour and food-ingredients companies. Based in Naarden, Netherlands, and with manufacturing operations in 28 countries, Quest is dominant in its sector. Such is the strength of its brand name and its record of product and service quality to its food industry customers that they are unlikely to switch business if approached by a lower priced rival.

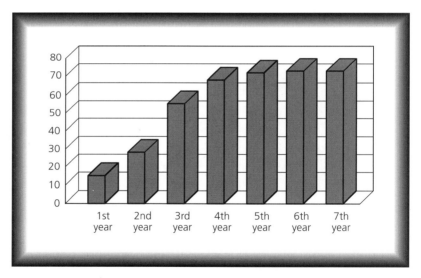

Figure 15.4 Increasing purchases – comparing first-year buyers with later years

How are we doing? Comparing against indicators

Selecting the right measures is the first part of the exercise. Having chosen these indicators, stage two is to establish comparable data. If the important factor is queueing time, how many seconds or minutes feels reasonable to the customer? How quickly do competing vendors serve key customers?

How are you doing compared with expectations and competitors? A large UK mortgage lender learnt that there was dissatisfaction with waiting time for the lending decision, and made changes that reduced this by seven days. This met the expectations of customers surveyed at the outset. However, in the intervening period new lenders had entered the market with significantly shorter times, and therefore the performance of competitors must be measured alongside original customer expectations.

- **Comparing against customer expectations.** Many companies ask their customers to rate them on a scale, typically ranging from one to ten, where one is poor and ten is excellent. In these circumstances, suppliers should set themselves very high scores as the objective. In blunt terms, a score of less than eight out of ten is a fail – moving from poor to mediocre will not bring delight and loyalty.

  On the Dell company website (www.dell.com), there is a case history of the successful Dell installation of computers and equipment at John Deere. After each set of users made the switch, the technology team conducted a user survey to gauge satisfaction levels with the new Dell environment. Users were asked about training, systems deployment requested software, etc. The project received a five-out-of-six rating, with six being perfect.

- **Comparing against competitors.** First Direct, the pioneering UK telephone bank, employs a research agency to interview 500 of its own customers and 500 customers from competing institutions. Only by doing this, can First Direct be confident that rivals are not out performing it. According to press reports, 90 per cent of its own customers describe themselves as extremely/very satisfied. Figures for competitors are substantially lower than this.

World-class comparisons

World-class customers expect world-class performance. Therefore many leading companies are now benchmarking outside their own industry to establish standards of operation. This may mean identifying your customer's best suppliers from any category and learning from them. Nissan and other automotive manufacturer encourage suppliers to do this.

World-class customers expect world-class performance.

Alternatively, for any given dimension, companies can seek a world-leading performer and measure themselves against this operation. For example, 3M has a division focusing on products for the dental industry.

According to the website, the customer response time of 3MDental matches that of Eastman-Kodak, an industry leader in customer service. For plant safety it benchmarks itself against the major chemical company, Dupont, which is recognized as a global leader in safety.

Conclusion

In conclusion, calibrating the strength and effectiveness of relationships with the Customers that Count is a vital part of understanding trends, expectations and future priorities. It is established business practice to take account of customer views in boardroom analysis of performance. Leading companies are now extending this overview to focus specifically on the measures of relationship quality with their top customers.

Case example   Theme: measurement

Motor Neurone Disease Association

The Motor Neurone Disease Association is a charity in the UK with a close interest in the quality and range of its relationships. For its comprehensive approach to understanding relationships, the MND Association offers lessons beyond the voluntary sector.

Motor neurone disease is the name given to a group of related diseases affecting the motor neurones in the brain and spinal cord. Motor neurones are the nerve cells that control the muscles; as the motor neurones die, the muscles stop working. MND is rapidly progressive and always fatal. It leaves people unable to walk, talk or feed themselves, but the intellect and senses remain intact. Average life expectancy after diagnosis is just 14 months.

I spoke to Chief Executive, George Levvy, about the way the MND Association manages and measures its relationships:

> Our antennae are vital in shaping the way we turn our face to the outside world. We need to know how we are seen by people with MND, by carers, by donors, by the medical profession, by researchers and grant awarding bodies, by Westminster and Whitehall and by members of the public.

The MND Association has some formal measures of successful relationships with its various constituencies. Understanding of MND by health and social care professionals, other service providers, decision makers and the general public is crucial to those affected by the disease. Each year the Association commissions public surveys of awareness of MND and understanding of the nature of the condition. Large-scale surveys of people with MND and their carers have identified their concerns, their experiences, their satisfaction with services from statutory providers and the MND Association. The relationship with donors also begins with awareness and understanding of the disease. Tracking of donor relations is done through monitoring the number and value of donations and legacies. Other measures, such as the number of new research grant applications to investigate the disease and media tracking, are also important tools.

Interestingly, the MND Association also deploys a range of more perceptual measures. Jane Burns, Director of Fundraising, told me that for every key contact the MND Association designates an individual who owns that relationship. He or she is responsible for identifying issues, ensuring the necessary frequency of contact, reviewing status and reporting on the durability of the relationship.

A key strategy is to build relationships with the medical research community. Brian Dickie, Director of Research, explained to me the drivers of positive perception: scientific merit, continuity of research grants on which jobs depend, and enthusiasm for sharing knowledge. Each of these is reviewed. As a commitment to extending scientific knowledge, the MND Association sponsors the annual International Amyotrophic Lateral Sclerosis/Motor Neurone Disease Symposium for neurologists, healthcare and research communities. Held in Aarhus Denmark in 2000, San Francisco USA in 2001 and Melbourne Australia in 2002, the symposium hosts 600 delegates from 35 countries. Consultant Neurologist Dr Chris Shaw, of Kings College Hospital London, said, 'Simply by bringing like-minded specialists together under the one roof, the MND Association fosters collaboration between groups throughout the world and undoubtedly accelerates the rate of scientific progress'. For tracking perceptions, this two-day event provides ample opportunity for informal feedback on perceptions of the MND Association. Post-symposium, the feedback will be shared across the Association.

Finally, Laura Simons, Director of Communications, gave me an insight into measuring perceptions at Whitehall and Westminster. The MND Association works increasingly with politicians and civil servants, for example in the area of disability allowances. It is also clear that involvement and interest in the appraisal of Riluzole (a new treatment for motor neurone disease) by the National Institute of Clinical Excellence in 2000 positively raised the charity's profile in Whitehall. There is a single factor that counts above all others. 'Government is interested in whether your influence is waning, static or growing. When they perceive influence is increasing, things really happen.'

Exercises   **Exercise 15**

Construct your own relationship scorecard. Using the template in Fig. 15.5, select three measures for Customers that Count within each category.

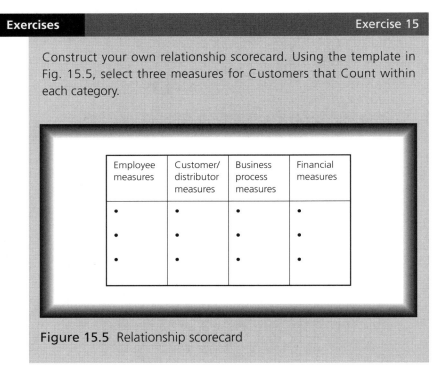

Employee measures	Customer/ distributor measures	Business process measures	Financial measures
•	•	•	•
•	•	•	•
•	•	•	•

Figure 15.5 Relationship scorecard

Further reading and references

Ambler, Tim (2000) *Marketing and the Bottom Line*, Financial Times/Prentice Hall.

Kaplan, Robert S. and Norton, David P. (1996) 'Using the Balanced Scorecard as a Strategic Management System', *Harvard Business Review*, January/February.

Reichheld, Frederick (2000) 'E-Loyalty: your secret weapon on the web', *Harvard Business Review*, July/August.

Van de Vliet, Anita (1997) 'Are they being served?' *Management Today*, February.

So, you're heading for a divorce?
   Yes, but it'll be painful, very painful
What will hurt the most?
   My wallet!

K eeping the Customers that Count relies on the eight human characteristics of good relationships described in Part III. These real virtues
build strong and constructive connections with important customers. Yet
relationships have ups and downs. As well as providing incentives to stay
with a relationship through difficult times, it is valuable to have some disincentives to separation. These are hurdles that make customers think long
and hard before they terminate. Often called switching costs, there are two
types of barriers to exit: financial penalties and psychological switching
costs. Successful organizations identify potential barriers to exit and build
them discretely, ensuring that customers become subtly aware of them.

Relationship disharmony

The blueprint of eight human characteristics provides a recipe for successful relationships with major customers. All things being equal, these will
support enduring relationships. Yet all things never are equal: problems
never arise singly. Queueing theory indicates that they will tend to arrive in
clusters. Thus a company will find that the customer appoints a new purchasing director, when a supply shortage impacts, and coincidentally a
competitor offers an uneconomic discount. As with human relationships,
commercial connections have their harmonies and discords.

What happens if there are no barriers to exit?

Normally the harmonies outweigh the discordant notes. But occasionally
the combination of circumstances may cause a customer to review the con-
tinuation of a long-standing business relationship. At these times it is
essential to have some hurdles that have the effect of restraining the departure of the customer long enough for the benefits to overcome the
temporary dissatisfaction (*see* Fig. 16.1).

Incentives to stay
- Reliable products and services
- Knowledgeable people
- Effective two-way communications
- Recognition, personalization
- Collaboration and shared insights

Disincentives to leave
- Barriers to exit

Figure 16.1 Retention

Where there are no barriers to exit, valuable customers may defect without hindrance. It can occur quickly. For example, in the three months to 30 September 2000, customers of Egg, the UK-based internet bank owned by Prudential, switched £443 million of funds out of their Egg accounts. The average balances of these customers were between £50 000 and £100 000, and with no barriers to retain them, they responded to better deposit rates elsewhere, by moving their money.

What barriers can you build?

There are two categories of exit barrier (*see* Fig. 16.2). One barrier is an actual financial penalty, which may be direct, such as a charge, or indirect, in the form of an additional cost the business would then have to bear. The second type is a psychological hurdle, where the decision maker experiences fear, uncertainty or doubt about the prospect of a change in supplier. Both types can be effective in disincentivizing departure.

Real financial costs
- Long-term contracts
- Improving terms

Psychological costs
- Fear, uncertainty, doubt
- Power of information

Trend towards contract freedom

Figure 16.2 Barriers to exit

Actual financial penalties

There are 20 barriers that contribute to making it better value for the customer to stay.

1   **Extended credit.** Market-leading companies with high volumes and a significant heart of loyal long-term customers typically earn higher margins than their competitors. This allows them scope to compete aggressively, and they choose to do this in ways other than price-cutting. For example, they can afford the cost of longer credit terms. In effect they act as a bank to their customers. A major manufacturer of tents and camping equipment will deliver new-season orders in February, but accept payment 60 days later, allowing undercapitalized retailers to sell a portion of the stock before they need to pay their supplier. To switch means the challenge of negotiating the same deal from an alternative supplier, or the financial penalty of an increase in working capital.

2   **Penalty contracts.** Many suppliers tie the offer of discounts to a guaranteed time commitment. Britannia Music, the dominant company in UK music clubs, packages cut-price CDs as an initial offer and ties this to a minimum order of six full-price CDs over a two-year period. Cancellation means a penalty.

3   **Cumulatively improving terms.** The longer an account is with a supplier, the more profitable it should become, if all the lessons of the experience curve are applied (*see* Chapter 4). Hence, it is possible to create 'experience curve' pricing, where terms improve cumulatively. Costs are not strictly related to each cumulative doubling of purchases, but there is an assumption that terms continue to improve. A major supplier of contract staff created a fee structure that featured a management fee and open-book charging of all staff employment costs, with a commitment to seek constant efficiencies so that staff costs fell as the experience curve rose.

4   **Price guarantees.** In commodity and near-commodity markets, market prices fluctuate wildly in response to changes in supply and demand. For example Usinor, Corus and ThyssenKrupp found that world prices of steel fell throughout 2000 because new capacity came on stream in Asia and Brazil substantially faster than the market grew. There is every incentive for a customer to switch suppliers to minimize prices paid. To counter the disloyalty evident in commodity markets, one European cement producer offered a 'no disadvantage' clause. This meant that if the customer bought 100 per cent of their cement from this company, it would invoice every shipment at the prevailing market price of that

week. At one stroke this removed the incentive to play the market, and saved substantial time and trouble for the buyer. For the vendor it provided continuity that allowed economies of scale and business predictability that covered the cost of the price guarantee.

5 **Buy-back guarantee.** Where end-users' tastes and patterns of demand for perishable products vary markedly, leading suppliers may provide stock on a sale-or-return basis. Magazines and newspaper wholesalers have sold to newsagents on this basis. This encourages the newsagent to take more stock and thereby achieve a higher availability for the end-consumer. Costs of waste are borne by the manufacturer. If the customer closes the account then marginal sales will be lost, as stocks are cut to forecast levels.

6 **Forecasting service.** Small customers often have limited expertise and knowledge in areas like currency movements and interest rates. Yet rate changes can significantly impact buying or selling costs. A supplier who provides a forecasting service can save considerable sums for customers. It can be an expensive proposition changing suppliers and forgoing this service.

7 **Managing the inventory.** Providing an inventory management service to customers can also impose penalties on switching customers. Where a stationery supplier manages the inventory of paper, pens, pencils and ink cartridges, there is a saving in staff costs. Cancelling the arrangement would mean recruiting and paying a new staff member.

8 **Proprietary systems.** Some manufacturers extend their product range to include services such as software to manage inventory or to support the customer's manufacturing process. The proprietary software is often provided free of charge, subject to business continuing. Thus if the customer switches suppliers, there is a need to buy software on the open market to carry out the same function.

9 **Providing equipment/tooling.** Brand owners may loan merchandising units to retailers for a product category so that sales increase, with the loan dependent on continuing loyalty. Some suppliers of equipment and manufacturing processes create specific moulds, tools or presses for customers and then, rather than sell these, they provide a lease service. This benefits the customer's cash flow, but also imposes a cost of purchase with any change of supplier.

10 **Joint ventures.** In other industries it is the convention for tools and equipment to be jointly owned. This shares the risk of failure, but the joint ownership restricts the buyer.

11 **Creating industry standards.** When a leading manufacturer is the model for the national and international bodies who write industry standards, it can be difficult for an intermediate customer to sell to the end-user a product that does not follow the standard. Siemens, the European industrial conglomerate, has considerable expertise in working with German industry-standards institutes. Conformance to standard is a barrier to switching. Where a hearing aid manufacturer specifies a Varta battery, customers will be reluctant to use another manufacturer's equivalent.

12 **Ingredient brands.** Manufacturers like Dupont have created ingredient brands like non-stick Teflon and the lightweight material Kevlar. DSM, the Dutch-based performance materials company, has established Dyneema as the premier high-strength fibre for ropes, rigging and cord. Archers using Dyneema strings won Olympic medals in Sydney 2000. Now it is hard for a bow maker to specify an unknown string. The logo 'Intel inside' makes a computer easier to sell and suggests to a computer manufacturer that without Intel the profits would be lower.

13 **Common catalogue.** Faced with a powerful buyer, an ingenious Asian company approached two non-competing suppliers to this dominant firm. Jointly, the three suppliers devised a common catalogue for all their components, using a single part numbering system and provided on a single CD. With so many regularly used parts coming from these suppliers this CD became the *de facto* standard. The convenience and time saving locked out competitors to the three and provided a barrier to exit based around the cost of the customer's time.

14 **Electronic links.** Implementing e-procurement links that offer specification downloads and a complete purchase history provides convenience. This reference bank would be difficult to replicate and therefore acts as barrier.

15 **Mutual/reciprocal business.** Reciprocal trade is a barrier to exit. Even if the element of mutual business is not significant in monetary terms, the link demonstrates two-way commitments and will lead to hesitation before termination.

16 **Design for customer.** Acting as a design service can create reliance and a cost of switching, where designers have to be recruited, inducted, trained and equipped.

17 **Design for customer's customer.** Acting as a design service for the customer's customer has a more powerful impact, as it is linked to the customer's performance in their marketplace. There are examples in the fine-paper industry: the Swedish-based paper merchant Papyrus

offers design support to advertising agencies and assists them in building their own services to advertising clients.

18 **Help-line for customer's customer.** Many consumer brands provide customer care-lines and help-screens on their websites. A supplier providing support or managing this care-line has a presence that is difficult to remove.

19 **Staff training.** Training is a priority in fast-changing businesses, and it is also an expense. Where the supplier takes on the provision of staff training, this encourages business connections to continue.

20 **Out-source service.** When you take over a particular function of your customer's operation, for example inventory management of aircraft tyres, or waste disposal of oil products, then the customer has a real financial penalty in changing suppliers.

Financial costs of switching are increasingly featuring in annual client and customer reviews. This is a form of neutralizing a competitor's story before it is told. Customers see a value statement of the current relationship, which could even quantify the penalty of switching to another supplier.

Psychological barriers

A survey in the UK published by the government's Department of Trade and Industry (November 2000) identified the 'hassle factor' as the main barrier against switching. According to the survey, 32 per cent of customers had considered changing their mortgages in the past five years, yet only 12 per cent had actually done so. With thousands of different mortgage offers available, it is probable that borrowers could have reduced their financial costs. The hassle factor held them back. Somehow the logic of cost is overruled by an emotional reluctance to take the risk of a change.

Peace of mind is a powerful deterrent to switching.

There are 16 barriers that create reluctance in the mind of customers to leave your service and support system. Peace of mind is a powerful deterrent to switching.

1 **Service guarantees.** Major suppliers with recognized resources internationally are able to provide guarantees of service speed and product choice that local rivals cannot match. International photocopier brand Xerox used this as a way of underlining their global reach and comprehensive range.

2 **Satisfaction-based pricing.** Companies with very strong performance records demonstrate their confidence by offering a money-back in the unlikely event of failure. For example, in January 2001 Travel Inn, the UK's

leading budget hotel chain, launched a 100 per cent satisfaction guarantee at their 260 hotels. Guests who are not completely satisfied with their stay are offered their money back in full before leaving. According to reports, 30–40 customers per day (of over 10,000 guests per day) invoke the guarantee – mainly through inconsiderate noise from other guests. If rivals are unable to offer the same guarantee, then this can sow seeds of doubt and discourage customers from defecting, even when (especially when) prices are substantially lower.

3 **Back-up resources.** Providing comprehensive back-up resources can be another source of peace of mind for the customer. Some IT systems suppliers ask customers to classify their problems according to a pre-agreed scale of severity. Is it a system crash or a minor inconvenience? They set goals for resolution time and monitor and report. Support priority is matched to the assessment. Experience has shown that self-assessments are normally realistic and increase the sense of the customer being in control. Control is a desirable emotion and hence this is another barrier to exit.

4 **Training and education.** Training new consumers or a customer's new employees breeds a familiarity with equipment and processes. A first impression is often a durable impression. Sanitary protection brand Always works hard to provide information to mothers of teenage girls and influential healthcare staff who can recommend products as girls approach puberty. The company website (www.always.com) is an accessible reference source for girls, parents and advisers.

5 **Support of colleges and universities.** Linking a product to a training experience can associate the product with long-term best practice. Hair stylists who learn their craft with a particular brand of shampoo or conditioner develop a psychological connection between the brand and their own success.

6 **Information provision.** When customers rely on their supplier for particular types of information, this can lead to reliance. For example, the UK logistics company Unipart provides comparative data on how each of its many distributors is performing compared with an index of all distributors in the same size category. This management tool allows distributors to learn lessons from the products where they are out-performing similar operations and focus attention on lines with below-par sales.

7 **Brand image.** Customers value a brand image, particularly if the category is hard for the consumer to judge on technical dimensions, or where the brand is helping to make a statement about the individual. This applies to consumer and industrial markets. *The Economist* (25 November 2000) points to the success of branded companies on

the internet like Yahoo and Amazon. There is a dramatic contrast with the disappointing performance of generic names like pets.com and jewellery.com. The generic site, bike.com is suffering, whereas www.ducati.it claims to receive 150 000 hits per day and in 31 minutes achieved the sale of a year's production of the super-bike the MH900, named after legendary world champion, Mike Hailwood (*Financial Times*, 1 February 2000).

8 **Quality awards.** Recognition by outside bodies provides reassurance and can even instil a fear of going to a no-name alternative. Repeated awards for quality won by the BBC help to reinforce its international sales of UK-produced programming.

9 **Reputation for innovation.** UK-based RHM Technology, leaders in developments in food technology, offers innovation to customers across its business spectrum. For example, it can use isoelectronic focusing for variety identification of cereals, seeds, fruits and vegetables. Another innovative area is its support for rapid prototyping, with computer-aided design allied to three-dimensional wax printing for concept, consumer or packaging trials.

10 **Exceeding international standards.** Volvo cars have consistently provided safety features ahead of those demanded by national and international standards. This is a disincentive for a customer with young children to switch to an alternative family vehicle.

11 **Reminders of value.** In the UK, many charities have an annual 'flag day', when they are permitted by local authorities to make street collections. It was hard to imagine how this process could be extended to a barrier to exit for donors. The Marie Curie Cancer Care charity found a way. Their collection day in the spring is known as Daffodil Day. The bright yellow flower is a universal symbol of hope and renewal. As the charity says, 'What better emblem to symbolize the improved quality of life given to people with cancer by Marie Curie Cancer Care?' Thousands of volunteers take to the streets to hand out millions of distinctive fabric blooms in return for a donation. Attached to the fabric daffodil was a bulb tag, encouraging the donor to send off for a free bulb which could be planted after the summer in time to flower for Daffodil Day next year. This neatly captured the supporter's name for further communication and relationship building, and also provided a reminder to the person to support next year's collection.

12 **User group intranet membership.** A bonding technique with customers is the creation of a user group through an intranet. This means that customers are able to share comments, suggestions, criticisms, praise and ideas freely with other customers. Ending the business would mean the wrench of leaving the user group.

13 **Privileged access to facilities.** Airlines offer loyalty points, which provide privileged access to lounges. Defecting to other airlines would jeopardize continued access.

14 **Website links.** Many organizations link their own recognized website to those of their less well-known customers. For example, potential second-hand car buyers who visit the BMW website (www.bmw.co.uk) are able to input criteria for an approved used car. The search engine then locates close matches and provides the telephone number, address, e-mail and website of the BMW dealer who is holding this car. For the dealer, this is strong psychological barrier to changing franchise.

15 **Focus on risks.** Marketing communications that focus on hygiene, safety or embarrassment build psychological barriers to switching. Close associations with protection, security and peace of mind are strong disincentives to experiment with unknown suppliers.

16 **Stories of switching disasters.** An effective weapon in the communications armoury is a collection of stories of switching catastrophes. Word-of-mouth can spread illustrations of other customers who changed suppliers only to suffer as a consequence. When the cut-price gas and electricity supplier in the UK, Independent Energy, called in the receivers in September 2000, rival utilities highlighted the risks of low-cost competitors. London Electricity ran banner adverts featuring newspaper headlines announcing the collapse of Independent Energy. Their message was 'Don't panic, help is only a phone call away' and emphasized their own size and security.

Barrier building with psychological factors requires subtle marketing. If it appears too strident, it can provoke an adverse reaction. Often communications strategy will focus on an area of customer interest, highlight a feature, allude to a risk and then provide a benefit pay-off. The presentation is not threatening; rather it is simply an element of reassurance that is included in the overall proposition.

> **Barrier building with psychological factors requires subtle marketing.**

Creating higher barriers

Financial barriers are very effective. However, it should be said that they are hard to maintain. There is a technological trend towards open systems and away from proprietary systems that lock in customers. Governments around the world encourage transferability to increase competitiveness of industries. For this reason, there are arguments for contractual freedom, and the creation of higher psychological barriers. One heavy industrial organization is quietly moving away from fixed-term contracts, favoured by its industry peers, and replacing them with open-ended contracts. The Chief Executive observed that a time-bound contract means an automatic diary entry for the buying team to negotiate, whereas an open contract has no specified renewal date and hence no implied invitation to renegotiate. At the same time, he is crafting a comprehensive array of psychological barriers to exit. Let them 'lock themselves in'.

Case example   Theme: Retaining customers

Ashridge Management College

Ashridge Management College is one of the world's leading centres for management and organization development. For more than 40 years, it has operated as an independent, not-for-profit business school with executive MBA programmes, a range of executive development programmes, management research and organizational consulting activities. In the 2000 survey of executive education providers, the *Financial Times* ranked Ashridge in Europe's top seven. Based in Hertfordshire UK, Ashridge works with over 6000 managers each year helping them to learn, experiment and reflect. Many attend programmes designed specifically for their organizations. Clients include Alcatel, Bull, Deutsche Bank, Electrolux, Lloyds TSB, MCI Worldcom, PricewaterhouseCoopers and Volkswagen.

Ashridge has an enviable record for client retention. For example, Unilever, the multinational consumer-products company, has been running programmes at Ashridge for more than 30 years. Successful relationships with client organizations are based on the provision of value in tangible and intangible forms.

Chief Executive, Leslie Hannah, believes that three particular factors – the 'three Is' – are important in encouraging clients to keep returning: Ashridge's name for innovation, its international thinking and the business impact achieved.

First, the focus on innovation means that there is always a new aspect and a new angle for returning managers. Ashridge was the first to launch an executive MBA programme in the UK. The Ashridge Learning Resource Centre is Europe's leading business library and its Director, Andrew Ettinger, was recognized as European Business Librarian of the Year in 1998. Andrew extended the effectiveness and reach of the Centre in 1999, to launch the Virtual Learning Resource Centre. The VLRC offers worldwide remote access to Ashridge's learning resources and can easily be linked to the intranets of clients for desk-top 'just-in-time' knowledge.

Innovation occurs in many ways. Each year, for instance, there is the January 'development week' when Ashridge closes to all clients and focuses on development activities, idea-sharing and exploring new techniques and concepts. This is open to every member of Ashridge, embracing gardening teams, the international faculty members and residential services staff. Ashridge shares its new intellectual capital with clients through publications like *Directions* and exploratory workshops such as the 'Thinking Aloud' series of seminars.

International credentials are vital for clients seeking challenge and global best practice. This is reflected in Ashridge's 80-strong faculty who deliver programmes around the world for global clients. A particular strength is in cross-cultural working, where Ashridge can demonstrate good practice alongside helping managers to address issues in their own organizations. Almost two-thirds of the participants on the suite of MBA programmes are from outside the UK. For managers working in a domestic context in any country in the world, the international insights offer continuing value.

The final 'I' is impact and this aspect of Ashridge's appeal draws from its roots in 1959. Founded by visionary directors from large international companies, Ashridge was originally focused on the provision of practical skills for practising managers. Every member of the faculty has senior-level business experience in their own right, prior to joining Ashridge. This is mandatory and provides a rich fund of real-life personal examples. Ashridge is the only business school in Europe with its own consulting arm. The real world is continually changing and therefore its real-world focus makes Ashridge an attractive business partner for leading organizations.

Innovation, the international context and the business impact are powerful retaining forces for Ashridge clients.

Exercise 16   Exercises

1 Identify existing switching costs for your customers, both real and psychological.

2 How could these be increased? This may require customer research and financial modelling of customer business variables.

3 What new switching costs could you introduce to your industry?

Further reading and references

Buckingham, Richard (2001) *Customer Once, Client Forever: 12 tools for building lifetime customer relationships*, Kiplinger.

Did he fall, or was he pushed?

B usiness relationships may not always work out the way you hoped at the point when the account was first opened. One of the Customers that Count may decide to transfer business elsewhere after a period of time. What can you gain from being left? There are lessons to be learnt from analyzing defecting customers. For example, the reasons for leaving can prompt new procedures that will stem the departure of other customers. Additionally, the pre-departure behaviour may suggest more effective measures of relationship health. There are also other customers who are unprofitable, who may never be profitable and who are diminishing your ability to service the Customers that Count. How can you sack them? There are steps to take in identifying loss-making customers, seeking to change their behaviour, modelling the impact of their exit on the business and easing their departure to competitors.

Failing relationships

Ian Robinson, Planning Director at insight@TMW advises against over-complicating segmentation (*Marketing Direct*, February 2000). He recommends three primary segments: the best customers, the worst and those most likely to move to the competition. In this book we are focusing on the Customers that Count and how you can build their loyalty and the mutual benefit between your organization and these customers. Given the reality of desertion and divorce in the world of personal relationships, we need to review the lessons of customers who defect, and the process of 'divorcing' customers. Failure has a value – we can learn from it (*see* Fig. 17.1).

FAIL = **F**irst **A**ction **I**n **L**earning

Figure 17.1 Failure?

Defecting customers

It is normal to survey customers, especially Customers that Count, and it is important to gauge their satisfaction with the business, service and support. These surveys of customers show feelings. They can identify areas of delight and dissatisfaction. However, there are limitations to surveys. Halo effects may influence customer reponses. For example, popular acclaim or tradition can distract forgiving customers from commenting on service shortcomings. Alternatively, criticisms are levied purely with the aim of negotiating lower prices. A danger is that customer surveys often fail to discern intentions. Sometimes customers are not aware of emergent dissatisfaction in their subconscious. At other times they are reluctant to reveal this to suppliers. Observation may be a better guide to identify customers who may move to competitors. The best method of identifying potential defecting customers is to study lost customers.

Exit interview

It is a convention that resigning employees should go though an exit interview. They are asked what led to their departure, and lessons are sought for future improvement and the retention of other employees. Answers may highlight important areas for addressing morale, conditions or safety. Similarly, lost customers can offer insights through exit interviews. For retailers, this may be in the form of focus groups of customers who no longer shop at the store. Consumer-goods companies research lapsed users. Car companies learn from in-depth interviews with former customers who have moved to other marques.

In business-to-business markets the research often takes the form of a visit, perhaps one to three months after departure. A senior executive will explain that the aim is to learn, rather than to appeal for the return of the business, though they would be warmly welcomed back. The executive will go though a structured series of questions to identify the reasons for defection, the contributory factors and whether there was a final incident that triggered the ultimate decision. The executive will have a mixture of personal feelings just before the exit interview, yet the outcome is normally a positive stream of actions for improvement. Some of the actions are major, some minor in scope, but all are equally important in terms of customer perceptions. An exit lesson in the UK brewing industry was that the asides and comments of the delivery crews are accorded great weight by bar owners, restaurateurs and club stewards. Therefore it is important to brief delivery crews on company strategy, quality programmes and brand plans.

Were there any warning signs?

Observation and analysis of customer behaviour prior to departure may suggest more effective measures of relationship health. KPMG, the global consulting organization, takes a close interest in customer management. A survey by KPMG, reported in *Marketing Direct* (February 1999), showed that 43 per cent of companies with a turnover of more than £200 million are unable to identify why they lose customers. A higher proportion was unable to list customers at risk of defecting.

Customers' behaviour provides indicators that companies should observe and act upon.

There are techniques to spot early warning signs of customers who may move their business. When people fall out of love, their behaviour becomes less affectionate and more independent. Likewise, as customers' perceptions slip from delight to barely satisfied, their behaviour provides indicators that companies should observe and act upon (*see* Fig. 17.2).

An essential technique is to record customer practices and to analyze retrospectively lost customers – how did their behaviour change before they stopped buying? What did they cease doing, what did they take up and decline? For a credit-card company, frequency of use and amount billed each month are important measures, and any decline will be noted. However, before the balance begins to decline, the first warning that a rival card is gaining preference is when the gasoline transactions cease.

An investigation by KPMG Consulting, posted on their website (www.kpmgconsulting.com), illustrated a telecommunications company facing competitive activity. Rivals would entice business customers to switch with a three-month trial period. The trial, with a percentage of calls, demonstrated performance. Through a data warehouse, the company was

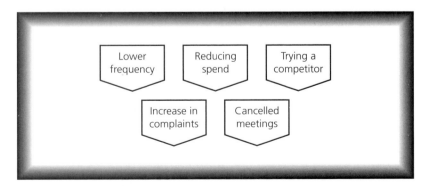

Figure 17.2 Early warning signs

able to make fine comparisons with historical call traffic, and identify fall-offs where trials might be taking place and then act appropriately to retain business.

Another warning sign is an increase in complaints. As a relationship fades, customers become less forgiving and will complain about minor matters they would previously have ignored. The UK bookseller and retailer of stationery, WHSmith, has a card-based customer loyalty scheme and the 38-strong customer relations team will scan in customer complaints and comments against the files of card members. Peter Crush, writing in *The Times* (25 April 2000) reports that if a customer complains about something specific, WHSmith will ensure that they do not send a further mailer on that topic which might frustrate them further.

In other industries, the early warning sign is a next-day rejection of invitations to social events and the cancellation of monthly or quarterly review meetings.

Intensive care

When early warnings are detected, customers so identified need to be placed in the commercial equivalent of intensive care. This involves:

- **Analysis.** Analysis means questioning users, buyers, influencers and contacts. It requires close observation of behaviour, and identifying changes in patterns.

- **Formulation.** Formulation is about resetting priorities for the customers identified at risk. This includes making changes in products, services, support, systems and records in response to concerns.

- **Implementation.** Implementation will embrace internal communication and possibly training. In many cases the customer will need to be advised of the new practices. It is often unwise to tell the customer they are seen as 'at risk' as the prophecy can become self-fulfilling.

- **Measurement.** As patients in intensive care are monitored more closely, so customers 'at risk', need much closer scrutiny with additional short-term measures. There may be a sign-off procedure where they can be taken off the list after a reassurance survey confirms that the relationship is back on track.

Unless you want the customer to leave

These are the responses to relationships failing, where the supplier wishes to retain the business. However, there may be customers identified in the defector analysis who are unprofitable, difficult to satisfy and whose departure would actually be a boon to the business, not a cost. In these circumstances the company simply takes no action, and allows the separation to occur.

Are there customers who don't suit you?

Two sides are able to initiate a relationship severance. We have looked at customers taking steps to end business relationships. There are other circumstances where the supplier may conclude it is in the customer's and its own best interests to part company.

Customer selection mistakes

Careful selection is critical, in gaining the profitable portfolio of best customers a business needs. We looked at this in Chapter 6. However, some customers may not live up to expectation, or their needs and style may evolve over time. Some customers do not fit your target profile. It can be hard for conventional thinkers to imagine not wanting a customer. The old philosophy is 'if it moves, shoot it' and that any and every customer is worth having. In businesses without relationships, where all transactions are free standing and there is no implied or actual service commitment, this may still be true. However, as the elements of service increase with every product proposition, more companies are finding that there are customers you do not want.

Disruptives

New thinking looks at the costs and consequences of serving customers. For example, a restaurant owner may want to discourage rowdy, roll-throwing 'Hooray Henries' who happily pay high prices, but whose behaviour drives away other customers.

Bad payers

Sprint, the US telecommunications business, announced in the *Financial Times* (21 September 2000) that its level of customer churn was in the range 2 to 3 per cent, higher than previous quarters. The explanation for this was the company firming its policy of cutting off late paying customers.

Negative profitability

A southern US bank allocated overheads to its customers based on their consumption of service support, and set this against the profit contribution of their product holdings. All customers were then ranked by profitability. The answer was in part expected. Eighty per cent of contribution came from the top 20 per cent of customers. The unexpected element was that a further 30 per cent of contribution came from the middle 40 per cent of customers. A simple mathematical calculation showed that the bottom 40 per cent of customers lost the bank 10 per cent of its gross contribution (*see* Fig. 17.3).

Tranche	Profit
Top 20% of customers	80%
Mid 40% of customers	30%
Bottom 40% of customers	(10%)

Figure 17.3 Customer profitability within a bank

Managing the loss makers

There are a number of strategies that are appropriate for loss makers.

Restricting customers

Sometimes lower-value customers cannot be allowed access to full facilities. This is the other side of giving priority to best customers. For example, Fidelity Investments is planning to restrict in the USA some customers' access to its phone representatives if they fail to provide sufficient income in fees and commissions.

Sacking customers

The Economist (9 January 1999) quotes the example of a large Texan computer maker who identifies unprofitable, service-intensive customers. When they place orders, the company dispatches compatible models produced by rival computer makers. Thus they export loss-making customers to competitors, driving down their own costs and penalizing competitors. Similarly, a British direct insurance company is exploring methods of forwarding calls from known high-risk customers to a competitor.

Can you change behaviour?

Sacking customers is, however, not likely to be the first step in the process, rather it will be a last resort. The first stage when customers are identified as unprofitable is to seek to re-shape their behaviour so that their contribution increases. This may be by increasing their level of payments or by reducing their service intensity. Australia's largest business is the Melbourne-based telephone company, Telstra. By law, it may not refuse connections to anyone. However, the company has discovered that young adults who move house frequently and request more frequent bills cost triple the amount to service as older subscribers. Therefore it has begun using its database to focus selling efforts for additional services on its most costly customers (*The Economist*, 9 January 1999).

Sometimes they have to go

There are circumstances where the ultimate consequence is that the company and customers need to go separate ways. Examples are customers who assault or insult staff, customers whose ethics are incompatible with company style, or customers who are and will continue to be unprofitable.

Jobless single mothers without assets or prospects are finding it increasingly difficult to obtain banking services. As companies perfect their customer profitability model, some customers emerge as a cost to their supplier, not a contribution. The Wisconsin-based door maker, Weyerhaeuser, has reportedly shed 5000 customers whose cost of supply was greater than their revenue. The era of cross-subsidization by other customers is coming to a close.

Some customers emerge as a cost to their supplier, not a contribution.

Customer shedding risks

There are real dangers to companies in moving down this track. Despite the profit attractions, there are risks. The media may champion unfortunates who are denied service and pillory the companies involved. Adverse word-of mouth messages may damage the company reputation. The approach must be carefully considered.

For companies there is a five-point process to assess the major risks (*see* Fig. 17.4):

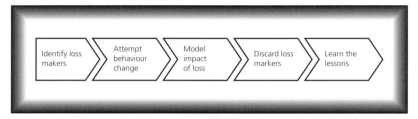

Figure 17.4 Sacking customers

Identify loss makers

Overheads of service, support, cost of delivery, inventory costs of variety and so on are matched as accurately as possible to individual customers to determine individual customer profitability. Trend data on the customer, and typical performance of customers in the same category, forecasts whether the customer will become profitable in time. For example, banks find that undergraduates become profitable two years after graduation. Customers who fall into the category of unprofitable today/unprofitable tomorrow are bad payers – those always seeking refunds or returning product, customers who use service support enormously and needlessly, customers who take up disproportionate amounts of time.

Behaviour change

Can you change behaviours or move customers on to an automated system rather than discard them? There may be ways of influencing customers to alter their usage of products or services to make them profitable. Customers made aware of the impact of their specification changes may willingly improve. Training packages on newly installed automation equipment can diminish subsequent call-outs for Rockwell Automation service engineers and make customers more profitable. Financial incentives can shape customer behaviours effectively, for example limiting the number of free calls to help-lines. Single orders are notoriously expensive to handle, so Books on Line (www.bol.com) encourages multi-buys with a delivery of £2.95 for up to ten books purchased at the same time.

Alternatively, where the expensive element in customer service is staff time, you may be able to automate some services. For example, the UK retailer Argos provides in-store terminals that allow shoppers to check product availability themselves. This transforms the profitability of indecisive purchasers of low-value items.

Financial modelling

When those customers who cannot be profitable have been identified as candidates for 'sacking', an important stage takes place. This constructs a financial model of the business without the costs and revenue of these customers. Savings are calculated for the future business without their consumption of service. For example, a brewery was able to close a distribution depot, downsize the workforce and reduce the delivery-fleet size, by eliminating low-transaction customers located in remote areas. It is critical to evaluate the extent to which low-value customers contribute to unavoidable overheads. Calculate the employee impact. What is the best timing?

Discarding customers

How can you sack non-profitable customers without a negative impact on company reputation? There are eight techniques to deploy (*see* Fig. 17.5) and it is critical that customer-facing employees are briefed and trained in executing these approaches. Role-plays may assist.

- Discriminary pricing
- Redirect customers to wholesalers
- Problem resolution
- Opportunity in change of circumstances
- Direct comparison
- New service priorities
- Withdraw service
- Promotion silence

Figure 17.5 Discarding customers

- **Discriminatory pricing.** Significant price increases imposed on loss-making customers can cause them to seek alternative sources. Builders will often quote high for work they would rather not take on. Service charges can be imposed. Where rebates are a part of the negotiation, these can be progressively withdrawn to create the effect of a higher price.

- **Wholesalers.** Redirect low-value customers to a wholesaler. Wholesalers traditionally operate on lower cost structures than manufacturers' operations and may be able to take over tranches of customers.

- **Problem resolution.** Use the opportunity presented when complaints arise to explain how an alternative supplier may meet the customer's needs better.

- **Review opportunity.** New circumstances such as the initiation of a new project or a change in personnel may create an opening for a review of the appropriateness of supply.

- **Direct comparison.** Seek a business review and provide comparative data that explains how certain of the customers' needs are better met by other suppliers. Recommend specific alternatives.

- **Establish service priorities.** Explain your service priority system, and help less valuable customers to select another supplier who is willing to respond more speedily.

- **Withdraw service.** Provide ample notice of cessation of service and recommend an alternative supply source.

- **Promotion silence.** Reduce communication. Do not prompt renewals. Exclude these customers from information bulletins about new ranges.

Learning the lessons

After the customer list has been cleansed, important conclusions can be drawn. These can identify patterns in desirable and undesirable customers that are then used in selecting new customers. They can also indicate how expectations of new customers should be shaped at the outset to ensure profitability. For example, new warranty conditions may be imposed on new customers initially.

Looking at the future

A final thought is that your competitors will be applying these principles to their customer portfolio. Be aware then, that they may be shedding unprofitable customers in your direction. Acquire new business with care. Learn these lessons and take heed not to replace loss-making old customers with unprofitable new customers. Identify customers you no longer wish to serve and smooth their transition to suppliers better able to serve them.

Case example	Theme: Lessons from failed relationship

'Singapore Services'

An Asian organization – let us call it 'Singapore Services', as I may not name it – showed me how to leverage learning from failed relationships. The market insight came not from the sales or marketing functions; rather it emerged from an analysis instituted by the Head of Information Technology. The company, based in Singapore, is a force across 15 Asian markets, providing a suite of related services to businesses, especially financial institutions. The business has grown dramatically over 25 years and is performing well, winning new accounts to compensate for some losses of customers to aggressive new competition.

The Head of IT explained to me how he created a file of five to eight formerly valuable customers who had not bought services in the last three months. Through curiosity, he had called up their records for the last year and graphed their performance, monthly, up to the point when they stopped buying. He had been expecting to see a steady decline, as usage dropped off. This was not the case; sales continued at close to normal levels and then suddenly ceased. In his words, he decided to 'go down the mine', and analyze a level of finer detail. He extracted and graphed the purchasing history for each of the five sectors of service that the company offers (*see* Fig. 17.6).

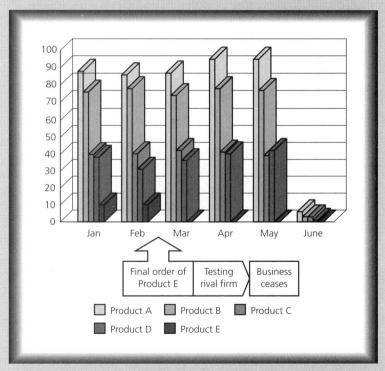

Figure 17.6 Trading patterns

When he saw the graphs, the pattern was the same for each lost customer. Volumes remained strong for the two major sectors and two medium sectors. But, between three and four months before the final order, almost all of the customers had stopped buying the least important sector (Product E). It was an 'aha' moment. He inferred correctly that dissatisfied customers had been trying out a competitor. To minimize the risk of the test, the trials had been conducted on the smallest part of the business. When the competitor had lived up to promises, the rest of the business had been transferred.

The Head of IT presented his findings at a formal meeting. Perhaps because he had only recently moved to Asia, perhaps because of his theoretical approach or perhaps for other reasons, his findings were politely received but did not lead to action. Patiently, he used his insight to create an 'at risk' list of current customers. These were existing customers who had, in the past four months, stopped buying the small fifth sector. He passed the list to his colleagues. During the next six weeks, two more customers were lost and, significantly, both had appeared on his 'at risk' list.

Now his findings were re-evaluated. Action was taken. Sales and service teams were made aware of the 'at risk' list and these customers are accorded service priority. Senior executives visit customers on the list and probe for areas of concern. Results are brought back into the company and practices are changed in response to customer comments. I was told that it is very difficult to win back a customer who has already moved the business away. Executives who reverse decisions quickly lose face. Customers who are wavering are different, and these immediate sensitive and practical approaches can keep them in the fold.

The organization has always been customer responsive, and now it has identified a further refinement: learning from lost customers how to identify and turn around disenchanted customers before they quit.

Exercises   Exercise 17

1 Create a defector project team representing all functions with customer contact.

2 Identify the customers who have ceased buying from your business over the past year.

3 Review their trading pattern for changes in the three to six months before the last order.

4 Review changes in payment performance.

5 Review the complaint log pattern.

6 Review the contact record for meetings and reviews.

7 Check the attendance pattern at company events.

8 Determine the three most effective indicators and use these to identify customers at risk.

9 Establish an intensive-care system for customers at risk.

10 Monitor results.

Further reading and references

Spector, Robert (2000) *Lessons from the Nordstrom Way*, John Wiley & Sons.

We're more than a customer and supplier.
   Yes, it's like a trading partnership.
How about 'reciprocal understanding?'
   I think it's more than that. I'd call it a mutual improvement society.

A successful relationship is more than a commercial transaction. The money exchange is only one aspect. Working together feels more harmonious. There are 12 ways you can support each other and create a mutual support system (*see* Fig. 18.1). We look at these methods of mutual support to bring together the concept of a living relationship with the Customers that Count.

- Reciprocal purchases
- Sister company trading
- Influencing governments
- Marketing support
- Mutual goals
- Shared facilities

- Sharing knowledge
- Benchmarking with customers
- Sharing human resources
- Induction for new employees
- Secondments
- Community activity

Figure 18.1 Building mutual benefits

Reciprocal trading

A sign that a relationship is working effectively is that each party is mindful of the other's best interests, and finds ways, small or large, to boost their commercial strength. One indicator is reciprocal trading. It is not always possible for a supplier to buy goods or services from their customer in return. Where it can be achieved, it is an attractive symbol of mutual support (*see* Fig. 18.2). Suppliers to the catering industry can be conspicuous in patronizing their customers for meals. Rolls Royce and Pratt & Whitney executives will prefer to travel with airlines whose planes use their aero engines. Electrical engineering companies use their wholesale customers as a source of outside components.

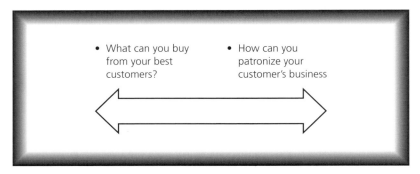

- What can you buy from your best customers?

- How can you patronize your customer's business

Figure 18.2 Reciprocal business

Sister company trading

An alternative element of commercial support is to build the business platform by working with or recommending sister companies. Where you build relationships with sister companies of your customer, a wider bond is created. Where you can encourage your customers to buy from your own sister companies, a broader canvas is created. UK-based Reality Group is a £400-million-turnover subsidiary of GUS PLC. With 20 000 employees, Reality is a major player in process out-sourcing, with 24-hour customer contact centres, 30 million cubic feet of storage, four fully automated parcel-sort centres, and 38 parcel depots within 60 minutes' drive of 85 per cent of UK homes. Company literature reports that clients begin by using one of the services offered, and then extend to other services. It quotes the Readers Digest, users of logistics services for several years, who went on to sign a contract for remittance processing.

Influencing governments together

Beyond the immediate commercial interests, there are longer-term aspects, such as in influencing future legislation. Here it can be valuable to approach the market together with the Customers that Count and work for your mutual best interests. Many examples exist in Europe of manufacturers and their suppliers lobbying Brussels for inclusions or exclusions in forthcoming directives.

An early example in the USA was Henry Heinz. Heinz, founder of the HJ Heinz company, spent his last years campaigning with some worried consumers for pure food legislation. At the turn of the twentieth century the practice of introducing chemical additives and preservatives was becoming an issue of concern. Other food manufacturers vehemently opposed the cause. Nevertheless, the Pure Food and Drug Act was passed in June 1906, 'preventing the manufacture, sale, or transportation of adulterated or misbranded or poisonous or deleterious foods, drugs, medicines, and liquors, and for regulating traffic therein, and for other purposes'. Section 4 decreed that 'examinations of specimens of foods and drugs shall be made in the Bureau of Chemistry of the Department of Agriculture, or under the direction and supervision of such Bureau, for the purpose of determining from such examinations whether such articles are adulterated or misbranded'. In concert with his customers, Henry Heinz had succeeded.

Marketing support

A shared market approach can provide mutual benefits where a company and its customers jointly enter a new market. In the 1990s with the opening of the markets in central Europe, many food companies prepared to set up manufacturing plants to serve new customers. Success often depended on collaboration with their packaging suppliers who invested in parallel and entered the market with them, providing consistent local supplies of wraps according to the brand standards.

In existing markets you can develop mutual word-of-mouth marketing strategies. For example, you can work specifically with your customers to help them to recommend the right kind of potential customers in the future. Provide them with the words, examples and statistics to be a convincing advocate. Listening to their recommending phrases can also bring out new and better forms of customer communication.

An obvious area of shared market approach is with advertising that benefits both parties. For example, Navision, a US-based software company with expertise in manufacturing and business management systems, features in its magazine advertising one of its customers: Steinway and Sons, makers of the finest pianos in the world.

Mutual goals

The growing relationship can be sustained when there are mutual goals: financial, technical and competitive goals that are shared. When Sony Computer Entertainment launched its PlayStation in the UK, ambitious goals were agreed mutually between the company and advertising agency, Simons Palmer Denton Clemmow & Johnson. The goals were all achieved, and Sony's European President appeared at the agency's Christmas party carrying a suitcase. He opened it dramatically to reveal £250 000 in cash. The agreement had included payment by results and this striking gesture illustrated to all the agency employees that success meant something to both parties.

The growing relationship can be sustained when there are mutual goals.

Another example occurs in the less conspicuous area of safety goals. Rockwell Automation has an enviable reputation for safe operations in its manufacturing plants. In 1999 it won the Safety Innovators award, which is given to only one industrial company each year by the Safety and Health Hall of Fame International. Rockwell Automation makes safety a mutual goal with its customers, helping it to reduce the number of sick days in customer workforces. A study in the USA indicated that repetitive manipulations on an operator interface, such as a push button on a machine, were the cause of every third absence due to sickness. For example, carpal tunnel syndrome can be extremely painful and take months to heal. One way to overcome this is to use touch-sensitive photo-electric switches. However, this creates the greater danger of unintended machine operation when dust, a cloth or a screwdriver, for example, break the beam and start the machine. Rockwell Automation found a safe solution to repetitive strain injury using field-effect technology. The Allen-Bradley Zero Force 800Z has two sensors on an ergonomically curved surface of the switch. Both sensors must respond within 0.2 seconds to count as being operated. Thus the sensor can distinguish deliberate operation by a person from an accidental operation by an object. Tests also show a reduction in operator injuries through repetitive actions.

Shared facilities

Facilities in common are a visible and effective way of providing mutual support in two ways. First, there is a practical resource saving. Second, the informal interactions that frequently result can lead to comradeship between individuals. Examples are giving suppliers a desk in the customer's offices, joint testing facilities and shared warehousing.

Beyond facilities, technologies may be shared. These may be communications systems or manufacturing processes. In logistics, Black & Decker the manufacturer of power tools and other electrical appliances, works with retailers on a shared approach to logistics aimed at reducing inventory in the process. This philosophy of 'sell one, ship one, build one' provides benefits of reduced working capital for both the company and its retailer customers.

Sharing knowledge

In living relationships, a significant reward comes from learning together, sharing knowledge and tackling challenges together. Increasingly, companies are offering information to customers and sharing knowledge with their customers. This occurs on a one-to-one level, for example with technological developments and competitive activity. An example on a larger scale is the Royal Mail in the UK, which offers customers a questionnaire to complete, identifying their interests and also subjects in which they

A significant reward comes from learning together, sharing knowledge and tackling challenges together.

have no interest. Royal Mail commits to pass this information to direct mailers so that households receive direct mail on topics they care about and are excluded from databases of suppliers in whom they have no interest.

Benchmarking with customers

The benchmarking approach is another collaborative method of achieving mutual benefit. Creative thinking can identify numerous areas of common concern for benchmarking between suppliers and customers. Examples are in usage of distribution, warehousing, information technology, introduction of system upgrades, staff training, suggestion schemes, staff communication methods and public-relations programmes.

The supplier–customer benchmarking process has twin objectives: learning together to improve both businesses and cementing personal relationships within the two companies. The process has the following steps:

1   Identification of an area for improvement by one party.
2   Definition of the scope to be achievable within the time-scale – usually within six to 12 weeks (longer than this and momentum may be lost or people may move roles).

3 Approach to the other party with an agreement on objectives.

4 Selection of a team – ideally four to six people with expertise in the area, credibility in their own operations and good ambassadors across the businesses.

5 Mapping the current process – team reviews and analysis of documents of the existing process.

6 Programme of visits agreed with the other party, to include process comparison and process challenge.

7 Review of conclusions.

8 Presentation of findings.

9 Agreement on implementation.

10 Measurement and communication of results.

Sharing human resources

For many small and medium-sized enterprises, trade-show attendance is an obligatory burden on their limited resources. Relationships can be built when their suppliers give a joint presence on exhibition stands. Suppliers can also offer items for display, exhibition material and contribute graphics.

Individual inductions

Learning together involves individual learning. Joining a new industry can be a challenging time for a recruit, and this period is crucial in forming first impressions of the industry and market. The induction is a formal process aimed at giving a balanced view. One way to broaden this and validate the perspectives is to extend the induction to the supplying company in the case of the customer, and vice versa. Joining a brewery might mean spending a week serving behind the bar of one of the accounts of the brewer. A new employee of a customer spent a day of induction with a supplying wholesaler. For the rest of his career in that business, the individual concerned never made a phone call to the distributor in the two hours after 8.00 am. He knew that until the vans had set out on their routes, chaos reigned, and a phone call was unlikely to be handled with calmness and only added to the pressure.

Secondments

Later in careers, learning is still important. The human resources director of a multinational organization noted that executives faced with a redundancy through mergers, acquisition and disposals often seized the moment to take a career break and study for an MBA. This observation led him to see the potential for learning breaks during management reshuffles. Where company reorganization left a talented individual without an immediate role, a secondment was arranged. In effect this was a loan to a small customer of an industry-hardened executive to handle a real project or issue in the customer's business. The multinational took back the executive after the three or four-month assignment. Naturally the customer benefited from an injection of resource. The individual learnt from a challenging test in a new environment and the large organization gained from the retention and development of some key individuals.

Citizenship – community activity

Finally, being a good citizen is a stated objective of a host of organizations. They strive to participate in community activity and be accepted as a good neighbour. When customers and suppliers are located in the same community it is possible for them to join forces in making a change or an impact on a local cause. Joint charity of the year is one avenue. Jointly supporting or creating employment opportunities in depressed areas is another. Retailers and suppliers in several countries have jointly set up fundraising initiatives to provide books or computers for schools. Mutual benefit can come in many guises and lead to better companies and better relationships. You cannot provide this mutuality with a million customers. Focus on the best customers.

Conclusion

The Customers that Count are in a real position to offer you benefits of a personal relationship. It is likely that the top 20 per cent of customers will account for 80 per cent of the turnover and profit of your business. They may account for 90 per cent of business-building ideas, innovations and market openings. With close attention to the lessons of human relationships, and the eight characteristics shown in this book, it is possible to create a living relationship with these customers. The crowning achievement of this is the mutual improvement society (*see* Fig. 18.3).

I wish you success with the Customers that Count.

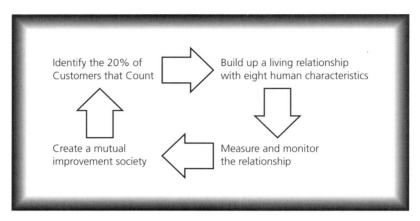

Figure 18.3 Customers that Count

DSM Polypropylene

Vestolen P is a leader in the business of sanitary pipes for transport-ing water, hot and cold, under pressure. Vestolen P is a granular material, supplied to pipe-makers to produce high-performance pipes that are long lasting and have no influence on the taste or smell of the water. Manufactured in Germany by DSM Polypropylene, part of the major Dutch life-sciences and chemical company, Vestolen P is a major brand with a European market share of 50 per cent and a strong presence in markets such as Argentina, Egypt, Kuwait and China. For 25 years the name has stood for relia-bility, security, safety and quality – Remko Goudappel, Business Manager Pipe Sheet for DSM Polypropylene, tells me that in the lab-oratory there is a pipe that has been running since 1975 and is still holding under pressure at high temperature. Vestolen P has a mutual interest in building this identity of quality together with its customers, many of whom use Vestolen P alone and take real advantage from the strength of the brand name.

Remko Goudappel has a strategy dedicated to mutual benefit right down the value chain, embracing pipe-makers and pipe-installers. He believes that when all sides gain something, the relationship is stronger and longer lasting.

The first plank of his strategy is to share knowledge and ideas so that everyone gains something from the relationship. For example, his team organized a seminar in summer 2000. Fifty people, representing 25 key accounts from all over the world, attended the two-day briefing. Vestolen P scientists communicated the research and development work carried out to support the product and its development, and production staff demonstrated the facilities. All the participants shared views on market issues, providing valuable insights to the DSM Polypropylene team. Goudappel adds:

By organizing such seminars for key accounts, one creates a discussion platform that helps us in defining the real issues faced by our customers. It creates customer intimacy that enables us to anticipate customer needs and create value for our customers, rather than just supplying a high-quality product.

The positive perception was mutual. One of the participants commented, 'You have so much know-how, sharing it with us will really help our businesses'. Naturally, there was also a social programme, including a visit to EXPO2000 in Hanover, and this helped to build personal connections between individuals facing similar issues in different markets. As a result of this seminar, each person has an international network of friends who are on call if they find themselves with an unexpected challenge. It is a perfect example of mutual benefit.

With one of the Turkish key customers, buying solely from Vestolen P, there is a plan to develop the relationship to a new level. This pipe-maker holds regular meetings with pipe-installers. Technical representatives of Vestolen P will attend and present an explanation of the characteristics of the product and how to make the maximum benefit from its capabilities. They will demonstrate how the installers can gain extra value for their own businesses through the performance of the piping. The technical representatives will also gain from their visits to Turkey – it will also be a useful testing environment for DSM products and the technicians will be able to take back experiences and knowledge highly relevant to other markets.

Providing resources that support the customer and also increase brand prominence is another form of mutual benefit. The customer's 20 top-performing sales people will win a welding kit, branded 'Vestolen P by DSM'. This incentive will no doubt create additional word-of-mouth awareness of the brand from highly credible sources of recommendation.

Exchange of staff is another example of mutual benefit, and Vestolen P can offer a cultural dimension through its international outlook. Two key production people from the Turkish pipe-maker are being invited to Germany for training in the Vestolen research and development section. They will also learn about the raw material and best ways to process it. Alongside the technical knowledge, there will be a broadening of attitude through visiting and working in another country.

As Goudappel says: 'By doing all this we intend to create value for both of us'.

Exercises   Exercise 18

1 Set up a joint creativity team with your customer.

2 Brainstorm all the things that you could do to support your customer in creating value for their enterprise (beyond the selling process).

3 Brainstorm all the things your customers might do to help you create value (beyond the buying process).

4 Jointly evaluate the most practical suggestions and select the best three. Also select one wild card (an impractical idea that appealed to both parties).

5 Seek to implement a balance of mutually beneficial ideas.